Hearing Enslaved V(

MW00323984

This book focuses on alternative types of slave narratives, especially courtroom testimony, and interrogates how such narratives were produced, the societies (both those that were majority slave societies and those in which slaves were a distinct minority of the population) in which testimony was permitted, and the meanings that can be attached to such narratives. The chapters in this book provide valuable information about the everyday lives—including the inner and spiritual lives—of enslaved African American and Native American individuals in the British and French Atlantic World, from Canada to the Caribbean. It explores slave testimony as a form of autobiographical narrative, and in ways that allow us to foreground enslaved persons' lived experience as expressed in their own words.

Sophie White is Professor of American Studies at the University of Notre Dame.

Trevor Burnard is Wilberforce Professor of Slavery and Emancipation at the University of Hull.

Routledge Studies in the History of the Americas

For more information about this series, please visit: https://www.routledge.com/Routledge-Studies-in-the-History-of-the-Americas/book-series/RSHAM

Hearing Enslaved Voices

African and Indian Slave Testimony in
British and French America, 1700–1848

**Edited by
Sophie White and
Trevor Burnard**

Routledge
Taylor & Francis Group

NEW YORK AND LONDON

First published 2020
by Routledge
52 Vanderbilt Avenue, New York, NY 10017

and by Routledge
2 Park Square, Milton Park, Abingdon, Oxon, OX14 4RN

Routledge is an imprint of the Taylor & Francis Group, an informa business

Library of Congress Cataloging-in-Publication Data
Names: White, Sophie, editor. | Burnard, Trevor G. (Trevor Graeme), editor.
Title: Hearing enslaved voices : African and Indian slave testimony in British and French America, 1700–1848 / Edited by Sophie White and Trevor Burnard.
Description: New York : Routledge Taylor & Francis Group, [2021] |
Series: Routledge studies in the history of the Americas; 14 | Includes bibliographical references and index.
Identifiers: LCCN 2020026051 (print) | LCCN 2020026052 (ebook) | ISBN 9780367541866 (hardback) | ISBN 9781003088127 (ebook) | ISBN 9781000172591 (adobe pdf) | ISBN 9781000172607 (mobi) | ISBN 9781000172614 (epub)
Subjects: LCSH: Slave narratives—North America—History and criticism. | Slavery—North America—History—18th century. | Slavery—North America—History—19th century. | African Americans—History. | Indians of North America—History.
Classification: LCC HT1048 .H43 2021 (print) | LCC HT1048 (ebook) | DDC 306.3/62097—dc23
LC record available at https://lccn.loc.gov/2020026051
LC ebook record available at https://lccn.loc.gov/2020026052

ISBN: 978-0-367-54186-6 (hbk)
ISBN: 978-0-367-54280-1 (pbk)
ISBN: 978-1-003-08812-7 (ebk)

Typeset in Sabon
by codeMantra

Contents

Figures

Introduction

Slave Narratives in British and French America, 1700–1848

Trevor Burnard and Sophie White

This book seeks to propel our thinking about how we understand the quotidian existence of enslaved people in the two biggest slave empires in the northern hemisphere New World—those controlled by France and Britain—over a long period of New World colonization, from around 1700, when the plantation system first became a dominant mode of economic production with significant cultural implications, until the end of slavery in French America in 1848. It does so through the examination of accounts originating with enslaved people—African Americans and Native Americans—that provide a different perspective on slavery than the usual documents and evidence that we have which derive from sources entirely produced by planters, slave-owners, or officials. Specifically, this book focuses on alternative types of slave narratives, especially testimony, and interrogates how such narratives were produced, the societies (both those that were majority slave societies and those in which slaves were a distinct minority of the population) in which testimony was permitted, and the meanings that we can attach to such narratives. The overall aim is to get more information about the everyday lives—including the inner and spiritual lives—of Native American and African slaves (including formerly liberated recaptives and others laying claim to freedom) in the British and French Atlantic Worlds, from Canada to the Caribbean. The ambition is to explore slave testimony as a form of autobiographical narrative, and in particular ways that allow us to foreground enslaved persons' lived experience as expressed in their own words.

The nature of slavery in the New World makes it extraordinarily hard to recapture the voices of the enslaved. The only place and time where written slave narratives are relatively abundant is the slave societies of the nineteenth-century American South, where a degree of literacy among slaves prevailed, leading to the production of a surprising number of complete literary texts that can be usefully analyzed using conventional literary techniques, and, to a lesser extent, nineteenth-century Brazil. In addition, for the twentieth century, there is rich source material showcasing the voices of former slaves in interviews produced by the Federal Writers' Project in the 1930s.[1] For the period and places that we study here—the French and British Atlantic Worlds in the period between 1700 and 1848—such materials are less plentiful, though see the qualification to this statement noted below. This relative scarcity of texts leads to a major problem for scholars of slavery in this period and place: We can usually only study enslavement from one perspective, that of the enslaver rather than the enslaved. Moreover, most of the voices of the enslaved within the archives of colonial slavery are heavily mediated, frequently taking the form of dictated texts or portraits and representations by others. Given how crucial slavery was to the success of these empires and to racialization in this period, the absence of the enslaved voice is a serious problem for truly understanding the dynamics of enslavement and what slavery did to the psyche of the enslaved.

There are, however, more potential slave narratives, by enslaved African Americans and Native Americans, than most scholars think that exist outside the conventional archive of slave narratives of the American South that are so often taken as emblematic of the enslaved experience in the Americas. Narratives that are often fragmentary, if revealing, are the ones that animate the chapters in this book, and (except for those discussed by Aaron Spencer Fogleman, which resemble the slave narratives of the antebellum American South) they consist almost exclusively of testimony presented in court or before some legal entity or another. They can be extraordinarily powerful narratives, as is shown consistently in the essays in this book. Both editors have a long-standing interest in expanding the canon of what might constitute a slave narrative. Sophie White, one of the editors of this volume, has shown, through a detailed examination of the testimony of enslaved people whose voices can be heard in the methodologically complicated but empirically rich records of judicial proceedings in mid-eighteenth-century New Orleans, how we can use such texts to overhear the fragmented yet compelling ways in which the enslaved communicated in often hostile settings their experiences of being enslaved. The enslaved lived in often frightening worlds in which people other than themselves set the rules and devised punishments for breaking rules that the enslaved had no part in making, yet they sought over and over to convey their values and, especially, to express their commitment to family and to the people they loved within institutional structures strongly opposed to their interests.[2] Similarly, Trevor Burnard, the other editor of this book, has worked extensively on rich records kept about enslaved people complaining to a government official about their treatment under enslavement in Berbice, in northeast South America in the second and third decades of the nineteenth century, illustrating that enslaved people in this time and place strived to voice their views, just like the Louisiana slaves studied by White did. The content of the complaints is itself mesmerizing, but it is the details contained within the complaints and how such complaints were fashioned—creating, as Cécile Vidal notes in an essay in this volume,

'Fiction in the Archives'—complex and multifaceted narratives out of testimony in often-charged environments. His work will lead to a book on enslaved women in Berbice which will complement work by Randy Browne using some of the same records on how enslaved people "survived" slavery.[3] Together, White and Burnard approach this subject from the vantage point of French America and British America, respectively. And their own work has led them to approach others interested in the same questions in order to compile the chapters in this book. Thus, one of the major ambitions of this volume is to have the enslaved people of the two most important empires in the Atlantic World in dialogue with each other, illustrating both commonalities in the enslaved experience and differences in the legal and institutional structures of each empire which itself helped shaped how enslaved people represented themselves in testimony and in how that testimony was recorded.

The aim in all the essays in this book and in all the investigations of enslaved (African and indigenous) testimony collected here is to try and get closer to the actual lived experience of the enslaved and to understand what concerned them and what they cared to articulate, and to try and uncover how they might have tried to create their own meanings. In doing so, we are conscious of how the 'archive' assists and hinders us in this task. We appreciate what Saidiya Hartman, drawing on Michel Foucault, argues about the impossibility of the archive yielding up its secrets about the lives of the inarticulate and the oppressed. Hartman states that "the archive is, in this case, a death sentence, a tomb, a display of the violated body, an inventory of property, a medical treatise on gonorrhea, a few lines about a whore's life, an asterisk in the grand narrative of history." As Foucault argues, "it is doubtless impossible to ever grasp [these lives] again in themselves, as they might have been 'in a free state." Marisa Fuentes has written movingly also about the impossibility of getting to 'truth' in archives which are hopelessly compromised by the ways in which they are constructed. Hartman asks an important question which all the authors in this collection address: "How can narrative embody life in words and at the same time respect what we cannot know? How does one listen for the groans and cries, the undecipherable songs, the crackle of fire in the cane fields, the laments for the dead, and the shouts of victory, and then assign words to all of it? Is it possible to construct a story from "the locus of impossible speech" or resurrect lives from the ruins? Can beauty provide an antidote to dishonor, and love a way to "exhume buried cries" and reanimate the dead?"[4] Yet as Leslie M. Harris reminds us, "The idea of silence, which is often used in discussions about early African American history, in fact can undermine the significance of our projects of historical recovery by implicitly positing a perfect archive."[5] As the authors of these essays argue, we do not want to give up in face of the methodological and epistemological problems that the archive produces in trying to recapture the lives of the enslaved, making our silence about their lives a further means whereby their experiences are ignored in the historical narratives we construct.

The focus in these essays is on narratives whose primary purpose was oral, and whose written afterlife was only secondary. Indeed, few of the narratives discussed here are the kind of published autobiographical texts which were produced by slaves themselves in the mid-nineteenth century or in ex-slave testimony collected long after the end of slavery from ex-slaves, and which are complete, lengthy, coherent and have been subjected to the tools of literary analysis. These texts are rare for early periods of slavery in North America and for the British Caribbean. For the French Atlantic, they are virtually nonexistent for different reasons, since the book-length autobiographical slave narrative is a peculiarly Anglo-American genre. As Sue Peabody notes, this is no accident, for, unlike British and American abolitionists, who "seized upon the older genre of the captivity narrative to recount the passage from slavery to freedom," this Protestant literary trope "of subjection (to sin) and redemption (as salvation) did not resonate with contemporary French political struggles" so that the French antislavery lobby did not seek out slave narratives to publicize the injustices of slavery.[6] Our project of juxtaposing the British and French Atlantic can be especially fruitful in bringing to light such disparities, while contextualizing why scholars looking at slave testimony in the places and times studied in this volume seldom have the canonical texts that have been customarily used to explore slave experiences—autobiographies that span the arc of a life in which a highly individuated self (usually male) is explained and asserted. Instead, the sources we have that provide indirect testimony about their experience are hybrid and polyvocal as well as at their core, oral. It is not lost on us that they originate in court records and legal systems that helped create systemic racism.

For some critics, as noted above, these multiple voices, or the fragmentary nature of their life stories proves an insuperable problem. We disagree. The literary theorist Nicole Aljoe has provided a useful overview of how we might look at textual representations of slave experiences, pointers that hold true for the types of sources analyzed in this volume, where oral testimony by enslaved individuals was transcribed by clerks of the court or mediated in other ways. It is difficult for a single voice, especially the voice of an illiterate enslaved person, to emerge from the cacophony of voices involved in the production of the fragmentary evidence we have available to recreate slave experiences. For some critics these intermediaries prove an insuperable problem, meaning that "the slave's voice does not yet control the imaginative forms which her personal history assumes in print." But just because we cannot recover the historical individual through the fragments available to us does not mean that the narratives need to be discarded. Aljoe urges us to move away from questions of the individual author (or deponent, in the case of courtroom testimony) and the vexed associated problems of authenticity and subjectivity to concentrate on the experiences narrated in the text as a means of teasing out the truths that may lie beneath the lives recorded by deeply invested writers. Enslaved people were involved in the production of their testimonies; and we cannot just discard these testimonies because they fail to fit the overly high standard of literary authenticity required by those who want to hear an unadulterated voice emanating from a slave's consciousness. As Aljoe argues, "calling the slave's dictation 'a mere body of data' from which the editor spins out another story seems woefully inadequate" and, it might be added, contrary to Mikhail Bahktin's instructive insights into how language cannot be owned by just one person and is always mediated in an active process of expropriation. It may be that the collaborative necessities that were involved in creating slave testimonies "violate the very notion of a singular, autonomous author." Nevertheless, they are what we have as evidence and if read sensitively (with what Aljoe calls "a method of strategic reading and critical hearing") then the testimonies embedded in the records we use here allow us to recuperate a little bit of the enslaved person's perspective.[7] Sometimes we can even hear them speak.

British and French America, 1700–1848

The essays in this book range widely thematically, but they take a common spatial and temporal orientation—the British and French American empires—over a long time period. The New World in the eighteenth and early nineteenth centuries were, of course, an arena of competing European empires, including the Spanish, Portuguese, Danish, American, and Dutch empires, as well as the British and French empires. This book concentrates on two of these worlds—the British and French Atlantic Worlds—and on both Native Americans and African Americans in a wide range of settings, from metropolitan France to New Orleans and New France, to New England in British America, and to parts of the British and French Caribbean. The two empires varied considerably in institutions, in attitudes to aspects of the enslaved experience, and spatially. The French Empire in the Americas was always smaller than that of the British and less variegated, especially after France's defeat by Britain in the Seven Years' War. It was also far more standardized with respect to slave codes and judicial procedure pertaining to slave testimony as Dominique Rogers shows, and this helps to contextualize the emphasis on the law in the essays on Louisiana, Montreal, and the French Caribbean. At the same time, French America was divided into two very different regions. The first region was Quebec in modern-day eastern Canada in which African slavery was limited (though not non-existent) and, as Brett Rushforth shows, where native slavery was significant. The second region was centered on the flourishing colony of

Saint-Domingue, one of the more complete slave societies in history, with less wealthy but still very important slave-based plantation societies in Martinique and Guadeloupe in the lesser Antilles and the North American mainland colony of Louisiana. As Cécile Vidal shows in a recent study of colonial New Orleans, the influence of the Antilles, especially Saint-Domingue, was persistent in shaping development in this vibrant Caribbean town throughout the eighteenth century, which is not to downplay the influence of New France on Louisiana, not least the presence of native slavery throughout that colony.[8] Consequently, when Saint-Domingue imploded as a result of the largest and most successful enslaved rebellion in world history between 1791 and 1804, the results for French imperialism in the Americas were especially catastrophic. By the early decades of the nineteenth century, the French empire in the Americas had been greatly diminished from a century previously though the French presence lingered long after.

The British Empire in the Americas was larger, longer lasting, and more heterogenous than that of the French, not least in terms of legal variations. It was considerably more ethnically diverse and had larger numbers of white people than in French America and was more obviously a place where settlers and settler colonialism had a place.[9] Unlike French mainland America, where growth was halted as a result of French defeat in the Seven Years' War, the British Atlantic World grew exponentially and continuously from its unpromising beginnings in early-seventeenth-century Virginia until it reached a peak in the 1760s. That decade, however, saw a decisive break in the empire, with the first successful colonial revolt in the Americas, the transformational American Revolution. That revolt split the slave-holding British Atlantic into two, with most whites in plantation regions and a substantial proportion of enslaved people breaking away from Britain to form the United States, a country that remained in its southern states devoted to the perpetuation of slavery. But Britain retained not just its colonies in Canada but also substantial slave-holding colonies in the Caribbean. Indeed, Britain added more colonies based on slavery to its empire during the French Revolutionary and Napoleonic Wars, including profitable slave societies in northern South America, as Burnard details in his essay in this volume. The birth of an abolitionist program which led to the abolition of the slave trade in 1807 did not lead immediately to the end of slavery, which continued for another thirty years and which, as Anita Rupprecht stresses, had significant legacies, even after it had ended. The British Empire in the eighteenth and nineteenth centuries was a diverse empire but one in which slavery and the slave trade was vital and where a very large percentage of the population were enslaved.

The differences between the two empires regarding slavery and the treatment of enslaved people were undoubtedly less important than the similarities. In both empires, there was a strong commitment to both slavery and to the plantation system, manifested most obviously in the Atlantic slave trade, whose horrors, Fogleman shows, were recorded more often than we might have thought by Africans caught up in its tentacles. That commitment was expressed in strong state support of planters and other settlers, especially in their almost untrammeled authority over enslaved people, and to the wealth that economic ventures dependent on slavery brought to colonists and to imperial coffers. It was shown also in fierce legislation (that built on earlier legal precedents in both French and British colonies) determined to keep enslaved people in their place, whether those enslaved people were Native American or, more frequently, of African descent. That legislation privileged white voices over black, authorized and normalized often horrific violence to ensure enslaved people were kept in order and in submission, and legitimated the extensive use of state power to maintain white supremacy and the integrity of plantation and other economic systems. Abolitionism in the British Empire and enslaved rebellion and abolitionism in the French Empire from the late eighteenth century onward complicated this state commitment to slavery, but at the level of interpersonal relations between the enslaved and enslavers, as governed by state rules and procedures, both the French and the British continued their resolution to favor the latter over the former throughout the period of slavery and into emancipation.

The broad similarities in the structural relations each empire evinced toward slavery, however, did not mean that there were not significant differences in how each empire decided to regulate slavery. These differences in regulation, notably how much latitude was allowed by each empire for the enslaved to talk back to enslavers and the colonial state, helped determine the extent of evidence that was collected containing slave voices. Here, the French, building on metropolitan legal procedure, were more willing than the British to be expansive about the extent that they allowed enslaved people to give testimony and, more importantly, in how they chose to record and preserve such testimony. The British occasionally had slave courts (from which little evidence has survived over time) but more often refused to allow enslaved people to testify in court either against others or in their own defense, and even when they did, seldom generated detailed record-keeping.[10] This is one of the key contrasts between the French and British empires, along with the fact that the British had no overarching slave policy that needed to be obeyed and which, in turn, produced evidence from enslaved persons that could be passed down into the archive. For most of the eighteenth century, the management of enslaved people was conducted at the level of the individual slaveowner, thus militating against enslaved testimony being produced or preserved. By contrast, the French governed enslaved people of African descent through both local and centralized laws, among these the so-called code noir. First promulgated in 1685, it was preceded and followed by a slew of local and metropolitan slave codes including Louisiana's 1724 code noir. The application of a code noir made it clear that the state had a stake in slave management and in controlling enslaved people's behavior and actions, including extrajudicial violence but also attempts at oversight over their spiritual and intimate lives, for example by mandating Catholic instruction and regulating access to legal marriage. Consequently, enslaved people were drawn into the law in the French empire in ways that were seldom possible in the eighteenth-century British empire. Though the code noir was clearly aspirational, the somewhat different relationship in the French Empire to how far the state could involve itself in supplementing and sometimes replacing the power of enslavers to dominate and control their enslaved property, allied to French judicial rules, made a difference in the quantity and quality of slave testimony that was permitted to be kept. This major difference between the French and the British attitudes to how much they were willing to hear—and then record—from slaves is a common theme in the essays in this volume.

Plan of the Book

This book divides into three sections, with a sweeping concluding essay by Emily Clark that points to the wider themes, conclusions, and future research directions that have arisen from the substantive chapters of the book. One major theme of this book is methodological, and this is the main concern of the first three chapters. The texts used by the scholars writing in this book are not easy of access or innocent of interpretation. The people we are interested in were in the main illiterate, often people as Native Americans or Africans firmly outside the polities in which they lived. They faced great struggles in their daily lives and lived lives that were dependent on the arbitrary whims of slave owners and states that had little interest in advancing their interests. Thus, the testimonies they gave and the narratives that a few of them wrote, or had written for them, must be understood within the difficult circumstances of their lives. Sophie White, Dominique Rogers, and Cécile Vidal use case studies from French colonies that consist of courtroom testimony by enslaved Africans such as Marguerite and Jupiter from mid-eighteenth-century New Orleans or Josaphat and others from the eighteenth- and nineteenth-century French Caribbean. While endeavoring to foreground these individuals whose narratives they analyze, they (along with Brett Rushforth in his essay on Native American slavery in Montreal) concentrate on the laws and court procedures that led to the creation of these texts—both the act of testifying and how it was recorded—and how scholars might usefully examine slave testimony bearing in mind the circumstance of their production and their inherent constraints.

The second section contains three essays, all concentrated on a single theme and thus each speaking to each other. Linford D. Fisher, Margaret Newell, and Brett Rushforth write on the relatively little studied subject of Native American slaves. Recent scholarship has shown that slavery was a more expansive institution than we used to think, not being confined either only to African Americans nor only in the plantation societies of the American South, the Caribbean, and northern South America. The three authors in this section, each of whom have been major figures in the recapturing of Native American slavery from the archives, look at different aspects of Native American slave testimony. Newell's chapter finds the voices of enslaved Native Americans and Africans in published conversion and crime narratives and in legal manuscripts in order to isolate the features of slavery in that region, showing the radical uncertainty of Native American lives lived in enslavement. Fisher provides a case study of a Native American in Connecticut named Ann and her four children of mixed ethnic descent. Ann and her children ran away from their master, but they claimed they were wrongly enslaved. The court case that followed shows how forced mobility and severed family connections were the reality for all enslaved people. He also investigates the differences between Native American and African American slavery in legal settings in New England. Rushforth tells the story of a thirty-year-old Native American enslaved woman called Manon accused of theft and whose testimony provides tantalizing details of her daily routine and webs of connections in Montreal.

Native American slavery existed in both French and British North America, but the processes of law and evidence were different in each place, shaping the testimony that Native Americans produced in telling ways. And Native American slavery operated in tandem with African American slavery. Comparing slave testimony given by Indians to slave testimony emanating from Africans shows that while in many ways Native Americans occupied a slightly more elevated position within colonial social and racial hierarchies than did Africans, and though their existence tends to be more amorphously documented in the archives, what is noticeable are less the differences than the similarities in slave narratives produced by both groups of enslaved people.

The final section comprises four chapters on the largest group of slaves (including recaptives and those petitioning for freedom) in the early modern French and British Empires: Africans and African Americans. These four essays range widely in time and place, from British North America, to Paris, to early-nineteenth-century South America and to the British Caribbean in the time of emancipation. After an essay by Aaron Fogleman on narratives produced by those born in some form of relative freedom in Africa who were enslaved by Europeans, an essay by Miranda Spieler examines in depth freedom suits brought by slaves in Paris, illustrating the contradictions inherent in a country both theoretically devoted to the idea that everyone became free once stepping on metropolitan soil and also a major slave power increasingly implicated in slavery not just in the colonies but in France itself. In such circumstances, ideological commitment to ideas of France as "free soil" faded in the face of the reality of the actual position of enslaved people in the metropolis. Two essays look at slave testimony from the perspective of specific groups and specific themes. The first, by Trevor Burnard, examines women in Berbice and how they shaped complaints to judicial authorities about their work conditions and aspirations. The second essay, by Anita Rupprecht, looks at testimony by recaptive Africans and by Caribbean slaves who were seized under the abolition laws in the British Caribbean during the final stages of slavery.

Themes in the Essays

In sum, these ten essays provide a comprehensive and exciting guide to the topic of slave testimony and narrative in a wide range of places and times and with much attention placed on methodological issues. Perhaps the most important point that can be made about the information provided by these essays is that they show that there is much more in the French and British colonial archive about the enslaved, either African or Native American, than is sometimes imagined. This material provides opportunities to gain special insights into how the enslaved lived, how they coped with periods of great tension (so often the theme in these essays, as they often concentrate on periods when enslaved people were in trouble, as when they had to come to court to defend themselves, to ask for more favorable treatment, or to seek redress), and what they had to put up with in structures and systems strongly biased against them. What we are able to do with the testimony that relates to the enslaved is not just to recover biographies which illuminate individual experiences but explore those testimonies, as Margaret Newell argues in her account of enslaved Native American testimony in New England, which "allow historians to make arguments about the origins and evolution of Indian and African servitude and slavery more generally and to make comparisons across racial and regional lines that can reveal variety in experience as well as common threads."

We understand that getting information about the enslaved from sources such as those in courtrooms or as part of petitions to lawmakers raises considerable methodological problems—all the writers of essays in this book are highly sensitive to biases and silences in the archive. But our belief is that we should emphasize the opportunities that arise from studying even very fragmented testimony from or about enslaved people in French and British America rather than concentrate too intensely on the problems inherent in such testimony. The skilled historians writing essays in this collection demonstrate amply just how much material of interest and importance can be wrung from seemingly unpromising archival materials. At bottom, it allows enslaved people to talk and thus enables us to hear what they had to say. That we can hear previously unheard voices is the major achievement of the essays in this volume.

And the stories that enslaved people tell as detailed in these essays are not just riveting but allow access to the worlds of people who have not been previously known within the historical record. One of the most important contributions that these essays make to the history of slavery is to give us some enthralling stories, about individual women, men, and children. Some involve, as in Cécile Vidal's lengthy exploration of the trial of Jupiter, a Louisiana enslaved man tried for running away and for theft, and in Margaret Newell's evocation of the trial of an enslaved woman, Patience Boston, enslaved people in an awful lot of trouble. Both Jupiter and Boston were executed despite their attempts to exonerate themselves. But, as Vidal shows for Jupiter, the unfortunate result of his court proceedings masks a long fight by the enslaved man to craft a defense for himself, a strategy based around constructing a story to explain away his problems, even though not assisted by lawyers and not kept informed of the legal procedures he was up against. Other essays tell detailed stories focused on one individual; still others present shorter accounts of some of the individuals who provided testimonies.

We say their names. Linford Fisher focuses on Indian Ann, a Native American enslaved woman in 1740s New England. Indian Ann was suspected of being a runaway but, as Fisher outlines, had a much more complicated tale to tell, one in which she claimed that she and her family had already been free. Brett Rushforth introduces us to Marie-Josephe, known as Manon, an enslaved Native American woman in Montreal, who in 1750 was accused of theft, linking her in interesting ways to Marie-Josephe-Angelique (the Luso-African enslaved woman hanged for supposedly burning down a large part of the city in 1734, and whom Manon may have been a hostile witness against) and urging us to think of the process of testifying and of being recorded. Sophie White presents the testimony of Marguerite who in 1764 was prosecuted for running away to the cabin of an enslaved man but used her acerbic wit in court to point out the flaws in how her masters treated her, not least by locking her up at night as if she were in the convent, words that reveal how mightily she disdained the Catholic conceptions of sexuality that she was confronted with. Dominique Rogers outlines, among others, the tale of Josaphat, a cook in 1826 to the governor of Martinique, in order to explore recurrent themes in the history of enslavement, such as what it felt like to be enslaved and how enslaved people coped with the constant violence inherent in the practice of Atlantic slavery in the Caribbean, but also how they maintained ties with family, kin, and others fulfilling the same skilled occupation.

Miranda Spieler tells us about Jacques Ledoux, a West Indian sailor heavily involved in the Seven Years' War whose petitions to a Parisian court demonstrated the 'picaresque vulnerability' that free people of color were forced to endure when challenged as o whether they were actually free or not. For Berbice, among other indignant complaints lodged before the Fiscal, Trevor Burnard quotes Laura, who was aggrieved that she couldn't take her breastfeeding child to the field as was customary. In a similar vein, Anita Rupprecht brings to light the testimony before the Royal Commission in Antigua of individuals such as Caroline Dewar, who launched into a furious reproach of her mistress's actions toward her. And Aaron Fogleman has unearthed several life stories by relatively unknown enslaved people alongside more famous Africans enslaved in the Atlantic World such as Jean-Baptiste Belley, thanks to which we see African writers during the Age of Revolution responsive to appropriations of Enlightenment, revolutionary, Christian, and Muslim ideals in order to challenge the situation they found themselves in as victims of the transatlantic slave trade. Almost every essay pays close attention to the stories of enslaved people, growing up in oral cultures in which telling stories was culturally vital, told, both in order to understand the structures of slavery in which enslaved people were trapped and to make visible people who were usually invisible.

Telling Stories

What comes out clearly in these tales of individuals are two things. First, the stories constructed by enslaved people to try and extricate themselves from punishment, to try to get an advantage for themselves, to explain their lives and experiences, and sometimes, just to be heard, without any hope of gain, show that enslaved people always had some degree of agency in shaping testimony and slave narratives. Enslaved people, when allowed to, were determined to make their own points, even when speaking up came with great risks. When the courts allowed, as Vidal, Rushforth, and White show for eighteenth-century French mainland colonies and Rogers shows for the nineteenth-century French Caribbean, as Burnard shows for nineteenth-century Berbice and as Rupprecht illustrates for Africans and Creoles who were indentured in the immediate years *prior* to emancipation in the British Lesser Antilles, enslaved and otherwise bonded people devised their own testimony unconstrained by too rigid legal formula, doggedly seeking to have their say. Judicial testimony, as White argues, could be capacious, as deponents veered off subject (adding details "without being asked"), their narratives brimming with character and personality. Indeed, while their current form is written, the fact that these narratives originated in the spoken word requires being attuned to the cadences and conventions of oral speech, not least its immediacy and its potential for impulsiveness, for changing tack along the way. Deponents did not always succeed in sticking to a pre-planned narrative (if they even had one), and the back and forth of interrogations, the performative aspects of judicial practice, the sheer stress of being on show, at risk, and in the hot seat, could lead to tangents and to narratives that were not always purely strategic but that are the richer for the glimpses they afford into the lives of complex human beings. This tendency to what can seem rambling or spontaneous testimony may have been difficult for lawmakers—and sometimes even for us—to contemplate, given the stakes, but it is a godsend for social historians. As Rogers insists, the main value of most of the slave testimony and incomplete and biased narratives that scholars need to work is not that they recreate cases from the past but that they provide insight into the quotidian lives and daily struggles of the enslaved.

Second, there is some unevenness in terms of the amount of narrative that was produced and recorded in different times, places, and legal regimes. Yet the accumulation of details in these stories help us appreciate the webs of significance which bound the enslaved and enslavers together and in which the enslaved were always at a distinctive disadvantage, as they were not holding the levers of power in ways that the enslavers did and always had to acknowledge the prejudices of those people who had authority over them, and who had the institutional mechanisms of the state to protect that power. The reality of unequal relationships within enslavement meant that enslaved people had to work within systems rather than outside them, employing tactics of day-to-day opposition more than direct confrontation, in ways that Michel de Certeau has described.[11] Sometimes these forms of indirect confrontation involved accepting the constraints on behavior that enslavers imposed on the enslaved and the totalizing power of the state as the agency guaranteeing the continuation of slavery. We need to remember that the enslaved people in many of the cases described in these essays knew that their chances of gaining any sort of freedom, or even redress, was very limited, given overwhelming support for the institution of slavery by imperial and state authorities. Their testimony must be read with this in mind, and with sensitivity to what else they might have hoped to achieve through their words, even if it was simply to be listened to for a short moment in time.

As Burnard shows in his essay, psychological tools of domination co-existed alongside the threat of physical violence and are a feature of the testimony collected in this volume: Few enslaved people "talked" without being very aware of how their words were being heard, interpreted, and acted on, though this knowledge did not necessarily curb them in what they chose to say. And they knew that the symbolic violence of how their words were shaped by the structures of enslavement they lived in was matched by the reality of actual violence which bubbled under or close to the surface for people caught within slavery's snares. All the testimonies put forward in the essays in this book show copious signs of being mediated by the context through which such testimonies were produced, though there is sometimes evidence of less adulterated testimony, seen for example in reported dialogue and turns of phrase. If there was a degree of complicity that enslaved people were forced to adopt in the process of testifying and having their words heard and recorded, this does not mean, however, that enslaved people had no say nor that they agreed with the systems that in some respect they were forced to accept. If we apply, as the authors in this volume do, the techniques of close reading, the willingness to bring together scattered anecdotes and multiple details into sorts of narrative, and an ability to read slave testimonies both with and against the grain, what we gain is something very special—an insight into the lives and views of people often silenced in history—enslaved people in French and British America.

Notes

1 "Born in Slavery: Slave Narratives from the Federal Writers' Project, 1936 to 1938," Library of Congress, https://www.loc.gov/collections/slave-narratives-from-the-federal-writers-project-1936-to-1938/about-this-collection/.

2 Sophie White, *Voices of the Enslaved: Love, Labor, and Longing in French Louisiana* (Chapel Hill: University of North Carolina Press, 2019).

3 Trevor Burnard, "A Voice For Slaves: The Office of the Fiscal in Berbice and the Beginnings of Protection in the British Empire," *Pacific Historical Review* 87, 1 (February 2018), 30–53; idem and Randy Browne, "Husbands and Fathers: The Family Experiences of Enslaved Men in Berbice," *New West India Guide* 91 (2017), 193–222.

4 Saidiya Hartman, 'Venus in Two Acts,' *Small Axe* 26 (June 2008), 2, 3; Michel Foucault, 'Lives of Infamous Men,' in *The Essential Foucault*, eds., Paul Rabinow and Nikolas Rose (New York: New Press, 2003), 284; Marisa Fuentes, Dispossessed Lives: *Enslaved Women, Violence, and the Archive* (Philadelphia: University of Pennsylvania Press, 2016).

5 Leslie M. Harris, "Imperfect Archives and the Historical Imagination," *Public Historian* 36, 1 (February 2014), 79.

6 Sue Peabody, *Madeleine's Children: Family, Freedom, Secrets, and Lies in France's Indian Ocean Colonies* (Oxford: Oxford University Press, 2017), 3–4 and Deborah Jenson, *Beyond the Slave Narrative: Politics, Sex, and Manuscripts in the Haitian Revolution* (Liverpool: Liverpool University Press, 2011).

7 Nicola Aljoe, *Creole Testimonies: Slave Narratives from the British West Indies, 1700–1838* (New York: Palgrave Macmillan, 2012).

8 Cécile Vidal, *Caribbean New Orleans: Empire, Race, and the Making of a Slave Society* (Chapel Hill: University of North Carolina Press, 2019).

9 Nancy Shoemaker and Jeffrey Ostler, "Forum: Settler Colonialism in Early America," *William and Mary Quarterly*, 3d ser., 76 (2018), 361–368.

10 Slaves and free persons of color in colonial Virginia, for instance, were not allowed to testify in court (trials against slaves for capital crimes being the only exception). See Philip J. Schwarz, *Twice Condemned: Slaves and the Criminal Laws of Virginia, 1705–1865* (Baton Rouge: Louisiana State University Press, 1988), 19. Slaves in the British Caribbean, on the other hand, could testify, but only for or against other slaves, not for or against free persons. See Natalie Zacek, "Voices and Silences: The Problem of Slave Testimony in the English West Indian Law Court," *Slavery and Abolition* 24, 3 (December 2003), 24–39, esp. 25.

11 Michel De Certeau, *The Practice of Everyday Life*, trans. Steven Rendall (Berkeley: University of California Press, 1984).

Section One
Voices in the Archives

1 "Said Without Being Asked"

Slavery, Testimony, and Autobiography

Sophie White

In 1764, Marguerite, a twenty-five-year-old enslaved African, was charged with running away from her master and brought before the Superior Council of Louisiana in New Orleans. She was first made to swear an oath to tell the truth before a crucifix and to identify herself to the court; then her interrogation began. Though she was the defendant in a criminal case, Marguerite placed the blame for her actions on her owners, complaining that she had become a fugitive three weeks earlier because "her master and mistress always beat her, that when she fell sick her mistress came to see her after four days and said 'Mademoiselle is playing at being ill, is she?' and right then beat her with a stick, made her work and clear the courtyard, and threatened that if she did not work she would call the slaves to take her to the public square to give her a hundred lashes of the whip." Marguerite concluded her narrative by adding to her list of grievances that "every night, they locked her up like in a convent."[1]

How do we make sense of Marguerite's testimony? Can we make sense of it? Should we even try? The answer to that last question is a resounding yes, for Marguerite's words do allow us, above all, to hear *her* voice. In her testimony, we see glimpses of her pain and her sense of outrage, but also flashes of her personality, character, and sense of humor. Her narrative also allows us to glean the dual ways she chose to respond to the abuse. She did so, first, with her feet, by running away, specifically to the cabin of a male slave, Janot. She identified him as Congo, like her, and he was in all likelihood her lover, or at the very least, a source of kinship, of emotional and material support. Janot's owner, Joseph Villars Dubreuil, was the son of the largest slaveholder in the colony, and the plantation where Janot lived was situated a few leagues downriver from New Orleans, requiring Marguerite to leave the town to reach him (Figure 1.1).[2] It was the overseer there who had her seized and taken to prison. Second, she signaled her displeasure verbally, in court, in the particular manner that she conveyed her disapproval of the way her masters treated her and her anger at the injustice of their actions.

Yet the court did not investigate her claims of abuse or her mistress's threat of a public whipping. Rather, it convicted her of running away

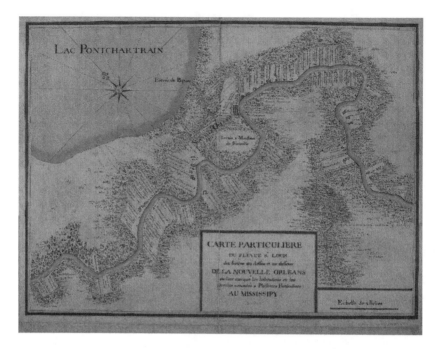

Figure 1.1 Unknown artist, *Carte particuliere du flevue [sic] St. Louis dix lieües au dessus et au dessous de la Nouvelle Orleans ou sont marqué les habitations et les terrains concedés à plusieurs particuliers au Mississipy.* Circa 1723. Edward E. Ayer Manuscript Map Collection. VAULT drawer Ayer MS map 30 sheet 80. Courtesy The Newberry Library, Chicago.

and sentenced her to have her ears cut and to be branded with a fleur-de-lis on her right shoulder. Finally, it ruled that she be returned to the home of her master, Mr. Guy Dufossat, a retired captain in the Marine, and his wife, Françoise Claudine Dreux, where she undoubtedly suffered more abuse. If Marguerite had planned her testimony tactically, the results were less than ideal, but then again, she was testifying while "black" (to cite the terminology of Louisiana's 1724 slave code) and the odds of getting justice were never going to be in her favor.[3] What else might she have hoped to achieve, the trial's outcome notwithstanding?

Her masters would not have been in the courtroom during her testimony but Marguerite probably realized that what she said in court could leak out to them. Madame Dufossat might have thought she was making fun of Marguerite, sardonically calling her "Mademoiselle" (Miss) and using the third person to address her slave, in imitation of the way that a servant, following convention, might address the person they were waiting on. But, in court, it was Marguerite who used her biting wit to mock her mistress, making fun of her behind her back by mimicking her words ("'Mademoiselle is playing at being ill, is she?'"). Marguerite also critiqued the behavior of the Dufossat-Dreux couple with a metaphor referencing New Orleans's Ursuline convent ("every night, they locked her up like in a convent"). Although court procedure required Marguerite to identify herself and, as an enslaved woman, to provide the name of her owner, she also volunteered that she was "of the Congo nation," stating that "she was named Margueritte belonging to M. Dufossat former Captain, aged twenty-five years old, of the Congo nation." Her purported origins suggest she might have been familiar with Catholicism as practiced in the kingdom of Kongo, which had converted to Catholicism in 1481. She evidently grasped the fundamental notion of the cloister, and of a Catholic model of celibacy, mediated by architecture, that segregated women from men. It was probably hard enough for any newcomer to understand this practice. But this African-born woman, who had herself been captured and then enslaved, likely could not even remotely fathom that cloistered nuns volunteered to be "locked" up.[4]

This level of detail, this range of experience, touching on labor, abuse, religion, sexuality, and surveillance, is one of the boons of working with eighteenth-century French judicial testimony. Seemingly extraneous at first glance, such tidbits are in fact deeply revealing and very often riveting. Certainly, testimony cannot tell us beyond any doubt whether the events described took place. Did Marguerite speak the truth? Had her mistress said those very words to her? We cannot know for sure, and perhaps we do not need to know. What we can say is that Marguerite answered the judges' questions and made an assertion about what she considered egregious in the way her mistress and master treated her, adding a flourish of sarcasm to her tale. It was the medium of testimony that gave her the opportunity to construct this narrative, one that was anchored in her own experience, temperament, wit, emotions, and ways of knowing, one that was autobiographical because it expressed how she looked at her world and how she evaluated it and made sense of it at that moment in time.

If not all enslaved defendants who appeared before New Orleans's Superior Council were as forthright or as expressive as Marguerite, others, like her, constantly redirected the court's focus away from the crimes at hand, crimes that were disproportionately centered on theft or marronnage (running away). And, when they did, in place of straightforward answers to questions posed, they proffered hints about their worldviews and gave glimpses of who they were. The result is an astoundingly rich archive of slave testimony that is unique in scope among colonial North American archives in allowing the enslaved themselves to let us hear their thoughts and their pronouncements.

In these narratives, it was the enslaved, ultimately, who chose what they wanted to reply in answer to interrogations, and it is their words that were recorded. After all, it was Marguerite, not her interrogators, who spoke of being "locked" up, and it was she who employed a simile to critique her masters' control of her sexuality—even using humor to do so. It was she who seemed genuinely put out that her masters did not treat her as she seemed to expect, for she surely had knowledge of, and had undoubtedly already internalized, what it could mean to be a slave in West Central Africa, where the concept of slavery allowed for a more flexible range of practices in the treatment of captives. It was also she who expressed her anger at being made fun of, she who described the forced intimacy created when her masters asserted physical and emotional control over her, not only beating her and locking her up but threatening her with the physical violence and humiliation of being whipped in public, in sight of all. A slave was supposed to submit, emotionless, to the constraints and violence inherent in such words and actions (and to be contrite if he or she failed to do so in the moment). Marguerite countered both of these notions, by running away but also by making a point, in court, of explaining her reaction and laying out her argument.[5]

The trial records of the Louisiana Superior Council brim with details about daily life and about inner lives. Like Marguerite, many deponents signaled that issues centered on intimate matters and on their emotional worlds lay at the core of their day-to-day responses to the yoke of slavery. For this reason alone, these documents are invaluable to those who seek to flesh out a richer understanding of the experiences of enslaved Africans. Certain linchpins undergird my approach to this extraordinary source material. Above all, it bears emphasizing that, though archives containing slave testimony in French colonies can be mined for empirical evidence about slavery, as other essays in this volume attest, testimony in and of itself does not necessarily enlighten us about the facts of a case: what happened, when, where, and to whom. But that is not the purpose of my analysis. Instead, I seek to make a couple of interventions, about the peculiar dynamic of oral testimony, and about autobiographical narrative.

First, I argue that we cannot presume a one-dimensional rationale (not even that of self-preservation) for the answers that deponents gave; instead, we must seek to anticipate a richer combination of explanations, ones with and without intent, for how and why, in the act of recalling and retelling, those who testified moved past the factual details of the court cases. Because of the inherent power dynamic in the act of testifying, there can be an expectation that testimony, especially that of a defendant, was inevitably framed by a hostile relationship to the law. This is not to underestimate the diametrically uneven power dynamics, the sheer terror of being on the stand, the fear and no doubt certainty of punishments to come. But though defendants could not speak freely (without fear of reprisals), and though their answers might end up putting them in jeopardy, the evidence suggests that testimony was not necessarily compelled or exclusively tactical and premeditated. Even when a court appearance was coerced or coached, there was room for unprompted narratives—clerks explicitly acknowledged as much when recording what one defendant might say "without being asked," then "again without his being asked," or what another "said, on her own initiative." Appearing before the court provided individuals with an opportunity to narrate their own stories, and they digressed, redirected questioning, and introduced unrelated matters in an arena where, temporarily commanding full attention, they had to be heard.[6]

Second, I suggest that we need to reorient and expand our notion of what an autobiographical narrative can look like. The rewards in doing so are many, for when the enslaved digressed from lines of questioning to introduce other topics that foregrounded their own viewpoints rather than the concerns of their interrogators, they produced a substantial corpus of narratives overflowing with personality, character, subjectivity, and humanity in which they seem to quite literally spring to life.[7]

In an article about the release of the film *Twelve Years a Slave*, Annette Gordon-Reed succinctly posed the familiar question, "Which historical voices should be deemed legitimate?" As she observed, "These questions are particularly fraught when one is dealing with past atrocities, like America's racially based system of chattel slavery." "Then there is history's cruel irony," she continued, that "the individuals who bore the brunt of the system—the enslaved—lived under a shroud of enforced anonymity. The vast majority could neither read nor write, and they therefore left behind no documents, which are the lifeblood of the historian's craft." In French colonies, no formal prohibitions existed barring slaves from reading or writing, but not many possessed these skills, meaning that few written sources were produced by the enslaved. The problem of source material is seen as especially acute in the period before the rise of autobiographical slave narratives. These published sources offer richly textured firsthand accounts of the experiences of individual slaves that showcase their voices, even when mediated by an editor or amanuensis. As a literary genre that emerged from Anglo-American Protestant abolitionist movements, however, they emphasize a trope of personal redemption that did not resonate with French or Catholic antislavery advocates, and no such narratives were created in France or her colonies.[8]

The evidence from French judicial slave testimony more than mitigates this void, offering an alternative set of historical voices and life stories that holds the potential to expand the canon of what we consider slave narratives. What made French law distinctive was that it hinged on testimony as central to judicial procedure. In particular, it privileged confession as the "queen of proofs," since only the defendant was deemed to know the truth. Accordingly, criminal trials in France and French colonies were subject to precise rules and strict guidelines to ensure the careful recording of proceedings. Answers that defendants and witnesses provided during questioning could be as expansive as deponents wished, and the written documents that resulted from this testimony, though not perfect mirrors of the spoken word, aimed to be comprehensive. Depositions were far more detailed, for example, than those of English colonial courts, where, in any case, the testimony of the enslaved was not always permitted, and where full transcripts of testimony were not produced as part of the court record. In contrast, both the legal purpose of testimony in French law and the strict court procedures that regulated how testimony was recorded meant that trials in French courts engendered exceptionally thorough written records. Although colonial and metropolitan officials remained committed to the broader project of subjugating enslaved Africans and imposed some limits on the circumstances in which slaves were permitted to testify, not least by excluding them from civil cases, they consistently upheld record-keeping requirements.[9]

More than eighty criminal trials involving slaves survive for French colonial Louisiana between 1723 and 1769, when France ceased its occupation of the colony. As a group, these trials preserve the voices of close to 150 enslaved Africans and some Amerindians who testified as defendants, witnesses, and, more rarely, victims. Most of the extant trial records from Louisiana are complete. There are some caveats; the judicial records for the period from 1756 to 1763 are lost, while the number of surviving trial records peaks after 1764.[10]

Louisiana's extant trial documents are just that—legal records of investigations and prosecutions. They represent only a fraction of the times that colonists and slaveowners sought to punish their slaves, which they could do extrajudicially, as Marguerite alluded to when she juxtaposed the endemic, quotidian violence of the in-house beatings with the relative anomaly of a *public* whipping.[11] Furthermore, this archive is a record of the mechanisms used by colonists to control what they deemed to be criminal and transgressive behavior in the context of their notions of social (and racial) order. Yet the very concept of slaves perpetrating criminal acts is a deeply problematic one, raising questions such as how enslaved persons could be guilty of theft, for example, when they themselves were stolen—their time, labor, and even family ties stripped from them. But it was not only those slaves accused of crimes who were brought to court to testify. According to Louisiana's Code Noir of 1724, which set the condition for slave testimony, slaves *had* to testify when accused, but they *could* in some circumstances testify in criminal and civil cases, such as when they were the sole witnesses. There were no constraints against women or children testifying, except when it involved testimony against a husband or parent. Therefore, we find slaves being interrogated because they were suspected of being accomplices or simply because they were privy to relevant information. Still others were brought in as innocent bystanders who had witnessed a crime. A few more testified because they had been victimized. For enslaved women in particular, these interrogatories constitute precious material, since fewer individual women than men were mentioned in records produced in the Atlantic world during the colonial period. In other words, a wide spectrum of enslaved individuals testified when accused, but also as witnesses and as victims. The resulting archive brims with the sound of their voices and their concerns, showcasing a multiplicity of voices even if those voices are fragmentary, their autobiographies patchy, their concerns those of the moment.

Their lives bear writing about, and their lives must be thought about, not least because their own words help us do so. Thanks to the richness of Louisiana's archives, which encompass testimony but also a multitude of other sources that can help us track the biographies of those who testified, the fragments are often enough to bring these lives back to the surface, even when we have only snapshots to work from.

Those snapshots were the result of a joint production: both court procedure and the format of judges' questions imposed a structure on these acts of public speech, necessarily framing the answers that the enslaved could provide. Judicial procedure also permitted coercive methods of interrogation that magnified the power of the court, such as judicial torture (*la question*), which could be triggered in the course of a prosecution though it was rarely invoked in Louisiana before 1764.[12] As in France, justice was rendered, not by juries, but by judges whose deliberations were sealed and never made part of the written record. With this one formal exception, virtually everything else that was said and done during court proceedings was methodically recorded, consistent with the French justice system's reliance on confession as the ultimate proof, which vested enormous importance in the recording of testimony.[13] This premise of French and French colonial judicial law—the accuracy of the trial record—is key: although trials were not devoid of biases both implicit and explicit, the trial record purported to be a truthful rendering of what had taken place and had been said in court. Certainly, court transcripts were selective soundscapes, not records of the whole performance of justice. They did not record defendants' reactions to judgments, such as whether they sat in stony silence, gasped, cried tears, or hurled insults when their sentence was pronounced. They were just as devoid, as Brett Rushforth's essay in this volume demonstrates, of references to interrogators' tone of voice and other nonverbal modes of intimidation. Nor did they make note of the noises produced during judicial torture. Court records omitted these sounds of suffering, just as they omitted descriptions of deponents' gestures, looks, mannerisms, facial expressions, accents, and intonation during their testimonies. These, too, were components of the performative aspects of court procedure, a performance shaped not just by verbal expressions but by sound, by the spatial environment, by sartorial conventions, by gestures, and by the rituals of the court. What testimony does offer is access to a close version of the words spoken, allowing the narratives of enslaved individuals to be uncovered virtually as they themselves spoke them.

The procedure for recording testimony was as follows. During questioning, the clerk of the court "hastily and in abbreviated form" wrote down the proceedings. At the close of the interrogation, this document, known as the plumitif, was read back in court to the deponent and his or her approbation noted—which means that the plumitif was accurate and intelligible enough to be read out, as surviving plumitifs confirm. The clerk then used the plumitif to produce the longhand version that would become the court record. Defendants, witnesses, and victims could be subjected to multiple interrogations, and the clerk repeated the process each and every time.[14]

Interrogatories were conducted in French, and, except where an interpreter was used, officials in Louisiana presumed that the enslaved could understand French since they were likely to be addressed in French (or Creole) throughout their work day. Further, after 1731 virtually all licit traffic in slaves from Africa ceased, meaning that the increase in population was largely due to reproduction, resulting in an increasingly creolized populace born in the colony and familiar with French and Creole.[15] The clerk's role was a crucial one. He did not write down testimony verbatim but usually formalized the French and used the third rather than the first person; no punctuation was included. At the same time, transcriptions consistently captured the words and tone of the speaker.

Given the convention for omitting punctuation, reported dialogue was not formally signaled as such, but it is easy to spot since it was almost always rendered as speech: that is, left in the first person (we, us) with metaphors, turns of phrase, passages in Creole, and other markers of syntax or forms of address intact. For instance, time after time, the clerk documented how colonists systematically used the familiar second person pronoun "tu" (rather than the formal "vous") to address slaves, but that the enslaved just as systematically responded using a more formal and deferential tone, addressing them as "Monsieur" or "Madame" and using the formal pronoun "vous." The clerk might also switch midsentence from formal French to Creole dialogue, as he did when writing down the reported words of the mother of the enslaved Charlot. It bears saying that, like all Creole languages, the Creole found in these archives is not a defective version of French but a rich language with its own vocabulary, rules of syntax, and grammar. This meant that, consistent with other examples of Louisiana creole, Charlot's mother omitted a pronoun, used the male rather than female possessive adjective, and did not conjugate her verb according to the rules of French grammar—yet clearly communicated her meaning when she asked him: "Why [you] turn your shirt [inside out] like that?" (pourquoy tourner ton Chemise Comme Ça?).[16] In hewing so closely to the spoken word and allowing dialogue to slip through, clerks enabled the immediacy and spontaneity of original testimony to be preserved, as it was in these passages, and as the record of Marguerite's testimony and that of so many others makes clear.

If what they said in court was painstakingly recorded, deponents did change their testimony over the course of multiple interrogations and each interrogatory must be contextualized on its own terms. Sometimes a deponent claimed outright to have lied in previous testimony. When Pierrot was asked anew, during a second interrogatory, where he had gotten the cowhide he was accused of stealing, "he said that he had lied previously and that he had taken it from his master." At other times, a change was explained away as a misunderstanding. When twenty-five-year-old Thomas was called out for giving testimony that conflicted with the previous day's interrogation, he "answered that he was telling the truth and that they had misheard what he had said yesterday." Deponents changed their testimony for a variety of reasons, including when they realized they needed to shift defense strategies or when they decided along the way to try to save (or betray) accomplices, as Cécile Vidal shows in her essay. But, in some cases, it could well be a simple act of miscommunication. Thomas had identified himself in court as Bambara, therefore as being born in West Africa. Though he had been brought to Louisiana from Martinique—suggesting he might have already learned some French—it is feasible that he did genuinely have problems understanding and speaking the language. Alternatively, he could have used his linguistic shortcomings (not to mention his accent) to his advantage in court. The point is that the court scribe took great pains to document these instances of altered testimony. In other words, even when testimony changed over the course of multiple interrogations, we can assume that the written record itself is largely reliable and that witnesses did indeed speak a close version of what they were recorded as saying in that interrogation.[17]

Judges and court scribes were assiduous in ensuring that the longhand redaction of the initial transcription was as accurate as possible, down to noting for posterity any errors that were corrected, or passages scratched out. The clerk also tried to mention any issues with the document, as seen in the final paragraph of this 1767 interrogation:

> Which is all that she has admitted knowing, her interrogatory was read back to her, said her answer contained the truth and persisted in this, and declared not knowing how to write nor read, this enquired of her according to the order. The following [changes] were approved: the word 'said' was redone, and one syllable was crossed out above.

Such attention to detail in recording a witness's words was an essential aspect of the process, an almost topsy-turvy judicial process that offered defendants a temporary seat at the table before reasserting the supremacy of the judges. Though clerks of the court necessarily mediated speech when providing a written record of testimony, they aimed for immediacy in transcribing words: the law required it, justice was believed to depend on it, and the records consistently prove it.[18]

The challenge, then, becomes one of interpreting courtroom testimony, a task magnified when testimony is that of enslaved persons.[19] Defendants in Louisiana (whether free or enslaved) had no legal representation, for lawyers were prohibited in the colony as part of an attempt by the crown to curtail litigation in its overseas possessions. Some coaching may have come from owners, since the conviction of a slave was of direct financial consequence for them, and in some cases, the enslaved found ways to coach each other. Yet others kept their own counsel. The young Estienne did so with respect to the elder Marion, an enslaved entrepreneur who leveraged her power over the minions who helped her with her illicit business dealings; according to his testimony, she had "forbidden him from talking about the theft, even to his mother, under threat of not letting him have any corn to eat; she had added that, even should the theft be discovered, it was best to suffer death than to talk about it." Where had Marion acquired this perspective—from observation, from fellow enslaved persons, from her master? In any case, Estienne ignored her command and provided detail after incriminating detail of his thefts on her behalf, but also, more unexpectedly, of the child-parent relationship he had with her.[20]

Testimony was a form of speech, and the familiarity of addressing (and being addressed by) masters and other colonists in a day-to-day context must also have inflected slaves' depositions. Enslaved persons quickly learned how they were expected to behave, including the necessity for verbal and nonverbal deference toward whites. Interpreting the testimony of enslaved Africans also requires us to acknowledge a different type of oral communication, that of storytelling. For the enslaved in Louisiana, Ibrahima Seck suggests, storytelling "eased the pain in their limbs and minds and allowed many to deal with their fate instead of crying or drowning in homesickness. Storytelling was also a means for the oppressed to create fictional situations where the weak could overcome the domination of the powerful," sometimes using humor, including trickster tales. At the same time, differences had to be negotiated. In West and West Central Africa, storytelling was chiefly reserved for the time of day after dusk. For witnesses appearing in court, choosing when to speak was not a luxury, but that was also the case for those subjected to divination rituals and judicial practices in West Africa that likewise required narrating a story. It is inevitable that the conventions of storytelling that developed in Louisiana (as well as their West African antecedents, including their inherent gender dynamics) informed deponents' conceptions of how to perform when asked to narrate their explanations. When Marguerite mimicked her mistress and openly mocked her, was she invoking a long-standing tradition of using humor to outwit an opponent? What other insights can testimony provide about the inner lives of individuals?[21]

Familiarity with West African laws is another piece of the puzzle, for it too could have influenced how deponents in Louisiana responded under questioning. West African judicial practices (including sentencing rules, questioning and divining rituals, and sentences for punishing activities deemed either criminal, immoral, or dangerous to society) might have differed in format, but they were not altogether unfamiliar, not entirely alien from the investigations and interrogations of French colonial courts. Since criminal activity was one mechanism that could lead to captivity and enslavement, it is also conceivable that African-born slaves were personally familiar with these practices, whether they themselves had been subjected to them or simply witnessed them. Knowledge of these judicial procedures, codes of conduct, and sentences were not eclipsed, especially for those born in Africa, and there is evidence that free and enslaved Africans found means to extend their native conceptions and forms of justice to Louisiana, for example, through secret male societies, or when they co-opted the law for their own purposes in handling internal affairs with other slaves or negotiating with owners in matters relating to manumission and sanctioned marriage.[22]

The records show repeatedly that deponents created parallel narratives that did not stay tethered to the investigations at hand and that it was on their own terms, ultimately, that they answered questions. Analyzing speech given in court requires us to recognize that, though deponents could have planned in advance what to say, the act of speaking is first and foremost a spontaneous performance that happens on the fly, shifting course along the way. As such, speech is also impulsive, subject to different rules and imperatives (not least the effect of adrenaline) than written autobiographical narratives, since it happens in the moment. This is especially important given that deponents did not know ahead of time what questions would be asked or what a prosecutor had uncovered in the course of his investigation or while questioning witnesses and suspected accomplices.

Sometimes deponents took the stage with purpose and intent, and sometimes they blurted out things they had not planned to or reacted in some other way in the course of testifying. We see this complicated process at work in other legal regimes. An observer in Suriname described the trial of a convicted runaway slave there who "beg'd only to be heard for a few moments," then proceeded to invoke memories of his honor in battle in Africa and his experience as a slave. His fate was already sealed; his compulsion to speak did not relate directly to the court case or the accusation of running away. Yet he launched into his autobiography, redirecting the narrative toward those selective aspects of his life experiences that were important for him to communicate at that moment in time. The enslaved often saw the occasion to testify, not as an antagonistic ordeal, but as an opportunity for expression. And, sometimes, as Leora Auslander, writing of Parisian Jews after World War II, describes such moments of veering off course, their words became "memory maps," a means of healing psychic wounds, of mourning lives, and of starting "the process of narrativizing loss." Though enslaved individuals were thrust into French colonial courtrooms under vastly different circumstances, they found in the act of testifying motivations other than a single-minded focus on pure self-preservation and it behooves us, in heeding their words and interpreting them, to honor their complexity as sentient and emotional beings.[23]

The work of interpretation rests on knowledge of the archive and of the law, it requires detailed linguistic analysis of the text, and it depends on the meticulous contextualization of the evidence against a broad array of other primary sources. These include slave inventories, probate documents, manumission records, official correspondence, parish registers of slave marriages and baptisms (there are no runaway advertisements of the kind found in British colonies since no newspapers were published in Louisiana during the French regime), as well as material culture, which can be especially valuable in giving contour to the lives of the nonliterate. Such an approach helps flesh out the lives of the enslaved in Louisiana so that their experiences come more clearly into focus. In the same way, the snatches of dialogue, the random colloquialisms and the imagery that seep through testimony are most revealing when they are set back into their larger historical and social contexts. Returning to the trial of Marguerite, we must first understand the built environment of New Orleans before we can grasp how she experienced the cityscape and her place within it. When she offered the simile of being "locked . . . up like in a convent" as one motive for running away to the cabin of her male friend, she had literally just been locked up, but in the town jail. How did that experience affect her choice of comparison, especially given the absence of these institutions in West Africa?

The prison was located on the Place d'armes (present-day Jackson Square), to the right of the Church of Saint Louis when facing the quay (Figure 1.2). It was the first major building constructed of brick without a timber frame, covered in masonry. Two stories high, consisting of two separate buildings linked by a walled-in courtyard for the use of prisoners, it contained communal cells as well as the criminal chamber, where special interrogations "on the sellette," so named for the low stool on which the defendant was made to sit, and interrogations under judicial torture, were carried out and recorded. Regular interrogations took place in the chambers of the Superior Council, which would have required a defendant to be led out of jail and taken under guard around the block.[24]

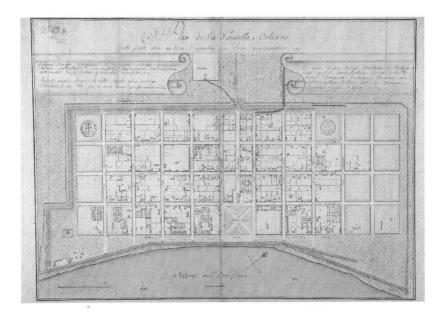

Figure 1.2 *Plan de la Nouvelle Orléans telle qu'elle estoit au mois de dexembre 1731 levé par Gonichon.* FR ANOM 04 DFC 89 B. Courtesy Archives nationales d'outre-mer, Aix-en-Provence, France.

That Marguerite had spent time in prison, however, was just one element of her narrative. She specifically mentioned that it was her master and mistress who had locked her up. Though we do not have information on where their residence was located, the architecture of New Orleans allows us to speculate about her experience. When Adrien de Pauger designed New Orleans in 1722, he laid out the city according to a straight grid anchored by the Place d'armes, with residential lots "of such a size that each and every one may have the houses on the street front and may still have some land in the rear to have a garden, which here is half of life." In other words, the town house lots consisted of dwellings set right on the street with rear courtyards, like the one that Marguerite was made to clear (see, for comparison, Figure 1.3).[25]

Courtyards were utilitarian, containing vegetable gardens for household use and sometimes cabins used as housing for the enslaved (though they also might reside within the house or more likely the kitchen, which was usually separate from the main house because of the risk of fire). Courtyards were also spaces of leisure for the master and mistress of the house. When the elderly Dame Elizabeth Real, Widow Marin, composed her will in 1769, the notary and his attendant had to wait on her at home. They "entered into the hall of the said House in which we have found the

Figure 1.3 Madame John's Legacy. 632 Dumaine Street, New Orleans. Photo courtesy of Philippe Halbert. The ground level was used for commerce and storage, the upper levels were residential, and the rear walled-in courtyard could be accessed either via the house or through the narrow side gate.

said [Dame] Widow Marin, seated between the two courtyard doors in the coolness." After Madame Dufossat beat Marguerite "with a stick, made her work and clear the courtyard, and threatened that if she did not work she would call the slaves to take her to the public square to give her a hundred lashes of the whip," did she, too, like Widow Marin, sit in the shade watching over her slaves? Accessed from the street via narrow side gates, courtyards were generally invisible to passersby, thanks to the high walls that enclosed the properties. Travel accounts emphasized that slaves customarily enjoyed a degree of mobility within the town, but perhaps such statements were hyberbolic. A master who really wanted to control his slaves' access in and out of these sealed-off residences could do so, as Dufossat and his wife seem to have done with Marguerite.[26] It may well have been unusual to do so though, and if it leaked out from the trial that they had been so stringent in locking her away, perhaps the town's rumormongers might have wondered why. As a result, the Dufossat couple might have felt pressured to change their ways, or been content to become the fodder for gossip, either way, amplifying Marguerite's message of disapprobation.

Why *did* they restrict her access quite so strictly, and were they more stringent than was broadly customary in New Orleans, or more so than what Marguerite might have anticipated? She was of childbearing age and perhaps they saw her as a short-term investment, one whose labor they did not want to see disrupted by pregnancy. Maybe she had made a habit of running away before—she did, after all, know how to make it all the way to Janot's plantation without being caught en route, though court officials did not probe whether he had assisted her in her journey. Or perhaps her master had other reasons to keep her at his beck and call under his roof all night, nefarious motives that his wife would have undoubtedly resented Marguerite for. Whether or not she was fleeing from sexual assault at the hands of her master (and the reference to the cloistered convent tempers such an interpretation in this particular case, especially in light of the fact that she blamed both her masters for locking her up), it is clear that Marguerite objected to being confined so regularly at night and that she actively desired the relative peace and the pleasures she derived from being in Janot's company.[27]

To plumb how Marguerite grasped the concept of cloistering ("locked up" like "in a convent"), particularly given that she identified herself as "of the Congo nation," we also need one final piece of the puzzle—that there was an Ursuline convent right in New Orleans, the buildings visible, the nuns closed off, covered from head to toe (Figures 1.4 and 1.5). In fact, the daughter of Marguerite's masters, Françoise Dufossat, would enter that very convent just nine years later to become a nun, suggesting that the household was a devout one that would have very likely sent Marguerite to the Ursulines for religious instruction as was customary in New Orleans. Approximately twenty-five years old in 1764, Marguerite could not have come to Louisiana on any known or sanctioned slave ships from the Congo (the only slave ship documented to have done so was in 1721). But there were other ways, licit and illicit, for a colonist in Louisiana (such as Dufossat, a Marine captain) to import enslaved individuals, especially through trade with the French islands. Given that Marguerite had enough command of French not to need a court interpreter, she was likely not new to the French colonies but brought in from the islands. Though the ethnonym Congo was ambiguous in terms of her actual origin in West Central Africa, it is possible that it was there that she first encountered Christian concepts and imagery given that its rulers had converted to Christianity. Yet there were no female convents in the kingdom of Kongo, meaning that it was in the New World that Marguerite initially encountered this institution and first saw nuns. If she had come via Martinique, and specifically Saint-Pierre, she might have seen the convent there, which was the only one in the French Antilles. More likely, her earliest glimpse of nuns living in a cloister was in New Orleans.[28]

Figure 1.4 Ursuline Convent. 1100 Chartres Street, New Orleans. Photo courtesy of Philippe Halbert.

This understanding of Marguerite's probable origins and the presence of an Ursuline convent in New Orleans helps us interpret her narrative and understand what it meant when, seizing the opportunity to voice her outrage, she expressed herself using this simile referencing the convent. In her interpretation, it was a comparison that evoked imprisonment but also a lack of access to men. It was an image that clearly resonated with Marguerite, who had certainly been to the New Orleans convent and who had the desire and wherewithal to escape that fate, even if temporarily, by running away from the urban center of New Orleans downriver to the cabin of a male companion.

And space for her was not abstract; it held meaning physically, culturally, and emotionally. Marguerite juxtaposed the convent-like confinement she felt at her masters' residence with the release of running away

Figure 1.5 Soeur Converse Ursuline de la Congrégation de Paris. From Pierre
Hélyot, *Histoire des ordres monastiques ...*, IV (Paris, 1715), x.
Wellcome Library, London. Credit: Wellcome Collection. CC BY.

to be with Janot at his plantation, though that space would not prove
safe to her since it was where she was captured. Her running away, her
insolence in mocking her mistress, and her sharp observations about
the incongruities of French (Catholic) society all point collectively to
the way she perceived *her* place in this world, and how she sought to
negotiate its horrors. It was not so much the fact of her enslavement
that she emphasized, though that too hung in the air. Instead, her words
illuminate, above all, the chasm between how her masters treated her
and how she herself wanted, dared expect, to be treated.

The archives do not reveal what happened to Marguerite beyond this court case, but if her testimony does not offer information about her future, it does offer tantalizing glimpses of her in that present moment, and it hints even at her past. Other enslaved individuals brought to bear their own frames of reference, their own motives, and their own ways of expressing themselves, based on their worldviews about the places, and roles, they inhabited. What is remarkable in Louisiana is that it is their own words that give us access to such insights.

Acknowledgments

Parts of this chapter are adapted from *Voices of the Enslaved: Love, Labor, and Longing in French Louisiana* by Sophie White. Copyright © 2019 by the Omohundro Institute of Early American History and Culture. Used by permission of the University of North Carolina Press. www.uncpress.org

Notes

1 Records of the Superior Council of Louisiana, (1717–1769), Louisiana Historical Center, Louisiana State Museum, New Orleans, hereafter RSCL, 1764/10/23/01 (year/month/day/sequence).

2 On the mobility of the enslaved in New Orleans, including the more common practice of enslaved men coming to urban New Orleans from the outlying plantations, see Sophie White, *Voices of the Enslaved: Love, Labor, and Longing in French Louisiana* (Chapel Hill: University of North Carolina Press, 2019), chap. 4; Cécile Vidal, *Caribbean New Orleans: Empire, Race, and the Making of a Slave Society* (Chapel Hill: University of North Carolina Press, 2019), chap. 2.

3 Sentences for *marronnage* (running away) were mandatory only for those who had absconded for longer than a month, which was not the case here, see Code Noir, March 1724, III 2852.23, Louisiana Historical Center, Louisiana State Museum, New Orleans, Article 32; RSCL 1764/11/03/01. For Dufossat's wife, see Emily Clark, *Masterless Mistresses: The New Orleans Ursulines and the Development of a New World Society, 1727–1834* (Chapel Hill: University of North Carolina Press, 2007), 128.

4 RSCL 1764/10/23/01, 1. On Dubreuil's father, Claude Joseph Villars Dubreuil, see Henry P. Dart, "The Career of Dubreuil in French Louisiana," *Louisiana Historical Quarterly*, 18, 2 (1935), 267. A "young negro named Jean" (Janot is a shortened version of the name) was purchased in 1758 by the younger Dubreuil from his father's estate for 3,050 livres (*ibid.*, 318). On Catholicism in the kingdom of Kongo, see Cécile Fromont, *The Art of Conversion: Christian Visual Culture in the Kingdom of Kongo* (Chapel Hill: University of North Carolina Press, 2014).

5 For an introduction to understanding the slave experience in West Africa with a focus on how to articulate slave voices, see Martin Klein, "Understanding the Slave Experience in West Africa," in Lisa A. Lindsay and John Wood Sweet, eds., *Biography and the Black Atlantic* (Philadelphia: University of Pennsylvania Press, 2014), 48–65.

6 Interrogation of Estienne, July 1757, Natchitoches Parish Conveyance Record Book 1: 1738–1765, 1757/7, no. 186, Natchitoches Parish Archives,

Natchitoches, Louisiana, microfilm, Family History Library of the Church of Jesus Christ of Latter Day Saints, Salt Lake City; RSCL 1744/03/12/01, 10.

7 On the challenges of producing slave biographies, see also Lindsay and Sweet, eds., *Biography and the Black Atlantic* (Philadelphia: University of Pennsylvania Press, 2013); Jeffrey A. Fortin and Mark Meuwese, eds., *Atlantic Biographies: Individuals and Peoples in the Atlantic World* (Leiden, Netherlands: Brill, 2014), Part 2; Sue Peabody, "Microhistory, Biography, Fiction: The Politics of Narrating the Lives of People under Slavery," *Transatlantica*, 2 (2012), n. p.; and the papers presented at the symposium on "Voices in the Legal Archives in the French Atlantic," organized by Nancy Christie, Michael Gauvreau, and Clare Haru Crowston held May 28–30, 2018, in North Hatley, QC. See also the series overseen by Marie-Jeanne Rossignol and Claire Parfait, which has consciously sought to bring together both "canonical" nineteenth-century published slave narratives and examples of slave voices from courtroom testimony, www.cairn.info/revue-francaise-d-etudes-americaines-2017-2-page-51.htm?contenu=resume; and Nicole N. Aljoe, "'Going to Law': Legal Discourse and Testimony in Early West Indian Slave Narratives," *Early American Literature*, 46, 2 (2011), 351–381. For the twentieth century, there is rich source material showcasing the voices of former slaves. See the transcriptions of interviews produced by the Federal Writers' Project in the 1930s, "Born in Slavery: Slave Narratives from the Federal Writers' Project, 1936 to 1938," *Library of Congress*, www.loc.gov/collections/slave-narratives-from-the-federal-writers-project-1936-to-1938/about-this-collection/ (accessed Aug. 24, 2018); and Zora Neale Hurston, *Barracoon: The Story of the Last "Black Cargo,"* ed., Deborah G. Plant (New York: Amistad, 2018).

8 Annette Gordon-Reed, "Slavery's Shadow," *New Yorker*, Oct. 23, 2013, www.newyorker.com/culture/culture-desk/slaverys-shadow (accessed Oct. 31, 2017). On slaves' access to literacy, see Sue Peabody, "'A Dangerous Zeal': Catholic Missions to Slaves in the French Antilles, 1635–1800," *French Historical Studies*, 25, 1 (2002), 56n. For a rare exception from Louisiana where one master wanted his slave Doucet, a young African man apprenticed to a cobbler, to receive instruction in how to read and write in the first two years, then taught the cobbler's trade, see RSCL 1741/08/09/01, 1741/09/02/02. On La Nuit, a favored slave of Jean-Charles de Pradel who was literate, see A. Baillardel and A. Prioult, eds., *Le chevalier de Pradel: Vie d'un colon français en Louisiane au XVIIIe siècle d'après sa correspondance et celle de sa famille* (Paris: Maisonneuve frères, 1928), 361. The literature on Anglo-American autobiographical narratives is vast; for a French perspective on these sources, see Michaël Roy, *Textes fugitifs: Le récit d'esclave au prisme de l'histoire du livre* (Lyon: ENS Éditions, 2017); and Marie-Jeanne Rossignol and Claire Parfait's series of works on slave narratives, www.cairn.info/revue-francaise-d-etudes-americaines-2017-2-page-51.htm?contenu=resume. On critiques of the dominance of the slave narrative as a peculiarly Anglo-American autobiographical genre, see Sue Peabody, *Madeleine's Children: Family, Freedom, Secrets, and Lies in France's Indian Ocean Colonies* (Oxford: Oxford University Press, 2017), 3–4; and Deborah Jenson, *Beyond the Slave Narrative: Politics, Sex, and Manuscripts in the Haitian Revolution* (Liverpool: Liverpool University Press, 2011).

9 On French law pertaining to testimony in France and her colonies, see Eric Wenzel, *La justice criminelle en Nouvelle-France (1670–1760): Le Grand Arrangement* (Dijon: Editions universitaires de Dijon, 2012), 91 (quotation); André Morel, "Réflexions sur la justice criminelle canadienne au 18e siècle," *Revue de l'histoire de l'Amérique française*, 29, 2 (1975), 242; and Jan Grabowski, "French Criminal Justice and Indians in Montreal, 1670–1760,"

Ethnohistory, 43, 3 (1996), 405–429. On French criminal law, see also Richard Mowery Andrews, *Law, Magistracy, and Crime in Old Regime Paris* (Cambridge: Cambridge University Press, 1994), Vol. I and François Serpillon, *Code criminel, ou commentaire sur l'ordonnance de 1670 ...*, 4 vols. (Lyon: Chez les Freres Perisse, 1767). There was no such consistency in English colonies. Slaves and free persons of color in colonial Virginia, for instance, were not allowed to testify in court (trials against slaves for capital crimes being the only exception). See Philip J. Schwarz, *Twice Condemned: Slaves and the Criminal Laws of Virginia, 1705–1865* (Baton Rouge: Louisiana State University Press, 1988), 19. Slaves in the English Caribbean, on the other hand, could testify, but only for or against other slaves, not for or against free persons. See Natalie Zacek, "Voices and Silences: The Problem of Slave Testimony in the English West Indian Law Court," *Slavery and Abolition*, 24, 3 (December 2003), 24–39, esp. 25. There were published accounts of trials, usually laced with preambles, asides, embellishments, and critical commentaries primarily aimed at entertaining or persuading the public; see Paul Finkelman, *Slavery in the Courtroom: An Annotated Bibliography of American Cases* (Union, NJ: The Lawbook Exchange, 1998), 21–22; Clive Emsley, Tim Hitchcock, and Robert Shoemaker, "The Proceedings—Publishing History of the Proceedings," Old Bailey Proceedings Online (www.oldbaileyonline.org, version 7.0, accessed Aug. 10, 2018).

10 On the records of the Superior Council of Louisiana from the French regime and the records of the Cabildo from the Spanish regime, held together in one archive (which includes the court records in which the enslaved testified), see Greg Lambousy and Emily Clark, eds., special issue on "Atlantic World Archives of Louisiana," *Collections: A Journal for Museum and Archives Professionals*, 11, 3 (2015). On the French records, see, in particular, Sophie White, "Notes from the Field: Lured in by the Archives," *ibid.*, 167–170.

11 On quotidian violence against the enslaved in Louisiana, see also Vidal, *Caribbean New Orleans*, 183–186.

12 On the rules regarding judicial torture in Louisiana, and the types of interrogation allowed under torture, see White, *Voices of the Enslaved*, chap. 1; Thomas N. Ingersoll, "The Law and Order Campaign in New Orleans, 1763–1765: A Comparative View," in Sally E. Hadden and Patricia Hagler Minter, eds., *Signposts: New Directions in Southern Legal History* (Athens: University of Georgia Press, 2013), 45–64.

13 Titre VI, Article 9, in Serpillon, *Code criminel ou commentaire sur l'ordonnance de 1670*, I, 478, and Titre XXIV, Article 3, III, 994; Letters patent for the establishment of a Superior Council of Louisiana, Dec. 23, 1712, Archives nationales d'outre-mer, Aix-en-Provence, France, hereafter ANOM, Ser. A22, fol. 11v–12r.

14 Title VI, Article 9, in Serpillon, *Code criminel*, I, 478. On the plumitif, see Antoine Furetière, *Dictionnaire universel contenat generalement tous les mots François, tant vieux que modernes, et les termes des sciences et des arts: Divisés en trois tomes*, 2d ed., III (The Hague, 1727), s.v. "plumitif." On the process of turning a plumitif into a register, see also Fréderéric-Antoine Raymond, "L'Ecriture au service de la communauté: Histoire des registres de délibérations de la communauté des procureurs au parlement de Toulouse (1693–1781)" (Master's thesis, Université Laval, 2005), 48–53, 76–77. Plumitifs rarely survive; for one example from 1578 to 1605, see Yves Metman, ed., *Le Registre ou plumitif de la construction du Pont Neuf (Archives nationales Z1f 1065)* (Paris: Comité d'Histoire de la ville de Paris, 1987). On the broader question of the importance of bureaucrats in Louisiana and how they were trained, see Alexandre Dubé, "Making a Career Out of the Atlantic: Louisiana's Plume," in Cécile Vidal, ed., *Louisiana:*

Crossroads of the Atlantic World (Philadelphia: University of Pennsylvania Press, 2014), 44–67.

15 Gwendolyn Midlo Hall, *Africans in Colonial Louisiana: The Development of Afro-Creole Culture in the Eighteenth Century* (Baton Rouge: Louisiana State University Press, 1992), Appendix A, "Basic Facts About All Slave-Trade Voyages from Africa to Louisiana during the French Regime," 382–397; Philip D. Curtin, *The Atlantic Slave Trade: A Census* (Madison: University of Wisconsin Press, 1969), 163–202.

16 For example, RSCL 1744/04/24/01; 1748/01/06/01, 4; 1744/03/13/01, 7; Kaskaskia Manuscripts, Randolph County Courthouse, Chester, IL, 48:7:16:2, 1. See also White, *Voices of the Enslaved*, 74–77. RSCL 1748/01/06/01, 5. On the lack of punctuation in court records, see Arlette Farge, *The Allure of the Archives*, trans., Thomas Scott-Railton (New Haven, CT: Yale University Press 2013), 3. On Louisiana creole, see Luc V. Baronian, "Au carrefour des Amériques françaises: Enquête sur les sources linguistiques du français louisianais," in Jean-Pierre Le Glaunec and Natalie Dessens, eds., *Interculturalité: La Louisiane au carrefour des cultures* (Laval: Presses Universitaires de Laval, 2016), 295–318; Baronian, "Une influence probable du créole louisianais sur le français cadien," *La linguistique*, 41, 1 (2005), 133–140.

17 RSCL 1764/01/04/01; 1752/03/27/02, 3. For a rich interpretation of the matter of changes in testimony over the course of a trial, see Cécile Vidal's essay in this volume. On the ethnonym Bambara (shorthand for non-Muslim), see Peter Caron, "'Of a Nation Which the Others Do Not Understand': Bambara Slaves and African Ethnicity in Colonial Louisiana, 1718–60," *Slavery and Abolition*, 28, 1 (1997), 98–121.

18 RSCL 1767/06/10/02.

19 On interpreting testimony in French colonies, see Dominique Rogers, ed., *Voix d'esclaves, Antilles, Guyane et Louisiane françaises, XVIIIe–XIXe siècles* (Paris: Karthala, 2015); Brett Rushforth, "The Gauolet Uprising of 1710: Maroons, Rebels, and the Informal Exchange Economy of a Caribbean Sugar Island," *William and Mary Quarterly* 76, 1 (2019), 75–110 and the relevant essays in this volume; see also Arlette Farge, *Allure of the Archives*, trans., Scott-Railton and the papers presented at the symposium on "Voices in the Legal Archives in the French Atlantic," organized by Nancy Christie, Michael Gauvreau, and Clare Haru Crowston held May 28–30, 2018, in North Hatley, QC.

20 Sophie White, "Marion, Eighteenth-Century French Louisiana," in Erica L. Ball, Tatiana Seijas, and Terri L. Snyder, eds., *Women in the African Diaspora: A Collective Biography of Emancipation in the Americas* (Cambridge: Cambridge University Press, 2020); Interrogation of Estienne, July 1757, Natchitoches Parish Conveyance Record Book 1: 1738–1765, 1757/7, no. 186, NP.

21 Ibrahima Seck, *Bouki Fait Gombo: A History of the Slave Community of Habitation Haydel (Whitney Plantation) Louisiana, 1750–1860* (New Orleans: University of New Orleans, 2014), 129–139 (quotation, 129–130). See also Alcée Fortier, *Louisiana Folk-tales in French Dialect and English Translation* (Boston, MA: American Folklore Society, 1895).

22 See White, *Voices of the Enslaved*, chaps. 4 and 5. For knowledge of West African judicial practices persisting in the colonies, see Emily Clark's book project "Noel Carriere's Liberty: From Slave to Soldier in Colonial New Orleans"; and Clark, "Noel Carriere, the Commander of the Free Black Militia, Deserves a Monument in New Orleans," *The Advocate*, New Orleans, LA,, July 8, 2015, www.theadvocate.com/baton_rouge/opinion/our_views/article_e3548cc4-6fb8-5837-8e5f-fe3128de4643.html (accessed Aug. 23,

2018). With reference to the Kongo in Saint Domingue, see John K. Thornton, "'I Am the Subject of the King of Congo': African Political Ideology and the Haitian Revolution," *Journal of World History,* IV (1993), 181–214, esp. 199–201. For specific examples of judicial procedures, see Paul E. Lovejoy, *Transformations in Slavery: A History of Slavery in Africa,* 2nd ed. (Cambridge: Cambridge University Press, 2000), 3–4; Boubacar Barry, *The Kingdom of Waalo: Senegal before the Conquest* (New York: Diasporic Africa Press, 2012), 48; and Robert M. Baum, *Shrines of the Slave Trade: Diola Religion and Society in Precolonial Senegambia* (New York: Oxford University Press, 1999), 53. Natalie Zacek points out how "a number of legal anthropologists have claimed that 'people who are relatively powerless in their relationships with others find courts to be powerful allies'" (Zacek, "Voices and Silences," *Slavery and Abolition,* 24, 3 (2003), 36. See also Mindie Lazarus-Black, "Slaves, Masters, and Magistrates: Law and the Politics of Resistance in the British Caribbean, 1736–1834," in Mindie Lazarus-Black and Susan F. Hirsch, eds., *Contested States: Law, Hegemony, and Resistance* (New York: Routledge, 1994), 267 and Trevor Burnard, *Hearing Slaves Speak* (Georgetown: Caribbean Press, 2010), http://caribbeanpress.org/caribbean-press-downloads/ (accessed May 7, 2019).

23 John Gabriel Stedman, *Narrative of a Five Years Expedition against the Revolted Negroes of Surinam,* eds., Richard and Sally Price (Baltimore, MD: Johns Hopkins University Press, 1988), 480–482, quoted in Davis, "Judges, Masters, Diviners," *Law and History Review,* 29, 4 (2011), 926–927. During interviews for her research, Zora Neale Hurston experienced a case of veering off script similar to that of the testimony of the runaway slave from Suriname; see Hurston, *Barracoon,* ed., Plant, 20–21. For the case study of Parisian Jews after Second World War, see Leora Auslander, "Beyond Words" *American Historical Review,* 110, 4 (2005), 1015–1045, esp. 1043.

24 Natalie Zemon Davis points out that "on the whole among the African polities, structures of incarceration for criminals were not built until the nineteenth century. Persons accused of crimes were kept from running away by their families in their compounds" (Davis, "Judges, Masters, Diviners," 937). On New Orleans's penal spaces, see Rashauna Johnson, *Slavery's Metropolis: Unfree Labor in New Orleans during the Age of Revolutions* (Cambridge: Cambridge University Press, 2016), chap. 4. On the New Orleans prison building, see Samuel Wilson, Jr., "La Nouvelle Orléans: Le Vieux Carré," in Jean M. Farnsworth and Ann M. Masson, eds., *The Architecture of Colonial Louisiana: Collected Essays of Samuel Wilson, Jr., F.A.I.A.* (Lafayette: University of Southwestern Louisiana, University of Alabama Press, 1987), 331–332. The building stood until 1769, when it was replaced by the first Cabildo building. Its foundations still lie beneath the Cabildo. See Jill-Karen Yakubik, Herschel A. Franks et al., "Archaeology at the Cabildo," Louisiana State Museum, www.crt.state.la.us/Assets/Museum/publications/Archaeology_At_The_Cabildo.pdf (accessed Oct. 12, 2018).

25 Adrien de Pauger to Le Blond de La Tour, Apr. 14, 1721, ANOM, Cartes et Plans, LXVII, no. 5, fol. 135, pièce 13, quoted in Shannon Lee Dawdy, "La Ville Sauvage: 'Enlightened' Colonialism and Creole Improvisation in New Orleans, 1699–1769" (Ph.D. diss., University of Michigan, 2003), 70–71. On the architecture of New Orleans, see Gilles-Antoine Langlois, "French Architect-Engineers of New Orleans, 1718–1730," in Erin Greenwald, ed., *New Orleans: The Founding Era (Charlottesville: University of Virginia Press, 2018),* 58–68; and Dawdy, "Madame John's Legacy (16OR51) Revisited: A Closer Look at the Archaeology of Colonial New Orleans,"

typescript, Greater New Orleans Archaeology Program, College of Urban and Public Affairs, University of New Orleans, 1998. See also Vidal, *Caribbean New Orleans*, esp. chap. 4.

26 RSCL 1769/04/27/02, quoted in Dawdy, "Madame John's Legacy," 36. For eyewitness accounts professing to have observed the too-free movement of slaves, see Samuel Wilson, "Architecture of the Vieux Carré: French Colonial Period, 1718–1768," in Farnsworth and Masson, eds., *Architecture of Colonial Louisiana*, 326–329, Wilson, "La Nouvelle Orléans: Le Vieux Carré," 330–335; and Dawdy, "Ethnicity in the Urban Landscape," 137–143.

27 On the importance of courtship, love, and committing to both short- and long-term affective and romantic relationships, see White, *Voices of the Enslaved*, chaps. 4 and 5.

28 On the Ursuline convent, see Clark, *Masterless Mistresses,* 128–129 (on Françoise Dufossat), 150–156; and Samuel Wilson, Jr., "An Architectural History of the Royal Hospital and the Ursuline Convent of New Orleans," in Farnsworth and Masson, eds., *Architecture of Colonial Louisiana,* 161–220. For an example of African-born slaves arriving in Louisiana via the islands, see the particularly well-documented case concerning the ship *La Roue de Fortune*. It docked in Martinique in 1765 with sixteen slaves (including two children) to be sold in Louisiana, many of whom were African-born, including four who identified as Congo or from Angola. The Superior Council interrogated the slaves but, predictably, given the demand for slaves in the colony, decided to permit the sale in spite of some clear irregularities. See RSCL 1765/11/12/03, 1765/11/13/01, 1765/11/16/04, 1765/12/04/01, 1765/12/06/02. On the challenges in interpreting the self-identification of African nations in Louisiana records, see, for example, Hall, *Africans in Colonial Louisiana;* Caron, "'Of a Nation Which the Others Do Not Understand,'" *Slavery and Abolition,* XVIII (1997), 98–121; and Jean-Pierre Le Glaunec, "'Un nègre nommè [sic] Lubin ne connaissant pas Sa Nation'": The Small World of Louisiana Slavery," in Vidal, ed., *Louisiana,* 103–122. On Catholicism in the kingdom of Kongo, see Fromont, *Art of Conversion.* See also Linda M. Heywood and John K. Thornton, *Central Africans, Atlantic Creoles, and the Foundation of the Americas, 1585–1660* (Cambridge: Cambridge University Press, 2007). On convents in the French Atlantic world, see Heidi Keller-Lapp, "Floating Cloisters and Heroic Women: French Ursuline Missionaries, 1639–1744," *World History Connected,* IV, 3 (2007) (accessed June 20, 2014), n. p. See also Sue Peabody, "'A Dangerous Zeal.'"

2   Fictions in the Archives

Jupiter alias Gamelle or the Tales of an Enslaved Peddler in the French New Orleans Court

Cécile Vidal

In the historiography of slavery, slave narratives refer to various kinds of testimonies given by men and women who had experienced slavery firsthand. The main focus was originally on biographies and autobiographies of former slaves published in British colonies or the United States in the eighteenth and nineteenth centuries and on interviews gathered by the Federal Writers' Project under the supervision of the Works Progress Administration in the United States in the 1930s.[1] The use of these slave testimonies from the 1960s and the 1970s decisively shaped slave studies and transformed the way slavery was viewed and interpreted on the basis of the paradigm of slaves' agency and resistance.[2] With the development of an Atlantic, hemispheric, and global history of slavery from the 1990s, the search for slave voices has been extended to other regions of the Americas and to other continents.[3] In the case of French American slave societies, historians cannot rely on the same primary sources as historians of British colonies and the United States. To offset this lack of reliable sources, they have over the last decades started to resort increasingly to slaves' interrogatories and testimonies kept in court records.[4]

One can wonder, however, if it is heuristically pertinent to include these documents within the category of slave narratives as they were produced with a different objective than slave autobiographies and interviews. They were not meant to reflect or collect slaves' personal visions and understandings of their experiences and lives retrospectively, once they had escaped from slavery. Even so, it does not mean that court records did not convey slave voices and stories, albeit in very different circumstances. To analyze the singular narrative quality of judicial interrogatories and testimonies, one needs to place these primary sources within a broader reflection about the production and forms taken by all kinds of judicial archives whether they concerned slaves or other categories of defendants.

In 1987, Natalie Zemon Davis published *Fictions in the Archives: Pardon Tales and their Tellers in Sixteenth Century France*.[5] She demonstrated how letters of remission narrated to royal notaries by admitted offenders in order to obtain pardon from the king took the form of carefully crafted stories. The analysis of their narrative techniques revealed the way crimes were interpreted and justified in the French kingdom, especially by people of the lower sorts. Drawing on this path-breaking study, this essay examines the fictional dimension of slaves' interrogatories and testimonies before the Superior Council of Louisiana in French New Orleans. Davis chose to focus on letters of remission rather than on judicial interrogatories because those she found for the sixteenth century did not let defendants express themselves at great length. In contrast, slaves who were tried or heard as witnesses in front of the Superior Council in French New Orleans were able to talk without being interrupted immediately. They carefully crafted stories in order to defend themselves and to convince judges to exonerate them. While Davis analyzed the sociopolitical significance of such narratives through the exploitation of a series of letters of remission, this essay is centered on a single trial which comprises several narratives, that of the enslaved defendant but also of other actors.

This suit concerns Louis Jupiter (or Jupiter Louis) alias Gamelle, a twenty-five-year-old slave of the Cerer/Sereer nation who belonged to Jean-Charles de Pradel and was accused of running away and theft by breaking and entering in 1744.[6] His master came as an ensign to the Mississippi colony in 1714, served the king for more than twenty years in various outposts, and climbed the military ranks, becoming a captain in 1720 before retiring in New Orleans in 1735. The following year, the former officer acquired a plantation in the vicinity of the Louisiana capital. Historians are familiar with Pradel because he left the only extant private correspondence from a Louisiana planter.[7] In his letters to his family residing in France, he wrote about the management of his plantation, but hardly mentioned any slave by name except for St. Louis alias La Nuit (The Night). Pradel and St. Louis maintained a complex relationship of proximity that allowed the privileged slave to obtain his freedom. Yet, except for some information included in the sacramental records, notarial archives, and documentation on the free colored militia, all we know about St. Louis comes from the words of his owner and other members of the Pradel family.[8]

In contrast, in his letters, Pradel never mentioned Jupiter who also served him as a peddler. Furthermore, during Jupiter's trial, Pradel was never heard as a witness while he played an ambiguous role in Jupiter's arrest. He only appeared once in front of the clerk, several days after the crime, to make a formal declaration that his slave was a runaway, and serve notice that he had had him arrested and abandoned to the court. Whereas for St. Louis alias La Nuit we are left with the words of the master and the silence of the slave, it is the reverse situation with Jupiter. We lack Pradel's view on the latter even though Jupiter reported some of his owner's alleged words. However, in addition to the defendant's multiple and long interrogatories, the suit includes the interrogatories of four other slaves who were suspected of having helped Jupiter in different ways, and the testimonies of sixteen whites who watched him flee and tried to arrest him after the burglary, or were engaged in commercial exchanges with him. Some of these whites' testimonies were taken during a second investigation after Jupiter's trial, that sought to determine whether Pradel owed financial reparations for his slave's wrongdoings as a huckster. The Council decided to grant the 2,000 *livres* of Jupiter's evaluation to three city dwellers in compensation for what had been stolen from them.

This series of judicial interrogatories and testimonies offers a window into the various social worlds in which Jupiter lived as well as into his mental world. Before analyzing the documentation produced by Jupiter's trial, his own interrogatories in particular, it is necessary to present more broadly the Records of the Superior Council of Louisiana to which Jupiter's case belongs and discuss the problems raised by the use of this kind of primary source. Probing Jupiter's case, the essay then shows how court records can be exploited fruitfully in various ways despite their biases. Historians can piece together multiple layers of microevidence unintentionally scattered in the interrogatories and testimonies and reconstruct the narratives of slaves' life stories through their own experience. They can also analyze the narratives intentionally developed by enslaved defendants to defend themselves in front of judges.

Located in the Louisiana State Museum in New Orleans, the Records of the Superior Council of Louisiana comprise thousands of legal, administrative, notarial, and judicial documents. A large number concerns civil and criminal law suits. The Superior Council was established temporarily in 1712 and permanently in 1716. It functioned as high court of first instance for New Orleans and its region and as high court of final appeal for the entire colony.[9] From 1731 to 1769 when Louisiana was ruled directly by the king, apart from the theoretical membership of the general governor and *intendant* of New France, the Council included the provincial governor, the *commissaire-ordonnateur*, the *lieutenant de roi*, the New Orleans *major*, five other councilors, an attorney general, and a clerk.[10] Both the governor and the *commissaire-ordonnateur* had the title of first councilor, but the role of the governor was mostly honorific and it was the *commissaire-ordonnateur* who acted as first judge and presided over the council. The number and power of the sword and pen officers balanced that of the five other councilors who were chosen among the local elite.[11] Like the *commissaire-ordonnateur*, these councilors had no legal training. Contrary to the situation in France, these judicial offices could not be purchased and were not hereditary; they came with annual wages. Instead, the king commissioned councilors, whose names had been suggested by colonial officials, for an unspecified period of time. As these commissions were few in number and hard to obtain, the process of nomination and the possibility of dismissal put the councilors in a situation of vulnerability and dependency towards the central power and local authorities. The Crown used these commissions to cultivate the loyalty of the colonial elite.

The Superior Council prosecuted people of all statuses, free and enslaved. Separate slave courts were never created in French colonies, as in Spanish and Portuguese ones, whereas a dual system of criminal justice was established in most British slave colonies.[12] Soldiers, however, were tried before a military court. The collection is incomplete, but, apart from dozens of declarations and requests which were apparently not followed by an investigation and prosecution and were probably settled by private agreement out of court, around two hundred civil or criminal suits over insults, assault, murder, theft, running away, desertion, and revolt have survived the ravages of time. Half of them concerned slaves and slavery. Each suit included several documents: sometimes declarations or requests written by plaintiffs (or someone else in their name) but mostly the orders to investigate a case given by the attorney general, interrogatories, testimonies, confrontations between defendants and witnesses, summing-up for the prosecution, and sentences.[13]

The individuals who were tried or appeared as witnesses belonged to all social categories, including slaves of African and Native American descent, free people of color and whites of the lower sort. In practice, plantation slaves of African ancestry quickly became the prime target of royal justice; urban slaves, in contrast, were rarely prosecuted. Enslaved men were also much more frequently tried than women. Although legal ordinances and judicial practice deprived many categories of the ability to testify in criminal trials, the social identities of witnesses were more diverse, and this fact partially compensates for the race, gender and class imbalance among defendants. In the metropole, over the eighteenth century, judges increasingly had the freedom to decide whether testimony could be received despite the legal incapacity of the witness as a relative, woman, convict, lunatic, and so on.[14] Likewise, despite the *Code Noir*'s prohibition—according to article 24 the enslaved could not serve as witnesses except in cases of necessity and if there were no white witnesses; they were also always forbidden to testify against their masters—some slaves appeared as witnesses in trials not only of other people of African or Native American descent but also of whites.

The judicial procedure was inquisitorial and secretive, and hearings were not public. The investigation (the "*information*") was left to one magistrate who questioned the defendant and witnesses in private. The whole council only gathered once the investigation was over for the prosecution case, the deliberations, and the sentence. The occasional recourse to judicial torture also implied the presence of all members of the Superior Council. The hearings in front of the judge in charge of the case were recorded by a scribe. In interrogation after interrogation, testimony after testimony, one can sense variations in the way the clerk transcribed the words of the defendants and witnesses—or, occasionally, of the interpreters—but it is impossible to identify the nature and to quantify the level of distortion and translation except for the use of indirect discourse most of the time—direct sentences or speeches were at times recorded. What is certain is that while not everyone shared the same ability to tell stories and to adapt their level of language to the judicial circumstances, especially when French was not their native language, most recorded statements were made intelligible. The clerk only occasionally transcribed incorrect grammatical sentences in direct speech.

The content of the interrogatories was oriented by the questions that were asked and that were prepared in advance.[15] They aimed at proving the guilt of the defendant, finding accomplices, and establishing aggravating or mitigating circumstances, for *ancien régime* justice was based on the arbitrary power of magistrates. Yet the judges let the defendants reply freely and at great length, and the latter told many more stories than what strictly concerned the offence or crime itself. Their responses were, nevertheless, also shaped by the issues at stake. Slaves risked terrible corporal punishment and even the death penalty. They were sometimes subjected to preparatory questioning (torture imposed before the final sentence in order to elicit the defendant's confession) or preliminary questioning (torture applied before the execution of the sentence to obtain the confession of other crimes or the denunciation of accomplices). Fear and the need to defend oneself could trigger omissions, distortions, or lies, but it could also lead defendants to say much more than they needed to. Moreover, explanations had to appear plausible. What men and women summoned in court thought could convince a judge is as much of interest for the historian as what really happened. The interrogatories and testimonies reflect norms public authorities wanted to impose, but they also reveal, through the stories the defendants and witnesses told and the manners they employed to express themselves, the representations, beliefs, and values of the speakers. Problematic as the use of these court records may be, they are also so fantastically rich that they cannot be easily dismissed.[16]

As Jupiter's trial exemplifies, slaves' interrogatories and testimonies are indeed so valuable that it is possible to profit from them in various ways. First, the myriad of anecdotes and details scattered in Jupiter's and other slaves' interrogatories can be mobilized to understand the way the slave system was experienced by slaves in daily life. Jupiter's case, for instance, gives a more nuanced view of the impact of the foodstuff trade between the plantations and the nearby city on the enslaved hucksters' social condition. It also offers a window into the way slaves perceived time, constructed narratives of their own life stories, and made sense of the permanent turmoil they faced. Their lives were marked by an incessant struggle to survive, escape violence, access resources, forge relations of solidarity, and build spaces of autonomy. Long-term security was an impossible quest in New Orleans as in any slave societies which were all characterized by a strong microinstability.[17]

Pradel employed Jupiter but also enslaved children as peddlers to sell the vegetables and milk produced on his plantation at the urban marketplace. Even though the estate was located on the other side of the Mississippi, they were left to their own resources to cross the river, paying other slaves who had pirogue boats if necessary. They were supposed to sell their merchandise on the levee, which was the only authorized and monitored marketplace within New Orleans, but they also offered their vegetables to settlers from door to door, to sailors on ships, and to soldiers in the barracks.

The *Code Noir* forbade slaves from participating in commercial exchanges without a certificate from their masters authorizing them to do so, but this practice was not well respected. Yet the certificate that Pradel initially gave to Jupiter stated that he was authorized to sell and buy on his owner's behalf. It set a limit on the amount of the commercial transactions that Jupiter could engage in. It also mentioned that larger bills could be given to him and that change would be given back afterward. The foodstuff trade largely rested on credit: some buyers did not pay on the spot or they gave larger bills than the requested price—since there were not enough coins in circulation, people used the cash vouchers and card money issued by local authorities as well as their own private bills and bonds. Jupiter's function consisted not only in selling plantation produce but also in collecting or paying the debts that this petty trade generated. In addition, Pradel also used Jupiter to collect other debts that were due for larger purchases, such as bricks. Jupiter thus exercised great responsibilities on his master's account.

On the one hand, the documentation seems to confirm the historiography that tends to describe peddlers as privileged slaves. Jupiter's functions gave him a freedom of movement and the possibility of access to material and social resources from which field slaves were deprived. As he came into town daily, he was able to interact with all kinds of people. In fact, most urban dwellers seem to have known him. While he seems to have kept his distance from soldiers, he maintained cordial relationships with white sailors with whom he drank and socialized. He apparently also shared a friendship with an urban domestic slave named Alexandre. He did not keep a mistress in town, but claimed that Marie Joseph who lived with her parents on Sieur Carrière's plantation "served him as a wife."[18] Significantly, all the slaves with whom he maintained the closest personal connections were of the Cerer/Sereer nation like him. In addition to maintaining these networks of sociability and solidarity, Jupiter also took advantage of his presence in the city to do many other things than selling his master's vegetables: he occasionally purchased some alcohol for the plantation's overseer while being often given free alcohol by his customers; he served as vendor for another white man who gave him one third of the profits; he sold his own poultry and eggs, and bought food, clothes, and jewelry for himself and his mistress; finally, he also frequently acquired goods and cash by stealing.

Pradel was not unaware of what his huckster was doing each time he went to the city. In fact, a white settler named Jacques Judice told the judge that before Jupiter's arrest he had come to Pradel's plantation to talk about some business they had together. He took advantage of their meeting to warn him: "your negro is on familiar terms with the sailors of the small ship before Mr. Prévost, I have seen them together round the table, they eat cabbages, say *tu* to each other, and he behaves with them as if they were relatives or friends. Keep an eye on him and don't trust him."[19] Pradel allegedly replied that he was not the kind of man to take offence when told such news, that Jupiter brought him the right amounts of money back, and that he was satisfied with him. Clearly, not all white colonists shared the same view on the need to repress cross-racial sociability.

In the same way, when Jupiter was caught by an enslaved child while he was stealing in the house of a merchant named Laissard, he ran away and went back to his plantation. He confessed what he had done to his master who told him that he would give the money back to Sieur Laissard and ordered him to work in the kitchen in the meantime. After the merchant came to visit Pradel on his rural estate, the planter put iron shackles on Jupiter's legs and locked him up, but the slave managed to free himself and to escape. He ran away, sleeping in various places for a few nights. When he came back once again to the plantation, he was finally arrested by soldiers. His master had first tried to conclude a private settlement with Sieur Laissard and to help Jupiter evade royal justice, but his position was made untenable as rumor of the burglary quickly spread among settlers and slaves in the city and the countryside. Although slaveholders collectively supported the repressive policy implemented by local officials and judges of the Superior Council against slaves who ran away or stole, it was another matter when their own laborers were concerned. Pradel knew that, if Jupiter was tried, he could be mutilated and even executed.

On the other hand, Jupiter's interrogatories also testify to the adversity and the many constraints that this so-called privileged slave had to face.[20] First, Jupiter not only worked as a huckster but was also employed as a domestic to help in the kitchen when he was on the plantation. Moreover, as the enslaved women who cooked for all the slaves were given their Saturdays and Sundays to work for themselves, Jupiter, who had to go to the urban marketplace every day, had to manage to feed himself on weekends and had only Sunday afternoon to take care of his own individual parcel and chickens. More importantly, the relationship that tied Pradel and Jupiter together was not only based on trust; violence also played a major role. His owner expected Jupiter to come back from the market with a certain amount of money, and when he failed, he whipped him. The slave repeatedly told the judge that his master threatened him with violent punishment in case he did not bring the expected amount. Despite the autonomy they enjoyed and the lighter tasks they fulfilled, enslaved peddlers were no less brutalized and exploited than other plantation slaves working in the fields.

The harshness of Jupiter's or other slaves' lives and the fragility of the positions and relations they tried to secure to survive also transpire from the many references to time scattered in the interrogatories. First, slaves' lives were divided according to the succession of masters to whom they belonged and the places where they worked. Marianne, for instance, who was interrogated because she had met Jupiter in the city while he was fleeing after he had been caught robbing at Laissard's, explained that she did not know what Jupiter had done because she used to work on the plantation and had only arrived in the capital recently. Yet she admitted that she had known Jupiter for a long time since they both belonged at some point to M. Vilenville when Jupiter was a young child. Slaves' lives were also marked by incidents related to conjugal and family relationships: Jupiter mentioned that he used to have a mistress, but that she had left with Sieur Lange.

Furthermore, slaves appropriated regular or exceptional events that at first sight seemed meaningful only for colonists. They corresponded to joyous or more dramatic memories. Margo, the mother of Jupiter's mistress, mentioned New Year gifts given "the day of good day good year" ("le jour de bonjour bonne année").[21] Likewise, Jupiter told the judge on two separate occasions that he went only once to the city at night, the day Governor Pierre de Rigaud de Vaudreuil de Cavagnal gave a ball for Mardi-Gras, and that he had only given his mistress a small silver cross since Vaudreuil had returned from Mobile. The slave also referred to the promulgation of an ordinance recalling the prohibition for the enslaved to purchase alcohol, admitting he had bought some for his overseer at the time before the prohibition. Finally, even more strikingly, Jupiter's mistress Marie-Joseph presented herself by stating that she "was born the year of the Natchez War or Nachtoches."[22] She referred to the Natchez Wars which started in 1729 and which could have destroyed the colony—at least it was what officials and settlers feared at the time. All these fragments about time are important because they reveal that enslaved men and women took part in the colony's sociopolitical life. They also suggest how slaves, as any other social actors, memorized their past with time indicators and in a narrative form that they could recount to themselves or to others, giving more importance to some events than others. These memories could then be mobilized to justify or to make sense of people' s actions.

Jupiter's interrogatories can also be exploited to analyze how slaves defended themselves in front of judges who used all the means at their disposal to create a climate of terror. Despite the ghastly circumstances in which slaves prosecuted by the Superior Council found themselves, they were not completely helpless and did seek to speak for themselves. Not all the enslaved shared the same ability to comprehend what was happening to them, keep their sangfroid, and articulate a thoughtful response, but they never remained passive and always voiced their perspective. Among all the slaves who appeared in front of the Superior Council, Jupiter was one of the best prepared for the ordeal of a trial. He had apparently arrived in the colony as a child and was raised there; he also knew the city very well and had learnt how to deal with all kinds of people and circumstances, and to navigate between various social milieus through his function as a peddler.

Still, it was very difficult for slaves to conceive of and plan a defense. They were not assisted by lawyers and were not kept informed of the procedure. Consequently, their interrogatories did not form long and coherent narratives in which the structure and every word had been carefully chosen as in the letters of remission studied by Davis. Each trial was preceded by an investigation and the investigation continued between the various interrogatories of the defendant. This investigation was not recorded. Yet its findings guided the choice of witnesses and the questions asked of the defendant. But the accused did not know in advance what the judge in charge of the case had against him. He had to respond to questions that were oriented by the ongoing investigation and that he discovered as they were raised; he did not have full mastery over what he could talk about. Moreover, defendants were not submitted to a single interrogatory. All in all, Jupiter was questioned five times, the last two times *sur la sellette* ("on the stool").[23] At one point he told the judge who had asked him why he had not told the truth in his first interrogatory "that he believed that things would be left at that and that he would not be asked twice or three times."[24] The difficulty for the enslaved was to sustain a strategy in the long run while not knowing exactly how judges were going to proceed. Time was a key element of the pressure imposed on the defendant, with several days between each interrogatory. Anxiety could grow along with uncertainty.

Jupiter needed time and skill to develop a defense strategy given that the stakes were very high. He had been caught by an enslaved child when he was breaking a cabinet in Laissard's house. During his trial he could not but admit his guilt for this burglary. He knew that he could be sentenced to the death penalty. During his second interrogatory, the judge reported a conversation Jupiter had with a military officer, Sieur Tixerant, when he was first brought to prison. The officer allegedly said, "Gamelle you have stolen, you have made a bad deal, don't you know that this deserves death?"[25] Jupiter claimed that he had replied to Tixerant that he would not be the first to die for having committed some crimes. Therefore, during his trial, he sought to escape from the death penalty. It was not a self-deluding strategy: although some slaves had been executed before 1744, magistrates were reluctant to use the death penalty even in case of theft or multiple escapes because the slave trade from Africa had nearly ceased in 1731 and it was very difficult and expensive to acquire new slaves.[26] The problem, however, was that the judge suspected Jupiter of having accomplices and, most of all, of being responsible for several other robberies which had happened in the city throughout the previous year. As a result, Jupiter needed both to explain and justify why he had broken in and robbed Laissard and to convince the court that it was his only crime.

Paradoxically, Jupiter used the risk of death as a stratagem to defend himself. For instance, in his second interrogatory, he denied that he had any accomplice, stating that "he was alone when he committed his theft. And that he will never say otherwise even if he was executed."[27] Likewise, in the confrontation between Jupiter and Alexandre, the former having accused the latter of having committed several other robberies, both men used the same argument: Alexandre claimed "that he had told the truth as if he was before God, that even if he was executed he would not say otherwise" when Jupiter later replied "that he is not a liar and that he does not need to look for a lie to exculpate himself since it is true that he has confessed that he had stolen at Sieur Henry's and Laissard's, that it would not cost him more to confess if he had stolen somewhere else since he must die and that he can pay only once with his body."[28]

The issue of accomplices put slaves' solidarity to the test. In his first and second interrogatories Jupiter denied both that he had any accomplice when committing the burglary at Laissard's and that he had committed any other robbery. However, in his third interrogatory, when he felt trapped and cornered as the pressure on him was growing, he accused Alexandre of having broken in and of stealing at Dumanoir's and Salmon's. He did not only accuse him; he also told the story about how he had learnt the information: Jupiter had come to the house of Alexandre's master to collect a debt; he asked Alexandre to pay "le filet" (a shot of alcohol); Alexandre went to buy some alcohol; while they were drinking Alexandre told him about the robberies and showed him the tools he had used and that Jupiter borrowed.[29] The latter also recalled another scene with Alexandre coming to see him on the bank of the river, talking to him about jewels to be sold to slaves at Dusigné and asking Jupiter to buy some for him to give to his mistress. Alexandre who had already been heard as a witness at the beginning of the trial was then interrogated twice, the second time *sur la sellette*, and the two men were confronted. Each time Alexandre denied everything, developing his own narrative defense. Finally, in his last interrogatory *sur la sellette*, Jupiter exculpated Alexandre and took full responsibility for all the robberies. Likewise, while he had previously identified and denounced slaves who had helped him cross the river in their pirogues, he claimed that he did it by himself. Instead of his mistress Marie Joseph to whom he had given clothes and jewels, he mentioned another woman who had not been identified and interrogated. At the end, when he knew for sure that he was going to be executed, he tried to save all his fellow companions. He explained to the judge that he had wrongly accused Alexandre because "he believed that he would save his [own] life."[30]

The narrative component of Jupiter's interrogatories also appeared in his justification for having burgled Laissard's house. Jupiter's main argument was that Pradel gave him too much produce and that it was impossible for him to sell all of it as the goods were too expensive or too many peddlers were selling foodstuff at the same time. For a while he tried to borrow money or to use the cash he made with the sale of his own produce; yet one year before his arrest he felt he had no other choice but to steal to bring back the money his master expected and to avoid violent punishment. The slave's interrogatories included the narrative of the conflictual relationship between Pradel and Jupiter over a long period of time. He repeated the same justification over and over in each of his interrogatories even though he did not use exactly the same words and anecdotes each time. When he was interrogated *sur la sellette* at the end of his trial Jupiter summarized his situation by using a French proverbial sentence: "if he [Jupiter] had told him [his master] that he could not sell he [Pradel] would have beaten him hard for a servant is not a master."[31] It was a matter-of-fact acknowledgment of the domination Pradel exercised over him because of his slave status.

The constraint under which the slave found himself recurred each time he had to go to the marketplace. Jupiter mentioned that he had been whipped several times for having failed to sell all his vegetables—and also once for having slept outside the plantation without permission. At the same time, within his general statements, Jupiter included specific episodes to make his argument more vivid and striking. For instance, in his second interrogatory, he reported a dialogue with his master that the clerk recorded in direct discourse: "that he gave him bunches of turnips and cabbages and asparagus to sell on his behalf and 'Here is what you have for this amount, you have to bring me back the money,' that he replied saying to him 'Mr. I cannot sell them. They are too expensive. How do you expect me to do it? There are already a lot for sale in town.' His master told him 'I don't care, I want you to bring me back the money from the foodstuff, do what you like or you'll be whipped,' this is what forced him to go stealing [...]."[32]

In the same way, in his third interrogatory, Jupiter recalled another dreadful story to justify that he had to give or throw away the vegetables he could not sell: "that often he was compelled to throw them in the water or give them away as he did not dare to bring them back to the other side, out of fear of being ill-treated, his master always telling him that he wanted his money, that he did not care if he sold anything, and that that was how Sieur Lange [Pradel's business partner] treated a little girl who is dead, who sold for him, that when this little negress brought back herbs or asparagus he forced them down her throat and made her eat them."[33] The way Jupiter talked about the many times he had had been whipped demonstrates that the use of corporal punishment was seen as being part of a daily routine on plantations, which does not mean that slaves did not seek to be spared from punishment. However, some incidents of extreme violence marked slaves more than others: In that case, the age and gender of the victim and the uncommon form of the violence appeared particularly scandalous and reprehensible. While most slaves were underfed and had to constantly struggle to find the food they needed, this young child was brutalized with the very foodstuff she had to sell at the marketplace on her master's behalf.

Finally, Jupiter did not only defend himself by recounting dramatic events such as the death of the enslaved girl. The peddler and the four other slaves—Alexandre, Marianne, Margo, and Marie Joseph—who were also interrogated during his trial all kept referring to a religious and eschatological time to justify themselves and to give weight to their words. They knew that they were considered untruthful. Among them only Margo was not baptized. Yet all mentioned God. Both Alexandre and Margo claimed that they were telling the truth as if they were before God. Likewise, in his first interrogatory when the judge asked if he had committed previous robberies, Jupiter said "that no, that he has never stolen, that it is the first misfortune that happened to him and that he is telling the truth as if before God and that even if he must be chopped in pieces he will not say otherwise." In fact, he described several times what had happened as a "misfortune" and claimed that he was telling the truth as if before God. He also added at some point "that he does not fear death because he says the truth."[34] During his second interrogatory, when he was asked in the first question if he had robbed Delaunay, Jupiter declared "that it would cost him nothing to say if he had done it since he gives his soul to God and his body to justice."[35] Slaves seemed to have appropriated the Catholic faith, the providentialist perspective on life shared by colonists of European descent, and a conception of royal justice as a delegation of the immanent justice of God. Although it is impossible to determine if they genuinely adhered to these politico-religious beliefs, they used them to defend themselves. It might have been all the easier for them to appropriate them since they conformed to the religious relationship to justice of many African ethnic groups, that often involved different kinds of ordeal.[36] Anyway, these calls to divine justice did not manage to save Jupiter. He was sentenced to be hanged and to be submitted beforehand to both the ordinary and extraordinary question (torture) in order for him to denounce his accomplices and confess to other robberies.

Jupiter told the Superior Council many stories. It is in that sense that one can speak of the fictional dimension of slaves' narratives in their interrogatories. The search for truth was an important issue for both parties as judges sought to determine the facts and the culprits and the defendants tried to exculpate themselves. Nevertheless, it is impossible to always know what really happened although some facts, events and stories could be corroborated by several persons. Even if everything that slaves told did not really happen, it had to look plausible, which means than historians can use this material because it fit what judges at the time knew about the way the slave system operated.

Whether the stories the enslaved told were authentic or not, they knew that they had to construct a narrative. This consciousness was reflected in their very words. In his first interrogatory, Jupiter explained that when he came back to his plantation after the robbery "he immediately came to find his master to whom he recounted his misfortune."[37] In his second interrogatory, he reported that during his escape he spent one night with Marie-Joseph; she asked him about the rumors that he had robbed Laissard and he told her that they were "tales" ("contes").[38] Forged narratives and tales were purposely deployed by slaves.

It may seem surprising at first sight that in French colonies slaves' trials were not expeditious and that magistrates took the time to interrogate, listen to and record what enslaved men and women had to say at great length. But several explanations can be suggested for this situation. They were partly related to the fact that the monarch felt responsible for the slave order—the French Empire differed from all other empires before the second half of the eighteenth century because the *Code Noir* was promulgated by the metropole—and that the *commissaire-ordonnateur*, the second top official of the colony, was the first judge of the Superior Council, while the governor, who was the king's representative, was also a member of the court. These trials were occasions for local authorities to collect information about was going on in various social underground worlds that they could not keep watch on, that of the slaves but also of all the lower social groups. They also needed to understand the reasons for the evolution of slave unrest, including maltreatment from theirs masters, because slave revolts had to be prevented and because the search for runaways and the judicial repression of criminal slaves cost the crown money. Finally, except in the early 1760s in very specific circumstances, the Superior Council did not try to enforce a highly severe judicial repression of slaves.[39] Judges, who were all slaveholders, sought to make examples from time to time, and this was certainly what happened to Jupiter who not only stole but was guilty of multiple thefts by breaking and entering within the colonial capital, but they preferred to spare the life of slaves, who represented both labor and capital. Magistrates needed to find all the culprits, establish the facts, and balance the aggravating and mitigating circumstances in order to sentence to death only those who threatened the slave order. Although they spared the life of most offenders, they were prompt to sentence them to terrible corporal punishments including whipping, branding, and mutilations.

Taken together, all the tales told by enslaved men and women and included in the Records of the Superior Council of French Louisiana represent a slave counter-narrative to their masters' views. As they were asked by judges why they had run away or stolen, they were able to report many stories about their exploitation and maltreatment at the hand of their owners or of their representatives. Admittedly, the possibility for the enslaved to voice their standpoint had hardly any effect on the way the slave system operated inside and outside the court room. Except for the application of the death penalty, judges rarely took into account mitigating circumstances when they decided the sentences. Yet, even when defendants did not escape the death penalty, as in Jupiter's case, or terrible physical chastisements, since their claims asserted their dignity it mattered for their own sake that they had stood up for themselves to present their version of the story of the never-ending struggle between masters and slaves.

Paradoxically, the significance of slaves defending themselves within the judicial arena is revealed by what happened to judicial archives in Saint-Domingue. In French Louisiana slaves' criminal suits have been preserved to a large extent even if the Records of the Superior Council are incomplete and many trials have been lost or have suffered the ravages of time. But in the French Caribbean colony, local authorities implemented a policy of complete or partial destruction of criminal trials related to slaves from the first decades of the eighteenth century. These campaigns of destruction went along with the progressive reduction of the right of appeal for slaves.[40] As Marie Houllemare explains, "rather than an intentional policy of silencing slaves alive—as they are indeed heard by judges—, this is in fact a policy of elimination of their written memory. This is the past that is reduced to silence, since the selection operated within the judicial documentation prevents the historicization of slaves' penal repression: what has been judged cannot be contested afterwards for lack of archival evidence, which has been voluntarily destroyed on magistrates' order."[41] Beyond the possibility for appeal, the destruction of slaves' criminal trials constituted a form of symbolic violence that complemented and reinforced other forms of violence against the enslaved. Such a policy also had consequences for the perpetuation of their memory over the longue durée.[42]

Where judicial archives have not been destroyed, historians should make the most of them. Yet the heuristic value of this documentation does not lie only in the recovery of slave voices and the expression of their subjectivity. Jupiter's case reveals many more stories related to him than those he told himself. In addition to his five interrogatories, the court records include those of four other slaves and the testimonies of sixteen whites. We know more about Jupiter's experience than about many other enslaved men or women thanks to these multiple accounts. In that regard, Jupiter's case is exceptional because his criminal trial was followed by his owner's civil suit as some people looked for financial reparations for Jupiter's mischiefs and because he was a peddler everybody knew in town. Many people could report a memory about Jupiter. It would be possible to reconstruct a narrative of Jupiter's life through all these anecdotes, but a biography or a microhistory centered on one individual constitutes only one possible approach to apprehend the personal experience of slavery.[43] Resorting to microhistory to study slave societies could also take other forms than the narration of one slave's life story. As judicial archives offer a repertoire of daily interactions between people of all conditions, they call for a relational social history of slavery rather than for an impossible quest of individual subjectivity.

Notes

1 Charles T. Davis and Henry Louis Gates, Jr., eds., *The Slave's Narrative* (Oxford: Oxford University Press, 1985); Audrey Fisch, ed., *The Cambridge Companion to the African American Slave Narrative* (Cambridge: Cambridge University Press, 2007); John Ernest, ed., *The Oxford Handbook of the African American Slave Narrative* (Oxford: Oxford University Press, 2014).
2 David Brion Davis "Slavery and the Post-World War II Historians," *Daedalus* 103, no. 2 (1974): 1–16; Norman R. Yetman, "Ex-Slave Interviews and the Historiography of Slavery," *American Quarterly* 36, no. 2 (1984): 181–210; Kathleen Hilliard, "Finding Slave Voices," in Mark M. Smith and Robert Paquette, eds., *The Oxford Handbook of Slavery in the Americas* (Oxford: Oxford University Press, 2010), 685–701.
3 For studies or edition of "slave narratives" in other regions of the Americas, Gloria García Rodríguez, *Voices of the Enslaved in Nineteenth-Century Cuba: A Documentary History* (Chapel Hill: University of North Carolina Press, 2003); Juan Francisco Manzano, *Autobiografía del esclavo poeta y otros escritos. Edición, introducción y notas de William Luis* (Madrid and Frankfurt: Iberoamericana and Vervuert, 2007); Kathryn Joy McKnight and Leo J. Garofalo, eds., *Afro-Latino Voices: Narratives from the Early Ibero-Atlantic World, 1550–1812* (Indianapolis, IN: Hackett Publishing, 2009); Gunvor Simonsen, *Slave Stories: Law, Representation, and Gender in the Danish West Indies* (Aarhus: Aarhus University Press, 2017). For slave voices in other continents, see Alice Bellagamba, Sandra A. Greene, and Martin A. Klein, eds., *African Voices on Slavery and the Slave Trade, Vol. 1: The Sources, Vol. 2: Essays on Sources and Methods* (Cambridge: Cambridge University Press, 2013 and 2016); Sandra Greene, *West African Narratives of Slavery: Texts from Late Nineteenth and Early Twentieth Century Ghana* (Bloomington: Indiana University Press, 2011); Eve Troutt Powell, *Tell This in My Memory: Stories of Enslavement from Egypt, Sudan, and the Ottoman Empire* (Palo Alto, CA: Stanford University Press, 2012).

4 Dominique Rogers, ed., *Voix d'esclaves. Antilles, Guyane et Louisiane françaises, XVIIIe–XIXe siècles* (Paris: Karthala, 2015); Frédéric Régent, Gilda Confier, and Bruno Maillart, *Libres et sans fers. Paroles d'esclaves français* (Paris: Fayard, 2015).

5 Natalie Zemon Davis, *Fictions in the Archives: Pardon Tales and Their Tellers in Sixteenth Century France* (Palo Alto, CA: Stanford University Press, 1987).

6 Louisiana State Museum, Records of the Superior Council of Louisiana (hereafter RSCL) 1744/02/26/01, 1744/02/29/01, 1744/03/02/01, 1744/03/03/01, 1744/03/05/01, 1744/03/07/02, 1744/03/11/01, 1744/03/11/02, 1744/03/12/01, 1744/03/12/02, 1744/03/13/01, 1744/03/14/01, 1744/03/14/02, 1744/03/16/01, 1744/03/17/01, 1744/03/18/01, 1744/03/18/02, 1744/03/19/01, 1743/03/21/01, 1743/03/21/02, 1744/03/21/03, 1744/03/21/04, 1744/03/21/05, 1744/04/23/01, 1744/04/24/01, 1744/10/03/01.

7 Historic New Orleans Collection, MSS 589, Chevalier de Pradel Papers; A. Baillardel and A. Prioult, eds., *Le chevalier de Pradel. Vie d'un colon français en Louisiane au XVIIIe siècle d'après sa correspondance et celle de sa famille* (Paris: Librairie orientale et américaine Maisonneuve frères, 1928).

8 On Jean-Charles de Pradel and on Saint-Louis, see Cécile Vidal, *Caribbean New Orleans: Empire, Race, and the Making of a Slave Society* (Chapel Hill: University of North Carolina Press, 2019), 59–63, 77–78, 99, 124–125, 168–170, 209–210, 249, 302, 326, 338, 349–354, 357, 360–363, 402, 406, 432–433, 436; Sylvia R. Frey, "The Free Black Militia of New Orleans in the Mississippi River and Gulf Coast Campaigns of the American Revolution," unpublished paper, SAR Annual Conference on the American Revolution: "Slavery and Liberty: Black Patriots of the American Revolution," Baltimore, MD, June 24–26, 2011.

9 ANOM COL A 22 f. 10v–12v, December 23, 1712, "Copie des lettres patentes pour l'établissement d'un Conseil Supérieur à la Louisiane pendant trois ans;" ANOM COL A 22 f. 19–20, September 1716, "Édit pour l'établissement d'un Conseil Supérieur à la Louisiane."

10 After 1731, the governor and the *commissaire-ordonnateur* were the two highest ranking officials in the colony. Both men belonged to the navy. The governor was a sword officer and represented the king while the *commissaire-ordonnateur* was a pen officer. They were supposed to govern the colony together and their functions partially overlapped even though the governor was especially in charge of military and diplomatic matters and the *commissaire-ordonnateur* of administrative, judicial, financial, and commercial matters. The *lieutenant de roi* and the New Orleans *major* were both military officers, the former assisting the governor and the latter being responsible for the Louisiana capital's garrison.

11 As these permanent councilors were often absent when the Council was in session, some assessor councilors with voting rights were also nominated by the governor and *commissaire-ordonnateur* from 1733. Khalil Saadani, "Le gouvernement de la Louisiane française, 1731–43. Essai d'histoire comparative," *French Colonial History* 4 (2003): 117–132.

12 Diana Paton, "Punishment, Crime, and the Bodies of Slaves in Eighteenth-Century Jamaica," *Journal of Social History* 34, no. 4 (2001): 927; Betty Wood, "'Until He Shall be Dead Dead, Dead:' The Judicial Treatment of Slaves in Eighteenth-Century Georgia," *Georgia Historical Society* 71, no. 3 (1987): 380.

13 On the judicial procedure, see Benoît Garnot, *Justice et société en France aux XVIe, XVIIe et XVIIIe siècles* (Gap: Ophrys, 2000), 85–127; *Histoire*

de la justice. France, XVIe–XXIe siècle (Paris: Gallimard, coll. Folio histoire, 2009), 343–419.

14 Benoît Garnot, "La justice pénale et les témoins en France au XVIIIe siècle: de la théorie à la pratique," *Dix-huitième siècle* 1, no. 39 (2007): 99–108.

15 RSCL 1738/04/24/01, 1741/01/10/01, 1742/01/09/05, 1743/06/27/01, 1743/09/09/02, 1748/01/05/01, 1748/01/05/03, 1748/05/22/01, 1748/06/10/02.

16 In the words of Arlette Farge, it is impossible to resist the "allure of the archives." Among her many inspiring books which have developed a pioneering approach to the use of judicial archives while insisting on their flaws, limitations and bias, see Arlette Farge, *Vivre dans la rue à Paris au XVIIIe siècle* (Paris: Gallimard and Julliard, 1979); *La vie fragile. Violence, pouvoirs et solidarités à Paris au XVIIIe siècle* (Paris: Hachette, 1986); *Le goût de l'archive* (Paris: Seuil, 1989) [*The Allure of the Archives*, translated by Thomas Scott-Railton (New Haven, CT: Yale University Press, 2013)].

17 For all references to Jupiter's trial in this section, see note 6.

18 RSCL 1744/03/05/01.

19 RSCL 1744/04/24/01.

20 To my knowledge, there is no specific work on slave peddlers, but they are frequently mentioned in the vast historiography on the slaves' economy. See among many studies: Hilary Beckles, "An Economic Life of Their Own: Slaves as Commodity Producers and Distributors in Barbados," *Slavery and Abolition* 12, no. 1 (1991): 31–47; Ira Berlin and Philip D. Morgan, eds., *The Slaves' Economy: Independent Production by Slaves in the Americas* (Portland: Frank Cass & Co. Ltd., 1991); Mary Turner, ed., *From Chattel Slaves to Wage Slaves: The Dynamics of Labour Bargaining in the Americas* (Kingston, Bloomington, and London: Ian Randle, Indiana University Press, and James Currey, 1995). See also Daniel H. Usner, Jr., "Food Marketing and Interethnic Exchange in the 18th-Century Lower Mississippi Valley," *Food and Foodways* 1, no. 3 (1986): 279–310.

21 RSCL 1744/03/11/01.

22 RSCL 1744/03/11/02.

23 The interrogatory "*sur la sellette*" took place at the end of the trial when the conclusions of the attorney general tended toward the recognition of the defendant's guilt. The defendant was then seated on a small stool with all the judges who were on the verge of deciding his fate surrounding him. The organization was meant to impress and terrorize the defendant.

24 RSCL 1744/03/03/01.

25 RSCL 1744/03/05/01.

26 Vidal, *Caribbean New Orleans*, 400–406.

27 RSCL 1744/03/05/01.

28 RSCL 1744/03/14/02.

29 RSCL 1744/03/12/01.

30 RSCL 1744/03/21/03.

31 RSCL 1744/03/21/03.

32 RSCL 1744/03/05/01.

33 RSCL 1744/03/12/01.

34 RSCL 1744/03/03/01.

35 RSCL 1744/03/05/01.

36 Natalie Zemon Davis, "Judges, Masters, Diviners: Slaves' Experience of Criminal Justice in Colonial Surinam," *Law and History Review* 29, no. 4 (2011): 925–984.

37 RSCL 1744/03/03/01.

38 RSCL 1744/03/05/01.

39 Thomas N. Ingersoll, "The Law and Order Campaign in New Orleans, 1763–1765: A Comparative View," in Sally E. Hadden and Patricia Hagler

Minter, eds., *Signposts: New Directions in Southern Legal History* (Athens: University of Georgia Press, 2013), 45–64; and Vidal, *Caribbean New Orleans*, 138–139, 406–412.

40 In French Louisiana, this right of appeal did not exist locally for slaves of New Orleans and its plantation region since there was only one level of jurisdiction in this part of the colony as the Superior Council was both the high court of first instance and of final appeal for them. In theory, masters could appeal for their slaves in front of the king's council.

41 Marie Houllemare, "Vers la centralisation des archives coloniales françaises au XVIIIe siècle: destruction et conservation des papiers judiciaires," in Marie-Pia Donato and Anne Saada, eds., *Autour d'archives. Créer, organiser et utiliser des archives à l'époque moderne* (Paris: Classiques Garnier, 2018).

42 Michel-Rolph Trouillot, *Silencing the Past: Power and the Production of History* (New York: Beacon Press, 1995); Marisa J. Fuentes, *Dispossessed Lives: Enslaved Women, Violence, and the Archive* (Philadelphia: University of Pennsylvania Press, 2016).

43 Sue Peabody, "Microhistory, Biography, Fiction," *Transatlantica* 2 (2012), consulted December 22, 2018, http://journals.openedition.org/transatlantica/6184.

3   Slave Judiciary Testimonies in the French Caribbean

What to Do with Them

Dominique Rogers

What can we learn from and how can we use judicial materials concerning enslaved persons of the French Caribbean? The answer to these questions requires, first, taking into account the very nature of the documents, the number of documents that have survived, and their richness. It also means taking into account the purposes for using these archives and the ways in which they can be used. The "French Caribbean" is a vast territory, which in the eighteenth and nineteenth centuries referred to Martinique, Guadeloupe and the smaller territories of Saint-Barthelemy and French Saint-Martin. It also included Saint-Lucia, Grenada, Tobago, Louisiana, and Saint-Domingue (modern-day Haiti), with French Guiana also considered a part of the great French Caribbean zone (*la grande Caraïbe française*). This essay will focus in particular on materials from French Saint-Domingue, Martinique, Guadeloupe and French Guiana, and to a lesser extent, Louisiana. As the author of a dissertation on the free people of color of the two main towns in French Saint-Domingue, I am not *per se* a specialist of enslaved persons.[1] However, during the European project EURESCL (7e PCRD) (2007–2012), I was in charge of coordinating a research project on slave voices, which helped identify more than 200 pages of new archival material, excerpts of which were published in 2015 in *Voix d'esclaves, Antilles, Guyane et Louisiane françaises, XVIIIe-XIXe siècles*.[2] A new volume produced jointly with Myriam Cottias and Jean-Pierre Sainton will highlight voices of slaves who were newly freed in 1848, and will focus in particular on their views on their new status and especially how they articulated a position on the question of "reparations" and "justice." Other slave testimonies have been recently published that offer still more material, thereby further legitimizing the question of how to use such sources.[3]

The range of judicial material at our disposal for the French Caribbean is large. Some documents are strictly judicial and are composed of spontaneous declarations (*main-courantes*), police interrogations and judicial hearings or examinations.[4] Others are court records: tribunal awards and debates, partially published in the local press in the nineteenth century.[5] Finally, some documents are only related to judicial procedure or infrajudicial practices: petitions of mercy, requests for the commutation of sentences, complaints, and even, exceptionally, memoirs written by a magistrate, in which the voice of the enslaved can only be read indirectly.[6] In order to evaluate the reliability of those slave testimonies, it is important to first understand the juridical contexts in which they were produced, before highlighting certain precautions to be taken in using them.

The edict of March 1685 (the so-called *Code Noir* of 1685) was the fundamental legal reference for the status of the enslaved in the French lesser Antilles until 1848, from 1687 to 1793 for French Saint-Domingue and from 1704 for French Guiana.[7] Nevertheless, from the seventeenth to the nineteenth century, local regulations (*règlements*), royal ordinances and decrees (*arrêts*) of the *Conseil d'Etat* modified some of these provisions, through both local and temporary amendments that sometimes had wider application. Given the limited scope of this essay, we will highlight only a few of these.[8]

What does the fundamental law assert concerning the rights of the enslaved in the French Antilles and French Guiana? The oft-cited article 44 of the edict of March 1685 posits that slaves are "movable assets" (*des biens meubles*); therefore, it is most often assumed that they have no rights, no juridical capacity, and sometimes it is even believed that they were viewed like animals or things, because they could be sold, let, ceded etc. In fact, the situation is more complex. Articles 32–36, just like articles 38, 18 and 19, affirm the full penal capacity of the enslaved, who are criminally accountable for their actions before the king's law. This fact necessarily produces judicial material, in the many cases of revolt, conspiracy, marronage, poisoning, robbery, and even sexual relations of enslaved men with white women, relationships that the parties involved might consent to but that society rejected. The need to determine the reality of the facts, the extent of the responsibilities and the nature of the sentences led the justices and the clerks to record the views of the enslaved suspects, victims or witnesses alongside those of the white or sometimes colored colonists. In these cases, masters were as interested as judges in knowing the truth; slaves were property, and their loss, whether by confiscation or death sentence, was probably not completely covered by the financial compensation that was provided by law.[9]

In civil matters, conversely, the legal standing of slaves was extremely reduced. Their inability to assert their rights derived primarily from the fact that the articles of the edict of March 1685 were contradictory and the many complementary regulations issued after its promulgation were sometimes even more restrictive. For instance, articles 30 and 31 of the 1685 edict denied the slaves the right to testify, except in very specific conditions. Article 30 states: "Slaves will not be allowed to be given offices or commissions with any public function, nor to be named agents by any other than their masters to act and administer any trade or judgement in loss or witnesses, either in civil and criminal matters; and in any cases they will be heard as witnesses, their dispositions will only serve as a memorandum to aid the justices in the investigation, without being the source of any presumption, conjecture or proof." Article 31 specifies also that "Nor can slaves be party, either in judgement, nor in civil suits, either as plaintiff or defendant, neither in civil or criminal suits." The impossibility of defending oneself, except by having a white witness to support one's position, considerably limited the possibility for the slave to win his case and thus perhaps imposed limitations on the very desire to make his voice heard. Nevertheless, these articles, which very clearly limit the legal capacity of slaves, must be read while taking into account two other provisions: one extracted from the March edict of 1685; the other stemming from modifications requested by the locals and validated by the *Conseil d'Etat* as early as 1686.

The first point of contradiction concerns article 26, which allowed slaves to denounce their ill-treatment by their masters: "The slaves who are not fed, clothed and supported by masters according to what we have ordered by these articles will notify our attorney of this and give him their statement, based on which and even as a matter of course, if the information comes to him from elsewhere, the masters will be prosecuted by him, without costs, which we want to be observed for the cries and barbarous and inhumane treatments of masters towards their slaves." According to Antoine Gisler those denunciations did occur, and he provides many examples of these.[10] However, if we stick to juridical materials, the rights of the enslaved to complain against their masters seem to have been constantly denied. The fact is stated in a decree of 1686, mentioned below, but also in a decree from 1738 that echoed the slave codes of 1723 for the Mascarenes (article 23) and of 1724 for Louisiana (article 24) which had more flexible rules about slave testimony.[11] At the end of the eighteenth century, when the king decided to authorize slaves to complain against managers and overseers who abused their powers, the colonists refused forcefully.[12] They argued that such a regulation, which directly attacked the absolute power of the masters, undermined the principle of slavery and might provoke a major revolt. To the contrary, those reactions seem to suggest that the enslaved did not often attempt to denounce such abuse.

In August 1686, the members of the *Conseil souverain* in Martinique, who had been invited to record the edict of March 1685, asked for a modification. They wanted slaves to be allowed to testify, "as they used to," in affairs concerning slaves only or when there was no white witness. The counselors argued that "many crimes would remain unpunished if one does not receive the testimony of the slaves in default of that of the whites, most of the crimes being committed and being able to be proved only by slaves."[13] Despite articles 30 and 31, the *conseil d'état* accepted the modification in October 1686, and it was implemented in all the colonies. This modification explains why we find records containing interrogations by slave witnesses throughout the period. In fact, authorities often believed it was necessary to be more flexible than the law allowed. Thus, during the revolution of French Saint-Domingue after 1791, the police authorities were often forced to accept the word of slaves in order to authenticate the death of their master, far beyond what the code of 1685 provided for. That code was only supposed to take the words of the enslaved "as a memorandum to aid the justices in the investigation, without being the source of any presumption, conjecture or proof" (article 30).[14]

Nevertheless, during the nineteenth century, the situation changed again, even if it did so progressively and slowly. In 1805, the promulgation of the Civil Code in Martinique and Guadeloupe did not benefit the slaves, who remained defined as property, and were governed both by the edict of March 1685 and books 2 and 3 of the Civil Code ("Property and various modifications of the property; About the different ways in which one acquires property").[15] By 1833, however, slaves were no longer considered to be "movable assets," but were thought of as actual persons, although they were not freed: *des personnes non libres*. The decision to change their legal status was a major step forward in enhancing the juridical personality of the enslaved, though it was not until 1840 that the law on patronage required magistrates to conduct regular surveys to verify compliance with the laws in favor of slaves. It was only in 1845, with the so-called Mackau laws, that penalties were first issued against masters for not observing the new regulations.[16] In the meantime, between 1831 and 1839 slaves were granted new rights concerning manumission, civil status and filiation, while the 1840 patronage act and the Mackau laws of 1845 covered other provisions concerning health, clothing, food and primary education. All of these new rights could be invoked in court.

Which other precautions should we take? It is clear that the vast majority of the documents discovered for the French Caribbean were not written by slave people themselves, in fact none were written by slaves during the eighteenth century. Some documents, however, were dictated by the enslaved at their initiative, but this was done only in the nineteenth century, when the enslaved were allowed to take legal steps to redeem or free themselves or their family, or even to sue their masters. Most often, such documents were produced in constrained circumstances, often following a crime in which the enslaved person was sometimes a victim, but more often was a suspect, and where a witness could too easily be named an accomplice. Frightened by the situation they found themselves in and by the high stakes of criminal proceedings, the enslaved could be tempted to alter the truth in order just to survive. Frédéric Régent underlines also the importance of judiciary intermediaries, asserting that the testimonies of slaves usually result from a transcription made by a clerk who does not always meet the standards for integrity required by his function and further that these documents could be altered by the questions and suggestions of the justices confronting the slaves.[17] But even when the clerks were not biased, one should also remember the fact that they sometimes came from metropolitan France and were not always fully capable of accurately transcribing or translating the words of a slave, especially since in the Antilles and French Guiana at least, the enslaved mostly spoke creole, sometimes African languages, but very rarely French.[18]

Nevertheless, it is important to remember (given that the partiality of the justices has been often noted) that the slave testimonies we are dealing with were not excerpted from the sentences, but were taken from other kinds of sources, recorded by clerks and sometimes by policemen, during the process of deciding whether the court case would proceed. In this respect, they seem less likely to be partial. For the nineteenth century, it was also the case that many of the judges sent from metropolitan France in the 1820s–1840s were in favor of the abolition of slavery. Further, the minister required that administrators publicize the cruelty of the masters by publishing debates on slavery in the local newspapers.[19] Administrators were asked to check both the merits of the debates and how these were published in the press. They were asked to protect the enslaved witnesses by preventing a master or his family members from selling them or otherwise interfering with their lives.[20]

Despite the wide range of types of documents, the actual number of surviving documents is very small for the French Caribbean and especially for the eighteenth century. Apart for French Louisiana, where complete or nearly complete series of judiciary documents have survived, most of the extant slave voices for the French Caribbean come from isolated documents, with no information on what happened before or after their creation, making it hard therefore to evaluate if the strategies deployed by the enslaved were fruitful, or even original. This means that it is impossible to write a judicial history of servile delinquency for those territories, except maybe for the nineteenth century, where the sources are richer.[21] Given this, two methodological approaches can offer some clarity. Where related documents have survived, it is possible to use these to chart what likely happened in that particular case. Where only disparate materials survive, these require a different approach focused on the information contained in the document rather than the legal case itself, with a focus on the lives and the psyche of the persons mentioned. Notwithstanding these limitations, the qualitative information within these records is invaluable. While it is not possible to present here the whole range of information to be gleaned from such documents, this essay will focus on three topics in particular: first, the social and family lives of the enslaved in the servile community; second, the condition of the enslaved as they themselves saw it; third, the question of violence against the enslaved.

As a general rule, judicial testimony is invaluable because the enslaved often referred to events which happened when the master was not there, both day and night, both in or outside the slave cabins or huts. In some cases, the documents concern runaway slaves and their lives in freedom, far away from the masters' grip. Therefore, judicial archives offer rare evidence of the choices made by the slaves themselves concerning questions as varied as their material conditions (food, clothes, houses), their social lives (balls, social meetings, leisure activities); family or affective relationships (how to court a girl, how to get engaged or married, but also conflicts and violence between partners). As regards material culture, the sources offer a level of detail that legal regulations and planters and managers' letters cannot match. Where the law speaks of flour, cassava, salted cod or sardines, the enslaved speak of recipes, of pigs stolen from the curate's garden, of fishing techniques and alternative sources of food.[22] They speak of culture, inherited from Africa or learnt through adaptation to their creole surroundings, but above all they speak of real day-to-day life. As regards religious practices, the testimonies offer nuanced information. Thus, in 1748, the testimony of Louis, a young runaway from Tonnegrande in French Guiana, evoked the spiritual life of his fellow companions, who followed, not African ceremonies, but those of the Corpus Christi's celebration twenty kilometres away in Cayenne.[23] Conversely, in 1757, Medor in his confession spoke of what contemporary readers would called sorcery or witchcraft: of potions for love, or for getting a master to grant freedom, and sometimes to poison him; of medical or magical substances, some of them clearly resembling Congo power objects (Minkisi).[24]

Slave testimony is especially precious where social matters, interpersonal relations, and especially family ties, are concerned. In 1757, the confession of the aforementioned slave Medor reveals the network of solidarity created or reactivated to kidnap Marie-Jeanne, servant of sieur Delavaud, who had refused to sell her to her father. To capture the girl and keep her out of the reach of her master, three slaves from different plantations, a free black woman living in Cap-Français, and a number of other accomplices were involved, illustrating solidarity across status and color constraints. Another case, that against Josaphat, the cook of the governor of Martinique, is even more instructive on this question of social networks.[25]

While narrating the routine of the day in 1826 when he was arrested, accused of obtaining arsenic in order to commit a crime, Josaphat evoked his ordinary links with his extended family and his social life:

> On the seventh of February eighteen hundred and twenty-six, in the civil and military prison of the city of Fort Royal in which we had transported ourselves, we had brought before us the said Josaphat, who, after having sworn to tell the truth, was asked to state his surnames, first names, age, occupation, qualities and religion.

He answered: his name was Josaphat, slave cook, about thirty years old, in the service of Monsieur the Governor, and of the Catholic religion. After which we asked him the following questions:

ASKED, OF THE ACCUSED. – Who are your parents in Saint Jacques?

ACCUSED. My father was Louis dit Sauterre, and my mother Ursule was a field worker (négresse de jardin). I was raised by Adrien, another *nègre*[26] living with my mother. He is a caretaker of a cassava field (gardien de maniocs). My godfather is Jean Jacques, cook. I was a relative of the Cautin family.

REQUEST. – Who are your friends in town?

ACCUSED. – I live with a *négresse* named Angèle, *patronée*[27] by her father François, a tinsmith. I have my brother Théophile at Monsieur Guillaume's house, my brother Zéphirin at the Attorney General's, and my cousin named Muscadin who is in the same house.

REQUEST. – Have you not other acquaintances?

ACCUSED. – I do not know any young men other than those I see at the ball. If they do not come to my house, I will not go to theirs. When it comes to dancing, I only trouble myself with them to have fun.

REQUEST. – What society (convoi) are you in?

ACCUSED. – I am not from any society, I go to the ball only by invitation.

REQUEST. – Did you used to dance with the société des Indes?

ACCUSED. – Yes, we were always invited to this ball.

REQUEST. – You had to know in particular the king of this company, who is a cook like you?

ACCUSED. – Yes, it's Leon, Mr. Bideaux's cook. He had us invited and showered us with courtesies.

REQUEST. – But do you have other acquaintances in town?

ACCUSED. – I do not have others. I go to Ezias, cook of M. Pinel, once or twice a year, because he comes like me from Saint Jacques. (...)[28]

While French historians have long asserted the disintegration of the slave family, Josaphat's case documents how family links could be maintained and social relations reconstructed in an urban context.[29] During his interrogation, Josaphat mentions his father and mother (Louis *dit* Sauterre and Ursule), but also Adrien, his mother's companion, and Jean-Jacques, his godfather. Despite his separation, for unknown reasons, from his biological family, he seems to have found substitute male figures who were important to him. Thus, he acknowledges the fact that it was Adrian, his mother's companion, who raised him, and not his father. His godfather's occupation as a cook, like himself, could also be of interest. Had he introduced him to the craft, as was very often the case? At the very least, this probably created a special link between the two men. Professional ties seem important in Josaphat's social life: twice, he mentions a cook among his close associates or relations (Leon, Mr. Bideaux's cook, king of the Société des Indes and Ezias, cook of M. Pinel). Although he was enslaved, Josaphat was by no means isolated, and his family was much larger than his ascendants. Beside his father and mother, Josaphat mentions the fact that he is a relative of the Cautin family, meaning he identified with the other members of that network. He also refers to his two brothers and a cousin, whom he seems to see quite often. They live in separate households, except Muscadin and Zéphirin, but they all live in the same town, which, despite having twenty thousand inhabitants, remained relatively close-knit. As for Josaphat's companion Angèle, she mentions in her interrogation that he used to receive a couple of hens from his parents, who were still living at Saint-Jacques.[30] Distance does not seem to be an impediment to the continuation of their family ties, even though Fonds Saint-Jacques, located in the territory of Sainte-Marie, is on the Atlantic coast, on the opposite side of the island (Figure 3.1).

Figure 3.1 Map of Martinique. Collection Géode Caraïbes. AIHP-GEODE EA 9292, Université des Antilles.

The desire to denounce the horrors of slavery has long led French historians to minimize, or even to ignore the question of the leisure time of the enslaved, despite the fact that many accounts of the seventeenth and eighteenth centuries frequently referred to clandestine meetings as well as sanctioned feasts.[31] Judicial archives highlight another set of social activities. Thus, Josaphat's interrogation documents the existence of dancing activities (balls) organized by societies ("convoi") by the first decades of the nineteenth century.[32] Most evidence pertaining to the existence of such alternative social activities dates to later periods. The first fraternal benefit societies (*sociétés de secours mutuel*) only appeared at the end of the nineteenth century in Martinique and the first mutual aid societies (*sociétés d'entraide*) only around 1848.[33] Thus the "société des Indes" mentioned above is not known to historians, though it seems very well known by the justices of the early nineteenth century. It could well be one of the numerous slave societies which appeared in 1793 and developed in the nineteenth century, societies that were tolerated by the administration as opposed to those of the seventeenth and eighteenth centuries.[34] The many regulations from the seventeenth to the eighteenth century aimed at regulating calendas, bamboulas and other slave gatherings illustrate the fact that the edict of March 1685 was not respected in this matter, like in many others. However, the interrogatories around the 1711 revolt of the Gaoulet are more useful, since they not only documented the fact that many of the enslaved of Saint-Pierre used to dance the Gaoulet in the Ursulines' semi-public garden (*enclos*) in 1711, but also provided many details on this activity.[35] Such information contained within judicial testimony is especially precious in this latter case.

Having access to slave voices offers the opportunity to understand what it means to be a slave, not according to what the law prescribed or the master said, but according to the enslaved themselves, speaking in their own ways and on their own terms, of who they are, of their place in society, of their dreams and aspirations. The richness of those rare texts is best exemplified by the 1780 testimony of a white man (his name is illegible) against Castor, a slave of the southern part of French Saint-Domingue, and whose words, spoken in Creole, are quoted by the man in his testimony.

> Yesterday, 23rd, between 9 and 10 at night being in the sugar quarters of the said estate as he is ordinarily, he had met a nègre who was defecating at the very door of the said sugar mill, of which the plaintiff (comparant) had disapproved and told him to go further away
>
> To which the said nègre responded with boldness and confidence:
> I am capable of doing what I want and where I want it (*Moi capable fait ça moi vlé et ou ti moi vlé*).
>
> After this very bold answer, the said nègre fled. However, the plaintiff, having asked the mill driver who could be this slave who

had just fled, and the driver having told him he did not know, the plaintiff had ordered him to watch more carefully and to prevent any foreign slave from approaching the quarters especially during the night.

But a few minutes later, a young nègre belonging to mister de Najac, and named Théodor or Thédor, who had come to ask permission from the plaintiff to cook some sweet potatoes in the sixth clarifier (*batterie*), he had allowed him to do so, as long as one of the sugar technicians was there, so that none were lost [in the syrup].[36] Then some minutes later, after this young slave had gone out, he came back immediately after and said to the plaintiff that the slave who had answered him with impertinence at the door of the sugar mill was about fifty steps away and had asked to talk to him: Hey, young nègre, is the white man still in the sugar factory? If you dare go back to the sugar factory: go, and tell him, that if has the guts, I shall be waiting for him, close to the water (*Jeune nègre, Blan- là, là, dans la sucrerie encore? Toi capable tourné dans sucrerie Si toi capable: alé, dy li que sy liy gagné cœur, moy après tende ly ici côté d'iau*).

After such an incredible report, the plaintiff said to one of the sugar technicians to go, close to the bridge to see if this nègre was still waiting for him, and, if he was still there, to arrest him. That this order was obeyed and the plaintiff had gone quickly on to the place where the slave had been seen, he saw that the said slave was being held and was defending himself against the sugar technician. Seeing this, he called the mill driver to give him a hand in order to capture this mutinous slave, who was still defending himself and kept on vomiting horrors, saying among other things: Thunder, strike me down! If ever you put me in the jail, I don't give a damn about anyone! I am a nègre of master Arnault, I am not the kind of slave a white surveyor can lay his hand on (Tonnerre, crazé moi! Si zam méné moi dans barre moi fou ban de zautres moi nègre maître Arnault, moi pas fait pour qu'un Blanc économe mette main en haut moi!)

The plaintiff [declared] that the aforementioned Dame Arnault is the spouse of Sieur Arnault, the young son of Dame D'Oloron, who had been on the said estate since two days. Since his will was only to repress the serious misconduct of the said slave towards him, a slave he heard was called Castor, and whose attitude could create much turmoil in the workshop he manages... he puts here an end to his declaration, although further consequences could only be more serious, because of the fears he might have for his own safety. He reserves the right to mention those facts, if necessary, declaring this situation to the King's Attorney General in this district in order for it to be denounced, and he asked us to give him the deed and a certified copy of it (one for him and one for the King's Attorney General). And the said plaintiff finally declares that the slave mentioned, against whom this declaration has been made, is detained and will be in the jail of the said estate, until the justices make their decision. The plaintiff signed with us.

Labrouche du Vin and (illegible).[37]

Three sentences pronounced in Creole by Castor exemplify the concept of agency and the difference between being a slave and an enslaved person. Although legally enslaved, and supposedly submissive, Castor asserts his personal agency to do what he wants to do: "I am capable of doing what I want and where I want it." However, Castor goes further, since he later posits his sense that he is equal to the white surveyor and therefore that he can compete with him physically: "Hey, young nègre, is the white man still in the sugar factory? If you dare go back to the sugar factory: go, and tell him, that if has the guts, I shall be waiting for him, close to the water." Then finally, he goes so far as to assert his superiority over the manager, "Thunder, strike me down! If ever you put me in the jail, I don't give a damn about anyone! I am a nègre of master Arnault, I am not the kind of slave a white surveyor can lay his hand on."

This case is unique for the French Antilles in terms of the audacity of the slave's pronouncements as quoted by Labrouche. It is unclear to what degree he was aware of the risks he was taking with his actions and his words, though there are some clues. First, the fact that it is difficult to choose a place busier than the very door of the sugar mill during harvest season suggests intent, whatever the risk. Second, it is not uncommon to hear that domestic slaves, who were at the top of the slave hierarchy, felt superior to many, especially field slaves whom they would not even marry. But they could also feel superior to poor whites (*petits Blancs*), whom they easily distinguished from the *Grands Blancs*, the more powerful big planters who themselves disdained the *petits Blancs*.[38]

It is not possible to draw generalizations from this unique example, and not all slaves would necessarily have reacted in the same way on a regular basis, yet the young man did transmit the audacious message, and the driver remained very evasive concerning the identity of the slave. Nonetheless, such a text demonstrates that being a slave did not automatically entail modeling a submissive attitude.

On a more general basis, judicial archives also allow us to deepen our understanding of the harsh conditions for the enslaved, especially as regards the arbitrary violence they suffered from colonists. The key sources for French colonies include the edict of March 1685 (especially clauses 15, 33, 34, 38, and 42, which were not always applied), as well as visual sources depicting instruments of torture or other physical constraints.[39] For French Saint-Domingue in particular, historians have placed too much attention on a few episodes, such as the Lejeune affair. They have also relied on memoirs written by travelers, whose accounts are so incredible as to be hard to believe.[40] For instance, Alexandre-Stanislas de Wimpffen evoked the case of a pastry maker thrown in an oven, while Girod de Chantrans insisted that masters conducted extrajudicial interrogations sadistically, using fire.[41] These two examples are so extreme that they seem to be motivated by abolitionist principles. Judicial archives offer a much clearer idea of reality. The many examples of crude violence but also the range of forms of violence (psychological, physical) help in the evaluation of what was day to day violence as opposed to what was considered extreme and exceptional. The context also helps illuminate the arbitrariness of violence. The interrogation of Lucile, a forty-year-old slave seamstress, offers a good example of the richness of the judicial testimonies on this matter.

Interrogation of Lucile, Guadeloupe, 1840

Lucile. (*She does not take an oath.*[42]) — I have always experienced the best treatment in my master's house until I incurred his disgrace. It was I who treated him in his illnesses. He promised me freedom, but the first time I asked him to fulfill his promise, he delayed it to another time, on the grounds that he was ill. After his recovery, my prayers became more pressing. I even offered him my ransom. He always refused, on the pretext that my care was indispensable to him.

One day, to my astonishment, he makes me stop without any reason:

"Go, miserable wretch! He said to me, "Go rot in the dungeon!"

And I was locked, my left foot and both hands in an iron ring. The left hand was superimposed on the left foot, so that it could not deviate from it. From the first day, the pain was so strong that, at my shouts, the iron was removed from my right hand. They gave me only a little food, the water was also spared, I received only one bottle a day. Deprived of air and light, my suffering repelled sleep and appetite. I only breathed when they opened my dungeon, which only happened once every twenty-four hours, when my food was brought. Without the help of my children, they would have left me in my garbage, and I was covered with vermin. The slimming of the chained hand allowed me one day to remove it from the ring which fixed it. My master having learned about this, brought a wheelwright, who tightened my chains again.

I remained twenty-two months locked up. When they came to free me, my eyes could not bear the light, my legs refused to carry me. The air was oppressing my chest and I vomited.

THE PRESIDENT. – During your captivity, did your master visit you?

R. – Never.

Q. – Did his daughters give you food?

A. – Sometimes. Most often, it was my children who brought me bread. It was cut into small pieces and passed under the door. I then drew them to me with a stick. Seeing me doomed to perish in the dungeon, I asked for a priest, to die at least as a Christian. It was refused. I never expected so much severity from a master so good.

THE PRESIDENT, TO THE ACCUSED. – What motive have you had in detaining your slave for so long?

THE ACCUSED. – I had proof that she was a poisoner.

LUCILE. – There was a great loss of cattle and slaves at my master's house, but it is not the only dwelling where mortality ravaged. At Bonne-Veine, the harm was as great. It was not the poison that was the cause, as I told my master, whom I saw worried and distressed. I reassured him in this way against his suspicions.

THE ACCUSED. – Ask Lucile if four of my slaves have not died in a few days for eating dead beef.

LUCILE. – Yes, no doubt, since they had eaten some corrupt meat. They died within hours of each other (movement in the audience). Quetty was also arrested and put in prison for poisoning. The goal was to kill me in the dungeon, just as other nègres died there.

THE ACCUSED. – Quetty, midwife of the estate, was put in jail for a few days for having forcibly delivered an unfortunate slave woman who died in pain. Her duty was to warn me to call the doctor. I was warned too late, and when the man of art arrived, the patient was dead. As for the death of any slave in the dungeon, it is a slander on the part of Lucile for her to add this to her slanderous deposition (...)[43]

Many of the realities evoked in the court records highlighted above could be more easily obtained by using slave autobiographies, such as those of Mary Prince, Gustavus Vassa (Olaudah Equiano), Frederick Douglass and many others, with, in addition, more complete records of life paths and less bias relative to the constrained nature of the production of some of our slave voices. Should we not therefore prefer them?

If morally speaking slavery is always unacceptable, opportunities and day-to-day conditions could vary immensely, according to economic activities undertaken, land ownership rules, different legal regimes, and colonial systems. Therefore, in order to explain rather than merely judge, it is worth drawing on archival materials that originated in the specific time and place being analyzed. Second, such slave autobiographies, though indeed precious, do not exist in the French context, or have yet to be found. Finally, it should be remembered that the slave narratives of the former British empire are also not straightforward documents. They have been constructed according to specific contexts (abolitionist or post-abolitionist), which requires that they be used with care.[44] Furthermore, they sometimes told the story of men and women, exceptional because of their origin (sons of kings participating in the transatlantic slave trade for the princes of Calabar, or a person close to a royal family for Ottobah Cugoano) or even more by their experience of slavery (domestic for Mary Prince, sailor and trusted manservant for Olaudah Equiano), and finally by their life paths, from slavery to freedom.[45] Narrated at a stage where the experience of bondage is sometimes far away, their life stories do not always seem completely reliable.[46] Stories of freed slaves or of exceptional men and women slaves, they are probably not characteristic of the daily life of the majority of slaves, and can be challenged for this reason. Conversely, documents from the French Caribbean give voice to ordinary men and women, who never had a plan to defend a cause other than their life or survival. Because of this, the judicial slave testimonies discovered were tested on school audiences and the general public, revealing the richness of their potential uses. What are those modern-day uses?

The events that these documents narrate are located in places (towns, villages, neighborhoods) familiar to the populations still living in those places, and they evoke men and women whose names are theirs today or those of "béké" families (descendants of the estate owners of the seventeenth, eighteenth and nineteenth centuries, still very present today). The slavery courses taught in school in these areas are no longer restricted to the history of North America or Brazil, but directly challenge these non-Caribbean accounts, entering into conversation with them. Colleagues in secondary education also emphasize the special status of slave voices for their pupils. They appear authentic and reliable, unlike the texts emanating from administrators or white and colored masters, disqualified a priori because they are presumed biased,[47] rightly or wrongly.[48] Even if the slave witnesses sometimes alter the reality, the study of their testimonies allows a dialogue with the youngsters to start, in order to lead them towards more complex discoveries, while helping them develop their capacity for critical thinking by means of deconstructing the sources. Slave autobiographies do not give such rich results.

Many American colleagues using Thomas Thistlewood's diary to explain slavery to their students testify to the difficulty of the process.[49] They usually evoke the rage that seizes African-American students, especially female students, in the face of the monstrosity of Egypt's manager and the sexual assaults committed, systematically and with impunity, in Jamaica in the second half of the eighteenth century. According to these colleagues, the extreme reactions generated can block any dialogue, and prohibit any attempt to understand the complexity of the slave system on estates and more widely in the slave societies of the eighteenth and nineteenth centuries. Conversely, the slave voices of the French Caribbean obviously make it possible to document the horror of slavery in the variety of its forms of aggression, but they also offer, and sometimes in the same text, the possibility of going further. Like in the interrogation of Lucile inserted above, they allow an understanding of the diversity of the relations between masters and slaves within the plantation or in towns, and make it possible to realize that the maintenance of the enslavement of slaves in the context of strong demographic imbalances cannot be explained solely by the use of extreme violence.

The most important virtue of those documents is their capacity to highlight the ability of some slaves to rebuild their family, to express their identity, despite all attempts to brutalize or treat them like animals. The few high school colleagues who tested them in Martinique stress the civic importance of documents that help to rebuild the young people in their charge. In a region of the world where most of the school population perceives itself as descendants of slaves, these sources allow the students to rise above more one-dimensional approaches, which sustain an emphasis on processes of victimization. Without ever denying the horrors of slavery, these documents offer alternative images of the enslaved, foregrounding them as subjects of their own life and not only as objects of it. Whether the enslaved made the choice of marronage, revolt or insolence, or even quiet stubbornness or solidarity, they transcended the place that had been assigned to them because of their status and of the racialization of slave societies during the eighteenth century. They sometime conquered another place, closer to their personal conception of life, family, etc. In this respect, these documents transmit positive values of humanity, but also simply of courage, and unwavering determination in adversity, values that are particularly valuable for the education of the youngest members of French Caribbean societies.

The evening events organized for adults do not give fundamentally different results, but offer other perspectives. The most effective ones have required a specific methodology, first putting the public in direct contact with the documents; second, letting the people speak freely, and finally reframing audience questions with reference to the historical context. The chosen approach was fruitful at each stage of the meetings.

Confronted with strong texts like the spontaneous declarations in creole of the slave Castor, the public most often experienced shock. Invited to ask their questions or give their interpretations of the situation, they first refused to accept that the characters mentioned were slaves. Although the event had been announced as dealing with slave voices, members of the public asserted that Castor and his fellow companions were not slaves, that they must have been freedmen after the abolition of 1848. Some struggled to find any solution coherent with their idea of what it meant to be a slave. Others accepted the idea that the persons evoked were slaves, but they placed the action in the revolutionary period, or in a period close to it, when the enslaved would have known already that another future was possible. The discovery of the fact that the action took place in 1780, eleven years before the slave revolt in the northern part of French Saint-Domingue and thirteen years before the abolition of 1793, provoked surprise, misunderstanding, but also curiosity and a desire to understand. Acceptance came through the careful unpacking of all elements of the scene (the little boy asking to put his sweet potato in the *batterie;* the driver pretending not to know the identity of the intruder) and also from the plurality of the interpretations proposed by the public (whether a stroke of madness, or an act of resistance and therefore a deliberate choice to defecate in a very busy place during the harvest season), carefully juxtaposed with contextual information. Little by little, the public discovered the plurality of attitudes and explanatory circumstances, and thus escaped from a univocal vision of the relationship between enslaved and enslaver. For most, it was just a seed that had been planted; for others, it was comfort that had been given; some others however felt confident enough to start challenging degrading images of themselves inherited from slavery and maintained by colonial post-abolition societies.

Such a process of engaging the public may seem strange in the twenty-first century, more than 150 years after the abolition of slavery in 1848, or 200 years after the independence of Haiti. Unfortunately, in French West Indian societies, slavery is flesh and bones, and not just a book on a shelf. It still permeates social relations, marked by subtle processes of racialization. It influences the construction of self-image, through clothing practices, hairstyle choices, work strategies, and so on.[50] What better illustration of this could I find than mentioning a dashing thirty-year-old man who asked me, during one of these evening events, "if I thought/ believed that the descendant of a slave could be a good father?" Here is encapsulated the trauma, and the importance of shedding it. The recent series of symposia on the psychological effects of slavery, organized in Guadeloupe and Martinique by Professor Aimé Charles-Nicolas, also reinforces this point.[51]

Therefore, in addition to the valuable information they offer on slave societies in the French Caribbean of the eighteenth and nineteenth centuries, the testimonies of slaves excerpted from the judicial archives of the French-speaking world are major tools in helping the reconstruction of those Caribbean societies. By, on one hand, bringing to the surface buried certainties, and on the other hand offering liberating perspectives, these sources seem to play a quasi-therapeutic role for those for whom the legacy of slavery is still a trauma. As one participant of this meeting said: "If my female ancestor managed to survive overwork and frequently being raped, am I not, as a woman, able to try to overcome day to day difficulties in the twenty-first century, and like her reconstruct myself, my family, and my social life the way I want it?" Beyond the horrors, the sufferings and the failures, the lived experience of the enslaved as found in these documents constitutes formidable reservoirs of strength and courage, which can more effectively help descendants take ownership of their lives instead of clinging to the long-term position of victimhood.

This perspective does not challenge the legitimacy of requests for reparation, whatever their form, but it allows each person to find in his/her own history and those of his/her ancestors the means of his or her own salvation. In a logical, obviously more civic than strictly academic way, I argue, as an historian living in a West Indian context, that all these elements fully justify the use of these judiciary testimonies of slaves for the historians of the French Caribbean.

Notes

1 Dominique Rogers, "Les Libres de couleur dans les capitales de Saint-Domingue: fortune, mentalités et intégration à la fin de l'Ancien Régime (1776–1789)" (Ph.D. diss., Université de Bordeaux III, 1999).

2 Jean Moomou, Jacqueline Zonzon and Céline Ronseray, who were not part of the slave voices project in the European project EURESCL, were kind enough to share their expertise in order to edit or complete the rare documents found for French Guiana.

3 Frédéric Régent, Gilda Gonfier, and Bruno Maillard, *Libres et sans fer, Paroles d'esclaves français* (Paris: Fayard, 2015); Caroline Oudin-Bastide, *Maîtres Accusés, Esclaves Accusateurs. Les Procès Gosset et Vivié (Martinique, 1848)* (Le Havre: Presses universitaires de Rouen et du Havre, 2015); and *Des nègres et des juges: La scandaleuse affaire Spoutourne, 1831–1834* (Bruxelles: Éditions complexe, 2008). Beyond the Antilles, see Charlotte de Castelnau-Lestoile, *Pascoa et ses deux maris. Une esclave entre Angola, Brésil et Portugal au XVIIe siècle* (Paris: Presses universitaires de France, 2019) and Sophie White, *Voices of the Enslaved, Love, Labor, and Longing in French Louisiana* (Chapel Hill: University of North Carolina Press, 2019), as well as the essays by Brett Rushforth, Cécile Vidal, and Sophie White in this volume.

4 The so-called declarations were recorded at notaries' or clerks' offices, but they were not official complaints.

5 La *Gazette officielle de la Guadeloupe* ou *l'Indicateur colonial* for la Réunion; see Régent, Gonfier, and Maillard, *Libres et sans fer*, 9; for the Gosset and Vivié cases studied by Caroline Oudin-Bastide, see also *le courrier de la Martinique*.

6 Infrajudicial pratices refer to a range of usages according to which disputes which might normally be resolved through the judicial process are settled by practices operated within or in parallel to the normal machinery and practices of the law. See Benoît Garnot, ed., *L'infrajudiciaire du Moyen-Age à l'époque contemporaine* (Dijon: Editions Universitaires de Dijon, 1996), 5.

7 For the edict of March 1685, currently referred to as the 1685 *Code Noir*, see the transcription and translations by John Garrigus, https://s3.wp.wsu.edu/uploads/sites/1205/2016/02/code-noir.pdf (accessed December 13, 2019), hereafter Garrigus, 1685 *Code Noir*. The status of the slaves of French Louisiana, like those of the Mascarenes, was governed by other codes (*Code Noir* of 1724 for the first, and of 1723 for the second) that we shall not discuss in detail here.

8 See also the works of Jean-François Niort, *Le code Noir: idées recues sur un texte symbolique* (Paris: Éditions Le Cavalier bleu, 2015); Frédéric Charlin, "Homo servilis: contribution à l'étude de la condition juridique de l'esclave dans les colonies françaises (1635–1848)" (Ph.D. diss., Université Pierre Mendès France, Grenoble, 2009).

9 The compensation seems to have been calculated according to the price of the slave, not the value of his or her work (article 40 of the edict of March 1685).

10 Antoine Gisler, *L'esclavage aux Antilles françaises, XVIIe–XIXe siècles: Contribution au problème de l'esclavage* (Paris: Karthala, 1981), 111–127.

11 Arrêt qui admet les témoignages des esclaves à défaut de Blancs, excepté ceux portés contre leurs maîtres, Bibliothèque Nationale de France; Code de la Martinique, 298, ordonnance du 15 juillet 1738, Archives nationales d'outre-mer, Aix-en-Provence, France, hereafter ANOM.

12 At the end of the eighteenth-century, Louis XVI tried to improve the status of the enslaved. The new regulations were sent to French Saint-Domingue by way of the ordinances of 1784 and 1785, and in Martinique and Guadeloupe with the ordinance of 15 October 1786. See especially Ordonnance du Roi concernant les procureurs et économes-gérants des habitations situées aux Îles sous le Vent, 3 December 1784, reprinted in M. L. E. Moreau de Saint-Méry, *Loix Et Constitutions Des Colonies Françoises De L'Amérique Sous Le Vent*. vol. 6 (Paris: Chez L'Auteur, 1784), 655 (www.eurescl.eu/images/files_wp3/textnat/17841203.pdf, accessed December 30, 2019).

13 See Arrêt du Conseil d'Etat en réformation des articles 7 et 30, de l'édit de mars 1685, et qui permet les marchés des nègres les Dimanches et Fêtes, et d'admettre leur témoignage à défaut de celui des Blancs, hormis contre leurs maîtres, 13 octobre 1686: "beaucoup de crimes pourroient demeurer impunis si on ne reçoit le témoignage des negres au défaut de celui des blancs, la plupart des crimes n'étant commis et ne pouvant être prouvés que par des negres," www.eurescl.eu/images/files_wp3/textnat/16861013.pdf (accessed December 30, 2019).

14 Requête de la veuve Pamelard du 11 août 1792 et auditions de Zemire, Catherine et Pernise du 13 août 1792, Greffes de Saint-Domingue, 6 DPPC, 166, ANOM.

15 Jérémy Richard, "Le statut juridique de l'esclave aux Antilles sous l'empire du code civil (1805–1848): d'un effort de civilisation à la réticence du parti colon," *Bulletin de la société d'histoire de la Guadeloupe*, 146–147 (2007): 60–61.

16 The so called Mackau's laws refer to two laws enacted on the 18th and the 19th of July 1845. Article 5 of the Law of the 18th of July 1845 posits the right of the slave to redeem or to free their parents (ascendants, legitimate or illegitimate children, spouse, and ascendants of their spouse). Articles 6–11 prescribe fines and imprisonment against masters having infringed their slaves' rights.

17 Régent, Gonfier and Maillard, *Libres et sans fer*, 14.

18 According to Cécile Vidal, the slaves were speaking French in Louisiana, and not creole.

19 Xavier Tanc and Adolphe Juston, *Les Kalmanquious, des magistrats indésirables aux Antilles en temps d'abolition* (Gosier: Éditions Caret, 1998); Oudin-Bastide, *Des Nègres et des juges*, 12–17, 29–30 and more specifically the conflict between Alexandre Belletête, justice of the peace, the commandant of Bellisle and the "white" estate owners in the district of La Trinité, on the one hand, and on the other hand, the justices Adolphe Juston and Hermé Duquenne in Martinique; see respectively 33–75 and 77–88.

20 See article 322 of the Code of criminal procedure (*code de l'instruction criminelle*) enacted for the French Antilles on October 12, 1828 and for French Guiana on May 10, 1829.

21 Valérie Gobert, "Le Droit matrimonial aux Antilles françaises XVII–XXe siècle" (Ph.D. diss., Université de Paris I, 2010); Régent, Gonfier, and Maillard, *Libres et sans fer*; Margaret Tanger, "Contribution de la Cour de cassation à l'émancipation des esclaves des colonies françaises d'Amérique entre 1828–1848," in Association des Professeurs d'Histoire et de Géographie de la Guyane (APHG) et la Société des Amis des Archives et de l'histoire de la Guyane (SAAHG), *Histoire et Mémoire, la Guyane au temps de l'esclavage* (Cayenne: Ibis rouge, 2011), 243–254; C. Oudin-Bastide, *Des Nègres et des juges*.

22 See article 22 of the edict of March 1685, in Garrigus, 1685 *Code Noir.*

23 According to Jean, when they would hear the gunfire announcing the beginning of the Corpus Christi procession, they would start a procession in their own village, holding crosses and singing hymns; see "Les marrons de Tonnégrande," in Dominique Rogers, ed., *Voix d'esclaves, Antilles, Guyane et Louisiane françaises, XVIIIe–XIXe siècles* (Paris: Karthala, 2015), 105.

24 See "Au commencement de l'affaire Macandal: la confession de Médor, Partie française de Saint-Domingue, 1757," in Rogers, ed., *Voix d'esclaves,* 73–84. David P. Geggus, "Haitian Voodoo in the Eighteenth Century: Language, Culture, Resistance," *Jahrbuch Für Geschichte von Staat, Wirtschaft Und Gesellschaft Lateinamerikas* 28, 1 (1991): 33; Hein Vanhee, "Central African Popular Christianity and the Making of Haitian Vodou Religion," in Linda M. Heywood, ed., *Central Africans and Cultural Transformations in the American Diaspora* (Cambridge: Cambridge University Press, 2002), 255.

25 Unless otherwise noted, all transcriptions and translations are the author's own. She thanks Sophie White for her help with translating and editing these passages.

26 The original terms *"nègre"* and *"négresse"* have been retained rather than translated as "slave" or "negro" since in French these are gendered terms that specifically denote males and females of African origin, whether born in Africa or not.

27 This term refers to a *statu liberis,* a slave who lives as a free person, despite the fact that his/her emancipation has not been ratified (or the process of his manumission is not totally completed). In order for this slave not to be arrested as a runaway, his/her name is mentioned on the census record of the sponsor *(le patron),* stating his/her intermediary (although not legal) status.

28 Martinique Geographic Series, carton 141 dossier 1270 (copie ADM, 1MI 1306), ANOM. My thanks to Stéphanie Belrose for sharing this document; the translation is my own.

29 Arlette Gautier, *Les soeurs de solitude, femmes et esclavage* (Rennes: Presses universitaires de Rennes, 2010), 104; Arlette Gautier, "Les familles esclaves aux Antilles françaises,1635–1848," *Population* 55, 6 (2000): 975–1001; Frédéric Régent, *Esclavage, métissage, liberté, la Révolution française en Guadeloupe* (Paris: Grasset, 2004), 114–115.

30 See the interrogatory of Angèle, in "Josaphat, empoisonneur à l'arsenic, 1826–1828, Martinique," in Rogers, ed., *Voix d'esclaves,* 131. The phrase "Saint-Jacques" refers most probably to Fonds Saint-Jacques Estate, which belonged to the Dominicans in the seventeenth and eighteenth centuries and was managed by Father Labat between 1696 and 1705. Like other clerical properties, the plantation was confiscated by the state during the French Revolution. All the slaves of the clergy were also confiscated, and therefore were called "esclaves du domaine." Some remained on the plantations (La Gabrielle in French Guiana, Fonds Saint-Jacques in Martinique, etc.), but some, like Josaphat, his brothers and cousin, were employed at the governor's house or at major officers' houses, or in administrative buildings (prisons, forts, courts, etc.).

31 No chapter in the masterful work of Gabriel Debien is devoted to this theme, nor does Jacques de Cauna's *Au temps des îles à sucre* fifteen years later show any interest in it; see Gabriel Debien, *Les Esclaves aux Antilles françaises* (Basse Terre: Société d'Histoire de la Guadeloupe, 1974); Jacques de Cauna, *Au temps des îles à sucre, Histoire d'une plantation à Saint-Domingue au XVIIIe siècle* (Paris, Karthala, 1987). The first dissertations on this question were written in the 1990s.

32 The words "convois" or "coteries" seem to refer to associations oriented towards providing magnificent, or sometimes just decent, burial to their members. Sometimes in Martinique, a convoy seems just a subdivision of a society or even another word to design a slave society. See Cécile Celma, "Les sociétés d'esclaves aux Antilles: une histoire comparative," in Marcel Dorigny, ed., *Esclavage, résistances et abolitions* (Paris: Éditions du CTHS, 1999), 85. See also Luciani Lanoir L'Étang, "Des rassemblements d'esclaves aux confréries noires," *Bulletin de la Société d'Histoire de la Guadeloupe* 152 (2009): 3–14.

33 For the first fraternal benefit societies (sociétés de secours mutuel) founded in 1882 at Saint-Pierre and for the mutual societies, see Cécile Celma, "Les sociétés d'esclaves aux Antilles: une histoire comparative," in Marcel Dorigny, ed., *Esclavage, résistances et abolitions* (Paris: Éditions du CTHS, 1999), 89 and Cécile Celma, "Deux formes de sociabilité de la population de couleur en Martinique et en Guadeloupe à la fin du XIXe siècle: la mutualité et le syndicat," *Revue Française d'histoire d'Outre-mer* 74, 275 (1987): 207–223.

34 Article 16 of the edict of March 1685 forbad slave meetings.

35 Rogers, ed., *Voix d'esclaves*, 15-53. See also Brett Rushforth, "The Gaoulet Uprising of 1710: Maroons, Rebels, and the Informal Exchange Economy of a Caribbean Sugar Island," *William and Mary Quarterly* 76, 1 (2019): 75–110.

36 On a sugar estate, the term "batterie" referred to the sixth copper of the series of clarifiers in the boiling house. It was a copper with a very small diameter, in which the syrupy sugar was close to crystallising. See Yannick Leroux, Réginald Auger et Nathalie Cazelles, *Loyola, l'habitation des Jésuites de Rémire en Guyane française* (Québec: Presses de l'université du Québec, 2009), 252–253; Sylvie Meslien, *La canne à sucre et ses enjeux aux Antilles françaises* (Martinique: SCEREN-CRDP, 2009), 37; and www.liverpoolmuseums.org.uk/ism/slavery/archaeology/caribbean/plantations/caribbean34.aspx (accessed December 13, 2019).

37 Déclaration du 23 avril 1780, greffe Saint-Domingue, greffe du Petit-Goâve, greffe 136, folio 36 recto verso, ANOM; see also Rogers, ed., *Voix d'esclaves*, 92–93.

38 See for instance Gabriel Debien, *Les esclaves aux Antilles françaises* (Basse Terre: Société d'Histoire de la Guadeloupe, 1974), but also Josette Fallope, "Les occupations d'esclaves à la Guadeloupe dans la première moitié du XIXe siècle," *Revue française d'histoire d'outre-mer* 74, 275 (1987): 189–205. www.persee.fr/doc/outre_0300-9513_1987_num_74_275_2590.

39 www.slaveryimages.org/s/slaveryimages/itemset/36?sort_by=created&sort_order=desc&page=1.

40 See Carolyn Fick, *Haïti, naissance d'une nation* (Cidhica: Les Perséides, Université d'état d'Haïti, 2014), 97, Pierre de Vaissière, *Saint-Domingue: La société et la vie créoles sous l'Ancien Régime (1629–1789)* (Paris: Perrin, 1909), 186–188; Gisler, *L'esclavage aux Antilles françaises*, 117–127; Jacques Thibau, *Le temps de Saint-Domingue* (Paris: JC Lattès, 1993), 17–93; and Malick Ghachem, *The Old Regime and the Haitian Revolution* (Cambridge: Cambridge University Press, 2012), 117–196.

41 Alexandre-Stanislas, baron de Wimpffen and Pierre Pluchon, *Haïti au XVIIIe siècle: Richesse et esclavage dans une colonie française* (Paris: Karthala, 1993), 181 and Justin Girod de Chantrans, *Voyage d'un Suisse dans les colonies d'Amérique* (Paris: J. Taillander, 1980), 64.

42 According to article 322 of the Code of Local Instruction, the statements of slaves against their master could only be heard, if the accused as well as the

Attorney General and the civil party consented; in this case, they were only heard for information purposes and without first swearing to tell the truth. In application of this article, Douillard-Mahaudière's lawyer accepted that Lucile testified but formally opposed her taking an oath as requested by the president of the *Cour d'assises*.

43 *Cour d'assises de la Pointe-à-Pitre, session d'octobre 1840* (Paris: A. Blondeau, 1841), 14–16; See also "Lucile de Guadeloupe, de l'intimité à l'empoisonnement, 1840," in Rogers, ed., *Voix d'esclaves*, 145–148. This document was found by Caroline Oudin-Bastide, as part of the EURESCL project.

44 For a synthetic analysis of these processes, see for instance Claire Parfait and Marie-Jeanne Rossignol, eds. and trans., *Le récit de William Welles Brown, esclave fugitif, écrit par lui-même* (Mont Saint-Aignan: Publications des universités de Rouen et du Havre, 2012), 19–26.

45 Randy J. Sparks, *The Two Princes of Calabar* (Cambridge, MA: Harvard University Press, 2005); Ottobah Cugoano, *Thoughts and Sentiments on the Evil and Wicked Traffic of the Slavery and Commerce of the Human Species Humbly Submitted to the Inhabitants of Great-Britain by Ottabah Cugoano, a Native of Africa. London, July 1787* (London: Sold by T. Becket, Bookseller, Pall-Mall; Also by Mr. Hall, at No. 25, Princes-Street, Soho; Mr. Phillips, George-Yard, Lombard-Street; and by the Author, at Mr. Cosway's, No. 88, Pall-Mall, 1787); Mary Prince, *The History of Mary Prince, a West Indian Slave: Related by Herself* (Baltimore, MD: Project Muse, 2017). *The History of Mary Prince, a West Indian Slave. Related by Herself, London* (1831).

46 The debates between Paul Lovejoy and Vincent Caretta could easily illustrate this point; see Vincent Carretta, *Equiano the African: Biography of a Self-Made Man* (Athens: University of Georgia Press, 2005); Paul E. Lovejoy, "Construction of Identity Olaudah Equiano or Gustavus Vassa," *Historically Speaking* 7, 3 (2006): 8–9; Paul E. Lovejoy, "Autobiography and Memory: Gustavus Vassa, alias Olaudah Equiano, the African," *Slavery and Abolition* 27, 3 (2006): 317–347; Vincent Carretta, "Olaudah Equiano or Gustavus Vassa? New Light on an Eighteenth-Century Question of Identity," *Slavery & Abolition* 20, 3 (1999): 96–105; Paul E. Lovejoy, "Issues of Motivation—Vassa/Equiano and Carretta's Critique of the Evidence," *Slavery & Abolition* 28, 1 (2007): 121–125; Vincent Carretta, "Does Equiano Still Matter," *Historically Speaking* 7 (2006): 81–92.

47 "Regards de Blancs, regards de maîtres" is the recurring criticism. In territories where the majority of the population's ancestors were slaves, the issue is important. Many French West Indian writers have made an argument for denying historians the ability to account for the history of these populations.

48 Evelyne Camara, Isabelle Dion, and Jacques Dion, *Esclaves, Regards de Blancs 1672–1913* (Aix-en-Provence: Archives nationales d'outre-mer, 2008) offers very good counterexamples.

49 Thomas Thistlewood papers, Beineke Library, Yale University. See also Trevor Burnard, *Mastery, Tyranny, and Desire: Thomas Thistlewood and His Slaves in the Anglo Jamaican World* (Chapel Hill: University of North Carolina Press, 2004) and Douglas Hall, *In Miserable Slavery: Thomas Thistlewood in Jamaica, 1750–1786* (London: Macmillan, 1999).

50 Juliette Smeralda, *Peau noire, cheveu crépu: L'histoire d'une aliénation* (Pointe-à-Pitre: Éditions Jasor, 2005).

51 See also Aimé Charles-Nicolas and Benjamin Browser, *L'esclavage: Quel impact sur la psychologie des populations?* (Paris: Idem Éditions, 2018) and Dominique Rogers, "Esclavage et réconciliation: les historiens ont-ils échoué?" in Matthieu Dussauge, ed., *Route de l'esclave. Des itinéraires pour réconcilier histoire et mémoire* (Paris: L'Harmattan, 2016), 27–43.

Section Two

Native Americans

4 A "Spanish Indian Squaw" in New England

Indian Ann's Journey from Slavery to Freedom

Linford D. Fisher

The new moon plunged the New England landscape into complete darkness on the night of October 3, 1743. The silhouettes of four individuals slipping into the inky nighttime away from a farmhouse in Norwich, Connecticut, went undetected. That is, until morning, when their labor and bodily presence were immediately missed. Their master, Stephen Gardner, had quite a surprise when there was no morning fire or breakfast, and no one ensuring the household ran smoothly. He immediately reported their absence to the local constable, who issued a warrant for their arrest. The relatively close-knit New England countryside could not hold secrets for long, however, and it only took three days for the four self-emancipated individuals to be dragged before a judge in Norwich.[1]

In court, the defendants admitted to running away, but they declared that they had been wrongfully enslaved and were, in fact, free individuals. They were a diverse crew: an older Native woman named Ann, two Indian girls named Ann and Phillis, and a man of mixed Indian and African ethnicity (called "molatto" in the records) named Caesar. The older Ann served as the group's spokeswoman. She declared unequivocally that she was a "Mohawk Squaw and born free." This identity was contested by white colonists, who affirmed she was, variously, a "Spanish Indian Squaw," a Carolina Indian, and even a Huron (from the Great Lakes region). Ann additionally declared that she was the mother of the other three individuals. The fate of all four rested on the elder Ann's identity, for if she was a free-born Native, then neither she nor her children could lawfully be enslaved.

Spanish Indian slave, Carolina Indian slave, Huron, or free-born Mohawk? John Richards, one of the Justices of the Peace for New London County, decided that the case was beyond the jurisdiction of the town court and referred the case to the Inferior Court of Common Pleas for a full jury trial, which was scheduled for early November, one month later. Richards and the other magistrates needed some time to get to the bottom of the situation, so they ordered the depositions of several additional individuals familiar with the Gardner household to help them understand the contested identity of Ann. But the supplementary information they learned only confused the situation, at least initially.

Ann was forcibly brought to New England in 1714 or early 1715, likely on a smaller 50–80 ton English merchant vessel that sailed into Newport, Rhode Island.[2] Like other New-England-bound ships from the American south and the Caribbean in this time period, it likely contained a small number slaves in its hold, along with other raw materials and trade items.[3] Ann would have arrived in chains, like the other enslaved individuals on the ship, and was sold through informal networks in Newport. In the opening decades of the eighteenth century, Newport was only slowly beginning to enter a centuries-old, bustling Atlantic African slave trade that forcibly placed enslaved Africans and Natives on plantations and in households throughout every European colony in the New World. Newport was already a major Atlantic trading port, rivaling its nearby neighbors of Boston and New London. By the end of the eighteenth century, Newport and its northerly neighbor, Providence, were known as the epicenter of the North American African slave trade, with more slave ships sailing from Rhode Island for Africa than any other port on the continent.[4]

A colonist named William Gardner purchased Ann and an enslaved Indian man in Newport at the same time in approximately 1715 and forced them to make yet another watery crossing, in a small boat from Aquidneck Island across the Narragansett Bay to the mainland, to where he resided on Boston Neck in South Kingstown, Rhode Island. Ann arrived at the home of Gardner in poor health, whether through a preexisting condition or, equally as possible, due to the experience of being enslaved and transshipped in the cramped quarters of the ship that brought her into Newport. William Gardner tried to sell off his sickly property to his sister, Abigail, but she refused due to Ann's unwell appearance. Instead, William sold Ann to his brother, Stephen, who also lived in Boston Neck. William held on to his male Indian slave but eventually sold him to Nicholas Gardner, a yeoman from nearby Kingstown (one wonders if Gardner was splitting up the family in the process). Within two years (in 1716 or 1717), Ann became pregnant by an unnamed local black man and gave birth to her son, Caesar, just before a massive snowy New England nor'easter.[5]

At some point in the next decade or two, Stephen Gardner moved thirty-five miles west to Norwich, Connecticut, and he took Ann and her growing family with him. By the early 1740s, Ann had four children: Caesar, Abraham, Ann, and Phillis. The father or fathers of these four are not recorded, but according to local observers, Ann's two girls were identifiably Indian. Because he was not involved with the self-emancipating crew, no additional information is given about Abraham. Caesar was apparently of mixed African and Indian ancestry, since he was designated a "molatto" in the records (although in much of the English Atlantic world such racial categorization was inconsistent and usually served the purposes of white magistrates and masters—often obscuring Indian ancestry).[6]

In Norwich, the elder Ann and at least three of her four children—Caesar, Phillis, and Ann—lived in the household of Stephen Gardner and functioned with the relatively ambiguous autonomy that slaves and servants of color sometimes did in eighteenth-century New England.[7] When the younger Ann developed an open sore, she spent three weeks convalescing at the house of the widow Elizabeth Rogers, who apparently served as a neighborhood doctor. A few months after the younger Ann recovered and returned home, the elder Ann also visited Rogers, likely to similarly seek medical treatment, where they had informal conversations that Rogers later related in court.[8]

The question remained in 1743: who was Indian Ann? Some family members and friends identified her as a Spanish Indian. Abigail Powers, who lived on Boston Neck (in Rhode Island) in 1715 when Ann first arrived at the home of Stephen Gardner, said that a group of enslaved Indians who arrived in Newport in the 1710s were all called Spanish Indians. Over twenty-five years later, Ann the elder (the mother) seemingly also self-identified as a Spanish Indian to Elizabeth Rogers, as did the younger Ann. Others claimed she was a "Carolina Indian." When William Gardner first purchased Ann in Newport in 1715, he told his wife that Ann was a Carolina Indian. Williams's son, John Gardner, also said Ann was known to be a Carolina Indian when she was purchased.[9]

But in court, in November 1743, Ann insisted she was a Mohawk Indian and had been freeborn, which would have meant she was originally from New York colony (or possibly New France), likely along the Mohawk River west of Albany, where the principal towns of the Mohawks were located. So, despite the testimony of white colonists that Ann was either a Spanish Indian or Carolina Indian, the justices called in local linguistic experts to test Ann's claims that she was a free-born Mohawk. To do so, they relied on Martin and Rebecca Kellog—brother and sister—who had been captured in the infamous raid on Deerfield, Massachusetts, by the French and Indians in 1704, and had somehow survived the arduous winter march—even as children—to Montreal. Although they were both adopted into local Mohawk families, Martin was ransomed a few years later. Rebecca, however, stayed for twenty-four years, taking a Mohawk husband and starting a family.[10]

Consequently, the Kellogs' testimony held great weight. They also took a thorough—one might even say distrustful—approach to investigating the elder Ann. Over the course of several hours, Martin Kellog asked Ann question after question in Mohawk and studiously wrote down all of her answers. To test the veracity of her responses, the next morning he met with Ann and asked the same questions, again in Mohawk, double-checking her answers for consistency. Both Rebecca and Martin affirmed to the court that Ann was fluent in "Mohawk," and identified her as a member of the Huron (Wyandot) nation, which they somewhat oddly identified as one of the Five/Six Nations of the Haudenosaunee

(Iroquois) Confederacy. The Kellogs' testimony left no doubt to the court that Ann was fluent in Mohawk, and seemed to confirm Ann's own testimony about her self-identification as a free-born Mohawk.[11]

After carefully sorting through the testimony, the jury assembled at the Norwich County Court ruled in favor of Ann. Rather spectacularly, Ann's own testimony about her own identity and community origins shaped the entire court proceedings. Because she had so eloquently and insistently insisted on her tribal identity, the court took the fairly radical step of testing her claims through the Kellogs. Having their confirmation, the court was satisfied. They decided she was, indeed, a free-born Mohawk, and that she had been wrongfully enslaved. Consequently, based on the informal legal precedent that the status of the children follows the mother, the jury declared that her children were also wrongfully enslaved. Ann, Phillis, Ann, and Caesar—four Natives all previously slaves for life—walked out of the Norwich courtroom in December 1743, free from the bondage of slavery. For Ann, her thirty years of enslavement had finally come to an end.[12]

These documents related to the freedom suit of Ann and her children reveal intimate, family, and everyday details about slavery that other kinds of records cannot offer. It would be interesting to compare the shipping records for the boat that carried Indian Ann from South Carolina to Rhode Island with these records, if we were able to find them. As Stephanie Smallwood has noted, clean and neat records like ledgers and invoices "effaced the personal histories that fueled the slaving economy."[13] By contrast, freedom suit records take what might have been one bland ledger line and fill in the details, bringing to life in vivid detail the histories and relations of an enslaved man or woman.

It is worth lingering over Ann's case because of what we can learn about the nature of Indian slavery and the testimony of enslaved Indians, especially those given by women, in eighteenth-century New England. Ann's case reveals a legal context in which Indian identity mattered a great deal, since there was growing awareness in the wider English empire about wrongful Indian enslavement.[14] Her case also sheds light on the Indian slave trade into New England in the early eighteenth century, and its legacies into successive generations. More broadly, cases like Ann's reveal the centrality of the status of maternal ancestors in determining whether enslaved people who sued for their freedom should be considered slave or free. Indian women's voices, ancestry, and actions are all on brilliant and full display in Ann's case, one that we could multiply by the hundreds and thousands over the course of the colonial period if the records provided it.

Ann's case is exceptionally detailed, but she was only one of tens of thousands of enslaved Indians in colonial America. From the beginning of English "exploration" of the Americas, merchants and adventurers routinely snatched Indians from the coasts and took them back to

London to parade around as curiosities. Captains relied on these forcibly captured Indians to provide knowledge of the landscape and coastline and to serve as translators on return trips. In all the places English colonists started colonies that survived—including Virginia (1607), Bermuda (1609), Plymouth (1620), Barbados (1627), Boston (1630)—they soon enslaved Indians locally or brought them in from other parts of the Caribbean. Through various wars with Indians, privateering in the Caribbean, and trading for enslaved Indians, English colonists soon utilized the slave labor of thousands of Indians, even as they began importing enslaved Africans.[15]

Ann was transported on a ship that was part of a wider world of trade, commerce, and slavery. As English colonies developed and grew in North America and the Caribbean, trade between these various points also flourished. Ships sailed from places like Rhode Island and Massachusetts to Bermuda and Jamaica and then back again, perhaps stopping at Virginia, South Carolina, or Pennsylvania. Colonists sent wood, vegetables, horses, and cattle to the Caribbean in exchange for sugar, rum, tobacco, indigo, and hardwoods of various sorts. Enslaved Africans and Indians were almost always part of this informal intercolonial trade that kept each colony supplied with what they lacked. This intercolonial trade intersected with the trans-Atlantic African slave trade as well, which by the 1740s was regularly bringing enslaved Africans to North American colonies as well as the sugar islands, such as Jamaica and Barbados.

Within these larger contexts, then, Ann's journey from freedom to slavery to freedom gives important insights into wider processes regarding colonial Indian slavery. At the most basic level of individual information and biographical details, this case reminds us of the many details of the lives of enslaved men and women that we will never be able to recover. Being an enslaved female of color in the colonial period ensured voiceless anonymity in the large majority of cases. Ann's act of self-emancipation and the court case it triggered ensured that future generations of historians would know far more about her life than many of her peers. Even so, the court records that survive suggest that Ann was not able to narrate her own past and history in a way that was meaningful for her. Instead, she and other deponents were shoe-horned into the narrow questions dictated by this particular legal context. The fragments of personal biographical information we get only serve to highlight the absences and silences in Ann's life as recorded in the archive.

Ann's experience of slavery also reminds us that forced mobility and severed family connections were the reality of all enslaved individuals. In a way that was different yet parallel to enslaved Africans, enslaved Indians like Ann experienced being sold as a slave and shipped to a foreign place.[16] Natives who were enslaved through warfare or outright slave-raiding were often shipped out of their home area as slaves, leading to the same kinds of family separation, culture shock, initial social death, and the need to reconstruct a new life and identity observed in black slavery. In all too many cases, shipping records do not accurately reflect the volume of Indians being shipped out key ports for the Indian slave trade, like Charleston.[17]

As harrowing as her transshipment and enslavement was, Ann was fortunate in some ways to be able to form a nuclear family and not have it be split up by masters. It is not clear how three of Ann's daughters were conceived, however. Her children might have been unchosen—they could easily have been the result of rape at the hands of her master, neighbors, or other slaves and servants. But it is significant that at least three of Ann's children were living with her in Gardner's household in Norwich. Many other enslaved people had to endure the injustice of enslavement and forced shipment as well as the continual and ongoing separation.

This court case also reveals some small but important intimate details about Ann. Abigail Powers recalled that Ann had a large "tattoo" on her leg that ran from her mid-thigh down to her shin, ornately crafted in a floral pattern after "the Indian fashion."[18] Native American skin art, scarification, and tattooing were commonly used by Native clans, tribes, and individuals in North America. They varied widely, and could be used to signify clan or tribal identity, tell stories, or serve as individualized artistic expression.[19] This is somewhat parallel to the "country marks" that "saltwater" (newly arrived) Africans often bore when they arrived in chains, naked, and were sold on auction blocks in Barbados, or Jamaica, or New York.[20] Other small details were recorded. Martin and Rebecca Kellog both testified that when Ann spoke Mohawk, she did so "without Shuting her Lips," which the Kellogs claimed was unique to Mohawk speakers. In giving some of these more intimate details, the depositions seemingly echo some of the physical descriptions contained in the self-emancipated (runaway) slave advertisements so common across the English colonies in the eighteenth century—descriptions designed to reduce, racialize, stigmatize, and other-ize.[21]

One of the many remarkable features of this case is that Ann herself is at the center of the action, and what she says shapes the emerging narrative of her identity and direction of the investigation. Cases like Ann's allow us to see enslaved men and women in action, to see them actively pushing back against structures of power, and asserting their own sense of themselves, their identity, and their rights within an oppressive colonial context. This includes a surprising permissible legal voice given to Ann by the justices. Courts in the wider eighteenth-century Atlantic were varied in terms of how much women of color were allowed to testify and provide their own perspective. Marisa Fuentes, in *Dispossessed Lives*, documents the silencing of enslaved women of color in Barbados courtrooms, in society, and in the archives.[22] Courts in other colonies, however, increasingly allowed people of color—including women—to testify.

Such was the case with Ann. Not only was she allowed to speak, but her side of the story and her own biography are taken seriously. Ann's voice comes through strongly, always mediated by the official summaries of the depositions, but it is still present. When the four Indians were brought into the Norwich court on October 6, 1743, Ann was the first of the runaways to speak. She made three strong claims. First, that she was "a Mohawk Squaw and born free"; second, that "Cesar and Ann the younger and Philliss were born of her"; and third, that her children, like herself, "ought not to be holden in Service." This last claim was especially poignant. Ann was demanding her freedom, but she was also looking out for her children. Of course, there are other ways in which local magistrates doubted and mistrusted Ann, but it is intriguing to note the power of her own testimony in the court's deliberations—and its presence as recorded in the archives. It does raise the question, however, of how much of latitude given by the court was due to Ann being Native, and whether an enslaved African woman would have been treated similarly.

In court, Ann asserted her Mohawk identity. What the records do not reveal is how she got wrapped up in the Indian slave trade in the Carolinas. If we take as a starting place Ann's own testimony about herself, that she was a "Mohawk Squaw, and free born," there are multiple historical possibilities. Although what follows is mostly conjecture, it is still useful as a way to understand Indian mobility, warfare, and even slavery practices in colonial America.

One strong possibility is that Ann could have been born in a Mohawk clan along the Mohawk River, west of Albany, New York. It is also possible she could have been born in an entirely different Mohawk community, at Kahnawake, just south of the St. Lawrence River near Montreal in Quebec. A third possible birth location is in a Native village in the southeast somewhere. Perhaps her mother was a Mohawk, but gave birth to Ann among the Tuscaroras, or perhaps even the Catawbas or Cherokees.

Given the centuries-old trading routes between the Haudenosaunee and Tuscarora Native villages in the Carolinas, it easily conceivable that Ann (or her mother) could have traveled as a child or as a wife to the Carolina region. Tuscarora and Mohawk are both part of the Iroquoian family of languages, and indeed, the Tuscaroras became the sixth member of the Haudenosaunee Confederacy in 1722. The connections between the two regions were strong. Slightly less probable but still in the realm of possibility is that Ann or her mother were taken as captives during Cherokee or Catawba raids on the Haudenosaunees. If she was taken this way, then she would have been raised (or even born) among "Carolina" Indians, which is perhaps where that designation came from.

No matter how she got there, it seems likely that Ann was in the region of the Carolinas between 1700 and 1715. Once in the Carolinas, she could have been enslaved by the English in any number of ways. The Carolina region was racked with warfare between 1701 and 1716, with Queen Anne's War (1701–1713), the Tuscarora War (1711–1713), and the Yamasee War (1714–1716) all taking place in quick succession. Colonists enslaved thousands of Indians during these wars, either claiming them as spoils of war, selling them within the Carolinas or Virginia, or shipping them out of Charlestown and into the wider Atlantic, whether to Barbados, Jamaica, Bermuda, or New England.[23]

Perhaps Ann was in Tuscarora country when war broke out in 1711. By the end of the war, the English enslaved approximately 700 Tuscaroras in the war and killed almost as many more. Approximately another 500–1,000 additional Tuscarora allies were enslaved by English Indian allies as well, although those are far more difficult to tabulate.[24] If this is when she was enslaved, Ann likely was forced to join the other enslaved Indians in being transported to Charleston, South Carolina, where she was loaded up on a sloop and sailed to Newport, Rhode Island, in 1714 or early 1715. In New England, such enslaved Indians shipped out of Charlestown were commonly called "Carolina Indians," but given raiding on Spanish Indian mission towns, it was not always clear which Indians were from which sites. If Ann had been born in a Mohawk or Tuscaroran village in New York or the Carolinas, she would have been born a free Indian, even if she was enslaved as part of wider colonial warfare and Indian slave raids. In the eighteenth century, colonial courts increasingly began freeing Natives who could prove they had a free maternal ancestor.[25]

Other aspects of this case reveal processes and questions related to Native (and wider enslaved) attempts to secure their freedom. As with many such cases in the colonies in this time period, running away was the best way to get the attention of local magistrates and be brought into a legal context where you could argue for your freedom. Perhaps Ann suspected she might get caught as well, thereby forcing local authorities to listen to her. We might be tempted to understand this as a runaway court case, for example, but one of the deponents calls it like it is: Abigail Powers says that Ann is "suing for her freedom."

Then again, it not entirely clear which laws the jury relied on when deciding Ann's case. Connecticut in particular, and New England in general, did not have any positive Indian slave laws that would govern this case. No New England law specifically stated clearly what should happen to the children of enslaved Indians (or even Africans). Instead, there were localized customs and practices that had existed since the Pequot War in the seventeenth century. Massachusetts included a generalized slavery clause in its 1641 Body of Liberties, and both Massachusetts and Rhode Island passed feeble attempts to limit slavery later in the seventeenth century, but nothing comprehensive or decisive emerged in the realm of the law. Instead, a pastiche of practices and customs ruled on the ground.[26]

This silence contrasts starkly with other English colonies that laid out precisely how slavery could be passed down to children, and under what circumstances Natives could be enslaved. The technical phrase for legal principle of slavery following the mother was *partus sequitur ventrem.* Although it was the bedrock of European slavery regimes in the wider Atlantic world, only some English colonies affirmed this in actual law; the rest, it seems, believed it to be self-evident and silently practiced it as a matter of course.[27] Virginia was one of the few English colonies to make this clear. In 1662, it passed a law that specifically stated that the status of children should follow the mother.[28] The purpose was to ensure that mixed race children (specifically, those who had a white father and black or Indian mother) could be easily and legally enslaved. Although the law formally imposed a fine for such "fornication," it inadvertently licensed and even incentivized planters to rape their female slaves, knowing such an act could result in enlarging his slaveholdings.[29]

The same was true in Jamaica. By the 1680s there was a law that stated that "all such Negroa or Indian slaves" which might be brought to the island from Africa, Asia, or America, should be slaves for life, along with their children.[30] There were precedents outside the English context, too. The French *Code Noir*, or Black Code, passed in 1685, was known by English colonists in the eighteenth century (Edward Long, for example, in his *History of Jamaica*, includes an abstract at the end of Volume two).[31] Article 13 of the *Code Noir* specifically stated that the status of the children should follow the mother, not the father.[32]

On the question of the enslaveability of Indians, New England colonies were largely silent in law but active in practice. This legal silence contrasts with other English colonies, especially Barbados, where by 1636 a law was in place that declared any Indians or Africans who were brought to Barbados to be slaves for life.[33] In 1661 Barbados passed a comprehensive slave code that governed all parts of slave movement, activity, mobility, labor, and punishment. As scholars have shown, this Barbados slave code became an important model for other larger-scale slave colonies, like Jamaica and the Carolinas.[34] In Virginia, too, a series of laws between the 1650s and 1705 in Virginia wrestled with the contexts in which Native Americans could rightfully be enslaved.[35] Compared to their French and Spanish counterparts, which legislated slavery at the imperial level for all of the empires, the ad hoc nature of English slavery in its colony-by-colony laws and silences is striking indeed.[36]

In fact, according to the laws on the books, Ann should have never been sold as a slave for life in Rhode Island in the first place. During the bloody and destructive war between most regional Indian nations and the English known as King Philip's War (1675–1676), Rhode Island passed a law prohibiting Indian slavery. A March 13, 1676, law stipulated that that "noe Indian in this Colony be a slave," with the important allowance that Indians could be forced to serve "to pay their debts or for their bringing up," that is, the costs of colonists to own and raise them.[37] Colonists soon found workarounds in any case by calling Indians servants and enslaving them for a limited time. Providence adopted a complex and graduated system of local, limited-term enslavement that assigned between seven and twenty-five years of service for surrendering Indians based on their ages.[38] Newport magistrates preferred a simple limited-term enslavement length of nine years.[39] As many Indians found out, these limited terms were not so limited, with many Indians serving for life, and having their children claimed as slaves as well.

By the time Ann was shipped to Newport from the Carolinas, Indian and African slavery were well-entrenched in New England practice, despite the absence of positive slave law. Perhaps as many as 1,500 Africans served as slaves in New England as a whole, in addition to 1,000–1,500 enslaved Native Americans.[40] But as hundreds of enslaved Indians were imported into New England from the Carolinas and the Caribbean in the early eighteenth century, colonial governments began to look around nervously, perhaps fearing an insurrection in their mist. The boat that brought Indian Ann, in fact, was one the last shipments of enslaved Natives from Carolina that arrived in Rhode Island before a law sought to suppress it. Ann likely arrived in 1714 or early 1715. By July of 1715, so many Carolina Indians had been imported that Rhode Island passed a law halting further importation of enslaved Indians, noting the outbreak of "conspiracies, insurrections" and other crimes perpetrated by recently imported Indians from the Carolinas.[41]

Rhode Island was not alone. In fact, every single New England colony had done or would do the same, but for differing reasons. Massachusetts had already passed a similar law in 1712, focused on Carolina Indians' reputation for causing trouble.[42] New Hampshire passed a law to the same effect in May 1715, noting the "Overgreat Number and increase" of Indian slaves in the colony and a generalized fear of "Conspiracies outrages Barbarities, Murders, Burglaries, Thefts and other Notorius Crimes" that had happened elsewhere. The colonial legislature levied a ten pound fine against every Indian imported after the passing of the law.[43] Connecticut did the same a few months later, in August 1715, giving the reason that the Indians brought from Carolina were "in open hostility" against the colonists there, and that they might cause "great mischiefs" in Connecticut if imported.[44]

Even so, hundreds (if not over a thousand) enslaved Indians from the Carolina region were imported into New England before and after these laws took effect. People found ways around the laws, of course. Indian cargo went unreported, or perhaps captains and buyers simply paid the penalty that governments imposed. Within two months of passing of Rhode Island's law, local officials made an exception for one shipment and—tellingly—referred to the fifty-pound fee as a "duty" (which implies importing Carolina Indians was a taxable instead of an illegal activity). When the sloop *Charles* sailed into Newport in late August, 1715, the captain George Wood had nine enslaved Indians from South Carolina on board. Three local Newport residents petitioned the General Assembly, noting that the nine Indian slaves were actually going to be given to a group of English refugees who fled the Carolinas due to the Yamasee War. The Indian slaves, the petitioners explained, were for this charitable cause, and therefore should be exempted from the duty. The Assembly relented and saved Captain Wood the hefty 450-pound duty on his enslaved Indian cargo.[45] This was at least the second time such an exception had been made for the supposed Indian slaves of English refugees from Carolina.[46]

"Carolina" or "Spanish" Indians continued to be listed in wills, inventories, and newspaper advertisements into the late 1710s and 1720s and beyond. Three Carolina Indian slaves ran away together from their masters in Boston in 1716. James, Robin, and Amareta belonged to Samuel Adams, Nehemiah Yeals, and Thomas Salter, respectively, likely living in close urban proximity. But on September 15, 1716, they ran away together, taking the clothes on their backs, along with other apparel. James and Robin, by their finer clothes, were likely house servants or skilled workers. James had on a leather jacket and black stockings. Robin was wearing a double-breasted jacket and leather breeches.[47] Others ran away, too. In July 1717, Willam Bourden of Newport, Rhode Island, ran an advertisement in the *Boston News-Letter* for two "Carolina Indian Men-Servants" who had run away from his estate. Both of were identifiable, in part, because William Bourden had his initials branded on their cheeks: one was branded with a "W" and the other with a "B."[48]

Ann's case also sheds light on the terminology applied to enslaved Indians. This is true regarding the archival imprecision between "servant" and "slave." Many New England masters and magistrates preferred to use the term "servant" for people they held as slaves, even African ones. This makes parsing the status of people listed in colonial documents difficult at times. In Ann's case, the both terms are used about her and her children, sometimes together: "servants and slaves." But as Martin Kellog stated outright, Stephen Gardner claimed Ann "as his slave."[49] Other deponents affirmed the same: that Gardner bought Ann "for a slave" and sold her again "for a slave."[50] These are important statements that should make us wary about soft-pedaling slavery when we see the word "servants" in the documents.

This case raises questions about the legal distinction between different kinds of Indians, and between Indians and Africans, particularly in terms of who was enslavable, and in what context. In the early modern English world, colonists saw Natives as enslaveable more generally, but they also had to almost always repeatedly ask about whether or not their

Indian slaves had been legally enslaved. There are dozens of cases in the wider Atlantic world where the legality of enslaving Indians was challenged in courts. Freedom suits for Natives were almost always based on this notion of wrongful enslavement. Although there are some cases in which African enslavement is seen as illegal, those cases are rare.[51] The more generalized assumption was that African enslavement was the result of "just wars" in Africa between African nations and needed no special defense.

But colonists at times distinguished *between* different kinds of Natives. In this particular case, is it possible that tagging Ann a Carolina or Spanish Indian made her more enslaveable, whereas her identity as a Mohawk would have made her less so? Margaret Newell has suggested in *Brethren by Nature* that, more generally, if enslaved Indians hoped to find freedom, they needed to first free themselves from labels like Carolina and Spanish—terms that implied legitimate enslavement.[52] Ann's claim to be a free member of one of the most well-known and feared Native nations in the northeast was especially powerful. In this case it seems highly likely Indian Ann knew exactly what she was doing to resist certain labels and appropriate others in court, and that the court similarly knew this given their involvement of the Kellogs to verify her claim.

The complexities of race are also revealed in the categorization of one of Ann's children, Caesar, as a "mulatto." Although the field has too often presumed individuals label as "mulatto" in the records are primarily African, this case reminds us that "mulatto" was a flexible enough racial descriptor to include Indians and those with Indian parentage. In this instance, we can see almost in real time the transformation of Indian identities into a more generic racially mixed identity. This was true in other parts of the English empire, and even up through the early nineteenth century in the United States. Calling people "mulatto" or "negro" or just "slave" who had a clear claim to Native identity and ancestry was an oft-used tool of magistrates and planters to make Indians and Indian descended people more enslaveable. Enslaved Indians sometimes raised legal questions; enslaved Africans and African-descended people rarely did. Most colonial Americans assumed Africans to be enslaved and enslaveable unless proven otherwise.

Indian Ann was just one of hundreds of "Spanish" and "Carolina" Indians forcibly brought to New England in the early eighteenth century. Spanish and Carolina Indians dot the runaway slave ads in New England's newspapers in the first two decades of the eighteenth century. Indian Ann was also not the only "Spanish" or "Carolina" Indian to run away and trigger a freedom suit. In 1749, an Indian man named Elisha ran away from his owner, William Marsh, of Plainfield, Connecticut.[53] When he was brought before the Windham court, he proclaimed himself to be "free-born and no slave." Marsh himself labeled Elisha as a "Spanish Indian," although Marsh also tried to label Elisha a "Negro Mulatto"—highlighting the African side of his mixed ancestry, which was common in English colonies by masters seeking to cast doubt on their slave's Indian identity.

What the court found in Elisha's case was a family history that could be traced all the way back to Spanish Florida. Elisha's mother was an Indian from Florida later renamed Betty. She was only a small child when Carolina English troops and Indian allies stormed the Spanish fort she and her mother were temporarily staying in, perhaps in the 1690s. Her mother strapped Betty to her back in typical Indian fashion and tried to escape by swimming away. English soldiers followed them by boat, shot Betty's mother, and took Betty captive. Betty and other Indian captives were taken to Charlestown, South Carolina, where they sold Betty to one colonist, who turned around and sold her to a merchant named William Crawford, from Newport, Rhode Island. Crawford brought her and presumably other enslaved Indians to Newport, where he sold her to a Rhode Islander named Edward Lillybridge. Betty was sold and bought by several different colonists before coming into the possession of Thomas Power.

In New England, Betty gave birth to Elisha, seemingly with an African man, in approximately 1715. He, too, was claimed as a slave by Power and eventually was sold to Marsh. Finally, at thirty-four years old, Elisha claimed his Indian heritage and his freedom based on his mother's former status as a free Indian. In an attempt to undermine Elisha's claims to freedom, Elisha's master tried to distinguish between "Carolina" and "Spanish" Indians. Carolina Indians were born and raised within English colonial jurisdiction and may have greater claim to unjust enslavement. Spanish Indians, on the other hand, were captured from the Spanish during a war that was justified, and so had no claims to freedom. Elisha's mother Betty fell into the latter category, Marsh argued, and therefore should not be freed. The court disagreed, and Elisha was given his freedom.

Such distinctions were apparently not important in Anne's case. There is a pattern among the witnesses and how they describe Ann that may provide a small clue as to the shift in how she was seen over time, perhaps in response to the changing legal context. Abigail Almy, who was married to William Gardner when he first purchased Ann in 1714 or 1715, said that her husband told her Ann was a "Carolina Indian Woman." William Gardner's son, John, said the same thing in court—he called Ann a "carolina indian woman." All the witnesses who interacted with Ann later called her a Spanish Indian. Although, there were some ambiguities of memory by the white witnesses who are called in. Elizabeth Rogers, who attended to Ann the elder (as she is called in the records) and one of her daughter, said that Anne's daughter told her one time that Ann was a "Spanish Indian"—but then admitted, "or what I understood to be a Spanish Indian."[54] The court never made anything of these distinctions, however, and the case really revolved around Ann's claim to be a free-born Mohawk. There is, of course, the possibility that Ann was being opportunistic in claiming to be a free Mohawk. The rigorous language testing undertaken by the Kellogs seems to rule that out in this case.

Despite the richness of the court records, there are still more questions than answers that emerge from this case. What exactly were the circumstances of Ann's original enslavement? Why did she wait so long to run away? Was this the first time she tried to contest her enslavement? If not, when were the prior attempts, and what did they look like? And we really have no details about what daily life looked like for Ann before her enslavement and transshipment or while she was enslaved.

After the case was closed in December 1743, Ann and her children seemingly disappear into the generalized silence and murkiness of the past. Ann and her children were free, but what did that mean in reality? How does one recover from half a lifetime of wrongful slavery? How does one begin to rebuild a life that has been shattered by forced relocation, separation, humiliation, likely abuse, and isolation? There is no record of any compensation from the court or Gardner for Ann or her children. Only their court costs were covered. The prospects for successful living in English society for a single mother of color were not good. It is possible, given the bleak outlook in Connecticut, that Ann either tried to make the arduous journey back home—wherever she felt that might be, or that she intermingled with local Native groups. Or she could have found gainful employment in local households or even bound one or more of her children to local colonists, as hundreds of other Native mothers did across New England in the eighteenth century. We just don't know.

In the end, of course, the countless additional details of Ann's life are lost to history. The information we get is shaped by the context in which that information was sought, and who was doing the seeking. Ann's experience, as we know, could be multiplied by the thousands in the eighteenth century. Still, there is a voice here, and there is enough to reconstruct a basic biographical outline. As we listen closely to such voices, we will understand more about the lives of individual enslaved people like Ann as well as the contexts that they shaped with their words and actions.

Notes

1 The details of this case are drawn from ten pages of court documents and depositions held in the Connecticut State Archives, CSL RG003, New London County Court Records, Native American, Box 1, Folder 44. My thanks to Jason Mancini for alerting me to these documents and providing me with transcriptions by Laurie Pasteryak.

2 Testimony of Abigail Almy, November 19, 1743. Connecticut State Archives, CSL RG003, New London County Court Records, Native American, Box 1, Folder 44.

3 For more on the intercolonial trade, see Gregory E. O'Malley, *Final Passages: The Intercolonial Slave Trade of British America, 1619–1807* (Chapel Hill: The University of North Carolina Press, 2014).

4 Jay Coughtry, *The Notorious Triangle: Rhode Island and the African Slave Trade, 1700–1807* (Philadelphia, PA: Temple University Press, 1981).

5 Testimony of Abigail Powers, November 28, 1743. Connecticut State Archives, CSL RG003, New London County Court Records, Native American, Box 1, Folder 44.

6 See, for example, Sharon Block, *Colonial Complexions: Race and Bodies in Eighteenth-Century America* (Philadelphia: University of Pennsylvania Press, 2018).

7 See, for example, Allegra Di Bonaventura, *For Adam's Sake: A Family Saga in Colonial New England* (New York: Liveright Publishing Corporation, 2013); Margaret Ellen Newell, *Brethren by Nature: New England Indians, Colonists, and the Origins of American Slavery* (Ithaca, NY: Cornell University Press, 2015); and Jared Ross Hardesty, *Unfreedom: Slavery and Dependence in Eighteenth-Century Boston* (New York: New York University Press, 2016).

8 Testimony of Elizabeth Rogers, November 28, 1743. Connecticut State Archives, CSL RG003, New London County Court Records, Native American, Box 1, Folder 44.

9 Testimony of Abigail Powers, Elizabeth Rogers, and John Gardner. Connecticut State Archives, CSL RG003, New London County Court Records, Native American, Box 1, Folder 44.

10 Testimony of Martin Kellog and Rebecca Kellog. Connecticut State Archives, CSL RG003, New London County Court Records, Native American, Box 1, Folder 44.

11 Testimony of Martin Kellog and Rebecca Kellog. Connecticut State Archives, CSL RG003, New London County Court Records, Native American, Box 1, Folder 44.

12 Court judgment, undated (but presumed to be November 1743). Connecticut State Archives, CSL RG003, New London County Court Records, Native American, Box 1, Folder 44.

13 Stephanie E. Smallwood, *Saltwater Slavery: A Middle Passage from Africa to American Diaspora* (Cambridge, MA: Harvard University Press, 2007), 98.

14 In 1741, for example, Jamaica passed a law against the Indian slave trade out of the Mosquito Shore. "An Act for recovering and extending the Trade with Indian Settlements in America, and preventing for the future some evil Practices formerly committed in that Trade," *Acts of Assembly, Passed in the Island of Jamaica, from the Year 1681 to the Year 1769 Inclusive. In Two Volumes*, vol. 2 (Kingston, Jamaica, 1787), 193–194.

15 Alan Gallay, *The Indian Slave Trade: The Rise of the English Empire in the American South, 1670–1717* (New Haven, CT: Yale University Press, 2002); Newell, *Brethren by Nature*; Wendy Warren, *New England Bound: Slavery and Colonization in Early America* (New York: Liveright, 2016).

16 Sowande M. Mustakeem, *Slavery at Sea: Terror, Sex, and Sickness in the Middle Passage* (Urbana: University of Illinois Press, 2016) and O'Malley, *Final Passages*.

17 Gallay, *The Indian Slave Trade*, 299–302.

18 Testimony of Abigail Powers, November 28, 1743. Connecticut State Archives, CSL RG003, New London County Court Records, Native American, Box 1, Folder 44.

19 Lars F. Krutak, *Tattoo Traditions of Native North America: Ancient and Contemporary Expressions of Identity* (Arnhem: LM Publishers, 2014);

Gordon Sayre, "The French View of Tattooing in Native North American Cultures," *Proceedings of the Meeting of the French Colonial Historical Society* 19 (1994): 23–34; and Jane Caplan, *Written on the Body: The Tattoo in European and American History* (Princeton, NJ: Princeton University Press, 2000).

20 Michael A. Gomez, *Exchanging Our Country Marks: The Transformation of African Identities in the Colonial and Antebellum South* (Chapel Hill: The University of North Carolina Press, 1998).

21 David Waldstreicher, "Reading the Runaways: Self-Fashioning, Print Culture, and Confidence in Slavery in the Eighteenth-Century Mid-Atlantic," *The William and Mary Quarterly* 56, no. 2 (1999): 243–72, https://doi.org/10.2307/2674119 and Block, *Colonial Complexions*.

22 Marisa J. Fuentes, *Dispossessed Lives: Enslaved Women, Violence, and the Archive* (Philadelphia: University of Pennsylvania Press, 2016).

23 Gallay, *The Indian Slave Trade*.

24 Gallay, 298.

25 Loren Schweninger, *Appealing for Liberty: Freedom Suits in the South* (Oxford: Oxford University Press, 2018) and Honor Sachs, "'Freedom by a Judgment': The Legal History of an Afro-Indian Family," *Law and History Review* 30, no. 1 (February 2012): 173–203.

26 *Proceedings of the Rhode Island General Assembly* 1 (1649–1669): 25. Regarding the 1641 law, see "A Coppie of the Liberties of the Massachusets Collonie in New England," in *Collections of the Massachusetts Historical Society*, vol. 7, 3rd Ser. (Boston, MA: Charles C. Little and James Brown, 1838); and Jerome S. Handler, "Custom and Law: The Status of Enslaved Africans in Seventeenth-Century Barbados," *Slavery & Abolition* 37, no. 2 (April 2016): 4, https://doi.org/10.1080/0144039X.2015.1123436.

27 Jennifer L. Morgan, "Partus Sequitur Ventrem: Law, Race, and Reproduction in Colonial Slavery," *Small Axe* 22, no. 1 (April 3, 2018): 1–17. See also Thomas D. Morris, "'Villeinage … as It Existed in England, Reflects but Little Light on Our Subject:' The Problem of the 'Sources' of Southern Slave Law," *The American Journal of Legal History* 32, no. 2 (1988): 95–137, https://doi.org/10.2307/845699.

28 William Waller Hening, *The Statutes at Large; Being a Collection of All the Laws of Virginia, from the First Session of the Legislature, in the Year 1619*, vol. 2 (Richmond: Printed by and for Samuel Pleasants, junior, printer to the commonwealth, 1809), 170, http://archive.org/details/statutesatlargeb02virg. See also Edmund S. Morgan, *American Slavery, American Freedom: The Ordeal of Colonial Virginia* (New York: W.W. Norton & Co., 2003), 335.

29 For the wider Virginia context, see Rebecca Anne Goetz, *The Baptism of Early Virginia: How Christianity Created Race* (Baltimore, MD: Johns Hopkins University Press, 2012).

30 David Buisseret, *Jamaica in 1687: The Taylor Manuscript at the National Library of Jamaica* (Kingston, Jamaica: University of the West Indies Press, 2008), 287.

31 Edward Long, *The History of Jamaica or, General Survey of the Antient and Modern State of the Island: With Reflections on Its Situation Settlements, Inhabitants, Climate, Products, Commerce, Laws, and Government*, vol. 2 (London: T. Lowndes, 1774), 487.

32 The Code Noir. http://chnm.gmu.edu/revolution/d/335, accessed May 30, 2019.

33 John Poyer, *The History of Barbados: From the First Discovery of the Island, in the Year 1605, Till the Accession of Lord Seaforth, 1801* (J. Mawman, 1808), 32.

34 Edward B. Rugemer, "The Development of Mastery and Race in the Comprehensive Slave Codes of the Greater Caribbean during the Seventeenth Century," *William and Mary Quarterly* 70, no. 3 (July, 2013): 429–458 and Edward B. Rugemer, *Slave Law and the Politics of Resistance in the Early Atlantic World* (Cambridge, MA: Harvard University Press, 2019).

35 For the 1705 laws that stated that Indians born in freedom in Christian countries could not be enslaved, see *Hening's Statutes*, October 1705—4th Anne, Chap. XLIX, 447–448.

36 Alan Watson, *Slave Law in the Americas: Alan Watson: 9780820311791: AmazonSmile: Books* (Atlanta: University of Georgia Press, 1990) and Brett Rushforth, *Bonds of Alliance: Indigenous and Atlantic Slaveries in New France* (Chapel Hill: The University of North Carolina Press, 2012), Chap. 2.

37 John Russell Bartlett, *Records of the Colony of Rhode Island and Providence Plantations, in New England*, vol. 2 (Providence, RI: A. C. Greene, 1856), 535.

38 *Collections of the Rhode Island Historical Society: Staples, W.R. Annals of the Town of Providence. 1843*, vol. 5 (Providence, RI, 1843), 170.

39 Bartlett, *Records of the Colony of Rhode Island and Providence Plantations, in New England*, vol. 2, 549.

40 Newell, *Brethren by Nature* and Warren, *New England Bound*.

41 See, for example, Charles J. Hoadly, ed., *The Public Records of the Colony of Connecticut*, vol. 5 (Hartford, CT: Case, Lockwood & Brainard, n.d.), 516; Bartlett, *Records of the Colony of Rhode Island and Providence Plantations, in New England*, vol. 4, 193.

42 Sanford Winston, "Indian Slavery in the Carolina Region," *The Journal of Negro History* 19, no. 4 (October, 1934): 435.

43 "An act prohibiting the importation or bringing into this province any Indian servant or slaves," passed May 15, 1714. New Hampshire, Henry Harrison Metcalf, and New Hampshire Secretary of State, *Laws of New Hampshire: Province Period, 1702–1745* (Manchester: John B. Clarke Company, 1913), 152–153.

44 Hoadly, *The Public Records of the Colony of Connecticut*, vol. 5, 516.

45 Rhode Island, *Records of the Colony of Rhode Island and Providence Plantations, in New England: Printed by Order of the General Assembly*, vol. 4 (A. C. Greene and Brothers, state printers, 1859), 197–198.

46 Island, vol. 4, 185–186.

47 *Boston News-Letter*, September 17, 1716. Database of Indigenous Slavery in the Americas, accessed May 14, 2018.

48 *Boston News-Letter*, July 15–22, 1717. Database of Indigenous Slavery in the Americas, accessed May 14, 2018.

49 Testimony of Martin Kellog. Connecticut State Archives, CSL RG003, New London County Court Records, Native American, Box 1, Folder 44.

50 Testimony of John Gardner; Testimony of Abigail Almy. Connecticut State Archives, CSL RG003, New London County Court Records, Native American, Box 1, Folder 44.

51 Warren, *New England Bound*, 37–42.

52 Newell, *Brethren by Nature*, 249.

53 The details for this case come from the Miscellaneous Papers, 2:64a, 71. See also Newell, 249–250.

54 Testimony of Elizabeth Rogers, November 28, 1743. Connecticut State Archives, CSL RG003, New London County Court Records, Native American, Box 1, Folder 44.

5 In the Borderlands of Race and Freedom (and Genre)

Embedded Indian and African Slave Testimony in Eighteenth-Century New England

Margaret Ellen Newell

Scholars interested in pre-1800 slave narratives face enormous challenges, but perhaps the biggest obstacle is that very few written sources exist in the British colonies. For decades literary and historical investigators, compilers of anthologies, and teachers tended to mine the same sources. These efforts enhanced our understanding of the experiences of enslaved Africans, of course, but heavy reliance on texts by Phillis Wheatley, Venture Smith, and Olaudah Equiano raises questions about how well these exceptional accounts represent the experiences of the voiceless many.[1] The "silence in the archive" regarding slavery has become a mainstay of conferences and theoretically sophisticated works on slavery in recent years. Scholars, particularly literary experts, have also inquired into questions of authenticity, authorship, fictionalization, and the influence of print capitalism and discursive conventions on the published narrative.[2]

If few African testimonies exist, even fewer Native American authors find voice in the current archive of early America.[3] Literacy and language created barriers to Indigenous communication with Euro-American audiences, but that is not the whole story. The Indigenous slavery archive is even less developed than its African counterpart because until recently scholars did not recognize Indian captivity and involuntary servitude as slavery. Crossing the boundary of race and ethnicity in slavery studies has produced an explosion of new works on Native American slavery. This research on Indigenous subjects will surely unlock additional sources for the slavery archive, but these may not necessarily be the same kinds of published autobiographies that formerly defined the African slavery narrative.

As we seek to broaden the slavery archive, crossing another border—the border of genre—offers a creative strategy for uncovering slave narratives and autobiography in the sources we now use to reconstruct the European-Native American encounter.[4] Published narratives featuring Indian slaves have been hiding in plain sight, often considered part of other genre categories: true-crime tales, the conversion narrative, the sermon. Other published and manuscript legal archives contain rich first- and third-person descriptions of Indigenous lives. Some subjects of these documents were biracial, offering insight into the racialization of slavery itself. Mining such sources for embedded biography and autobiography means identifying new genres of slave narrative, which in turn requires that we engage critically with issues of content, context, authorship, literary convention and production in the same way scholars who use the older canon have. Given an emerging consensus about the value of embedded slave narratives, it is also time to think comparatively about the insights narratives of Indian slavery offer.

The New England Indian archive is a good place to start exploring existing works for hidden slave narratives. A robust print culture in the region meant that contemporary published sources exist, and a law of slavery that permitted enslaved Indians and Africans to testify in court (unlike in other English colonies by the eighteenth century) generated many manuscript court testimonies and depositions featuring Indians. This allows us to compare a variety of source material on the slave experience, including unpublished petitions, depositions, and challenges to legal writs, as well as items from well-known published genres. Most involve Indians, but some feature biracial New Englanders and Africans.

Differences across these narrative formats are not as great as they initially appear. Ultimately, all were produced by Euro-American third parties. In the case of depositions and petitions, the level of English colonial intervention in shaping Indian testimony varied; it might include posing the questions and creating the menacing legal environment that shaped the narrative, or making corrections to language or translating, or providing legal advice that conditioned the ways in which enslaved persons described their experience.[5] It is impossible to tell whether this amounted to a more or less extensive alteration than the editorial intervention in the testimonies that appear in published conversion narratives and in execution or crime sermons. Meanwhile, published Native American accounts offer some surprises. Intended as something other than a slave narrative, they were bound by genre considerations which would seem to limit their utility. But, precisely because their creators had other intentions, they were not limited to the conventions of the classic published slave narrative. In addition, they offer elements that the typical legal manuscript does not: an entire life arc, insights into the role of religion, emotional content, and complex personal sentiments about enslavement and acculturation.[6] Taken together, distinct genres of published narratives and legal testimony allow us to construct individual Indian biographies and to make arguments about the origins and evolution of Indian and African servitude and slavery more generally.

Published Indian slavery narratives have typically been packaged as something else, both by eighteenth-century contemporaries and in recent scholarship. Two of the three most well-developed criminal conversion accounts published in America between 1701 and 1738, for example. involved New England Indians.[7] They were collected by Samuel Moody, a minister in York, Maine, who encountered both subjects in jailhouse visits, sometimes with his son Joseph. The Moodys and their Indigenous subjects essentially invented the American crime genre, making auto-biography of the perpetrator the centerpieces. Publishers hawked them to popular audiences and reprinted shorter versions that completely dropped the pastor's sermon and interpretation. The Moody narratives are well known and often included in literary anthologies, but they have been read as stories about criminality, Native literacy, and religion rather than as narratives of involuntary servitude.[8]

In fact, both of Reverend Samuel Moody's subjects were Indians from the Monomoy community on Cape Cod who experienced involuntary servitude and/or enslavement a very short distance from their homes.[9] These are slave stories without the Middle Passage or even the scenes of violent captivity that formed part of the experience of Indians enslaved during the Pequot War (1637–1638) and King Philip's War (1675–1676) decades earlier, although the victims' near total estrangement from nearby communities of Indians is a striking feature of both histories. These accounts, however, are not exceptional in other ways. Many New England Indians were enslaved or forced into servitude in close prox-imity to their homes.[10] In the 1700s, enslavement most often occurred through penal servitude, marriage, or the extra-legal extension of term servants into slaves for life. These accounts help illustrate such processes.

Of course, Moody did not highlight his characters' enslavement but rather the morphology of their conversions, and his editorial influence is apparent in how the stories were organized. He structured their accounts to conform to his audience's expectations of the conversion narrative genre—the good start, the fall from grace, the poor moral choices and alcohol consumption culminating in crime, and the eventual repentance before death. Still, he permitted his subjects an invaluable first-person narrative role.

Joseph Quasson entered servitude "voluntarily" at age six in 1704, following a pathway from freedom to debt peonage that many other In-dians paced. Although Moody was not aware of Quasson's background and so did not stress it, Quasson's elite connections even conformed to later slave narrative and theatrical genre expectations that slavery's vic-tims be of noble origins.[11] The Quasson family had been sachems and large landholders, and some of Joseph's relatives had even owned other Indians' indentures. But they had lost many of their assets by 1720.[12] When Joseph was six, he recalled, "my Father died five Pounds in Debt to Mr. *Samuel Sturges* of *Yarmouth*. I was bound out to him by my Mother on that Account." In other words, because Joseph's father died owing money to town clerk and occasional Justice of the Peace Samuel Sturgis, Joseph's mother offered the child to Sturgis as an indentured servant to clear the family's account. Sturgis was something of a broker of Indian labor and of penal indentures, and his brother Thomas had a similar history. Sturgis also oversaw the transfer and distribution of Indian lands to the Euro-American proprietors of Yarmouth, including his own family.[13]

Following typical household patterns, the mistress of the house, Mary Coggeshall Sturgis, taught young Quasson along with other children and dependents. As he recalled, "I was, as soon as possible, instructed in Reading and my Catechism ... I had then great Fear of Sin." Joseph acquired literacy and worked in the family's Yarmouth warehouse. Proud of his apparel and English appearance, he attended English church alongside the Sturgises and felt like a welcome member of the congregation. Despite physical proximity to the Monomoy community he did not attempt to escape, and later events suggest that he did not have much contact with his family.

As reported by Moody, Joseph Quasson described complicated feelings both of loyalty and resistance concerning the Sturgises and their acculturation project as an adolescent. He did not actively resist servitude, claiming "I don't remember that I then allowed myself in any external Way of Wickedness; such as Lying, Swearing, Stealing, &c." The Sturgises took no chances and kept Joseph under surveillance, "such strict and regular Government Night and Day that I had no Opportunity" for carousing or other independent activities. The child also felt affective bonds toward the people who had replaced his parents, complex emotions likely shared by many involuntary servant and slave children living in household environments. Joseph admitted that when fellow "'prentices" (apprenticed or bound youths, likely Indians) asked for gunpowder from his master's warehouse, the boy "suffered some of them to do it, which troubled me afterwards."[14] Reluctant to steal because of attachment to his master and mistress and to a moral code, he permitted theft by others. Possibly Joseph viewed his cohorts' theft of gunpowder as a form of resistance—to servitude and to English occupation of their lands without payment—an act to which he wanted to lend at least passive aid. Or perhaps he merely wanted to create independent relationships with people outside of the Sturgis home. At the end of his fifteen-year term at age 21 (longer than typical male apprentices), the Sturgises released him from their service with a suit of clothes and a Bible in his hand.

That the Sturgises freed Joseph at all, without attempting to extend his indenture through legal and extra-legal means, makes his story unusual. Many Indians who entered servitude as small children never exited from that status, as their masters claimed them and eventually their children as slaves. Still, Quasson's post-servitude existence reflected another common experience: the limits of freedom in colonial societies that denied Indians like him the political and economic privileges that former

English servants enjoyed. English people who passed from slavery to freedom might fail, but they might also become householders eligible to share in free land divisions. They could gain full membership in the town church, exercise the vote if male property owners, serve on juries and participate in an important form of governance, aspire to office and the respect and remuneration that followed officeholding, and even borrow money from colonial land banks. Connecticut was the only New England colony that made any provision for the future of former Indian servants in freedom, and the legislation there mainly concerned itself with requirements that freed servants carry freedom papers to prove their status. The highest form of citizenship freed Indians might acquire was that of "sojourner"—the right to stay in a town but not to become a full member community with privileges.[15] Massachusetts did even less to clarify the status of freed Indians in English towns. Thus, young men and women like Quasson faced uncertain economic futures and no clear entry into local English institutional and community life.

Quasson got some work but soon found it difficult to pay his expenses. Having pawned his clothes and bible, he felt embarrassed to attend the English church. "[W]hen I had brought myself into a poor and ragged Condition," he confessed, "I left the English Meeting through Shame, where *I* always used to appear well clothed: *I* went to the *Indian* Meeting (where *I* understood nothing) only to save my Fine."[16] Church attendance in Massachusetts was mandatory, so to avoid paying a civil fine he joined an Indian congregation. But Joseph did not understand the preaching there: fifteen years of service in the Sturgis household had left him fluent in English but ignorant of Wampanoag. He had lost touch with most of his kin. Unsuccessful at finding a place in the English community, and alienated from his Indian family, he suffered bouts of depression and began drinking heavily.

Broke and without options, in 1725 Quasson joined an expedition to Maine during Dummer's War, one of five conflicts that pitted New England and British armies against the Wabanaki Confederacy and their French allies between 1676 and 1748.[17] New England forces relied on the local Native American population, who at times composed upwards of a fifth of Provincial units in these so-called "Indian Wars." Southern New England Indians in military service might be servants enlisted by masters who collected their bounties and wages, or debtors anxious to avoid penal servitude, or clients of officials who pressed them to enlist in return for protection and kept their debentures. They might join town militia forces composed primarily of Euro-Americans or serve in all-Indian units with English officers. In Maine, Joseph's troop merged with other Massachusetts forces and he encountered Indians, including kinfolk still attached to their villages and serving in their own military company under their English "guardian," Captain Richard Bourne.[18] Quasson could not understand them, and they mocked him for his cultural ignorance and his English ways. One evening he got into a brawl with a soldier named John Peter, who turned out to be his cousin, and ended up killing Peter with the man's own gun.

The murderous finale made Joseph Quasson's story unusual, but his military service, and the economic, social, and cultural difficulties that attended his transition from the Sturgis household to freedom, formed a more common narrative thread for Native captives and involuntary servants. Quasson's account gives this experience, reflected in other legal documents, an emotional heft and poignancy. Native Americans raised in English households were no longer as "Indian" as their peers, but neither were they full English citizens with opportunities and connections to help them begin an independent life. Quasson entered a world of even less opportunity than the one that confronted Native American captives and servants from a previous generation seeking to consolidate freedom. The roles as leaders or cultural intermediaries that former captives such as Robin Cassacinamon of the Mashantucket Pequots had assumed among their own people a century earlier still existed in the eighteenth century, but in much diminished form and power. Few English needed intermediaries to deal with Indians anymore, given a century of acculturation and knowledge on both sides. Quasson had the lineage status to become a leader at Monomoy but lacked cultural capital and even acquaintance among his own people. Nor had his service with the Sturgises created sufficient social, political, and economic capital for him to achieve personal independence in English colonial society. Quasson managed to remain free for about a year. More typically, former servants like him ended up not on the scaffold but at the public vendue, being auctioned off in restitution for debt or crime and returned to servitude.

Patience Boston, the narrator/author of Moody's other converted convict story (*Taken from her Mouth*, the title blared) was also a child of two high-status parents, John Sampson and a Christian Indian woman named Sarah Jethro.[19] Her father bound her out at age three to the family of Yarmouth farmer and deacon Paul Crow[ell] and his wife Elizabeth Hallett Crowell. Unlike Joseph Quasson, who engaged in quiet subversion outside of the home, Patience used the household to stage acts of rebellion, resistance, and defiance. A self-described "mischievous and rebellious Servant," young Patience not only violated the Sabbath but committed acts of sabotage, such as driving cattle into the cornfields and eventually setting fire to the Crowell home three times.[20] Arson by servants and slaves was a capital crime, yet numerous court cases indicate that this failed to deter enslaved Native and African children and adults from burning their masters' houses and barns.

Patience described her complicated relations with her mistress, who employed "seasonable corrections" (corporal punishment), but also exhorted her to change her ways and achieve salvation. The Crowells could have stood by and seen Patience prosecuted for arson but apparently did not. Despite near-constant conflict Patience admitted that Elizabeth was "a Mother to me" and deeply mourned her death. Patience's complex attitude toward Elizabeth Crowell points to the ways in which English household life created powerful emotional bonds as well as lines of conflict between master and servant, even as these sentiments further separated Patience from her home community. She remained in touch with other Indians everywhere she lived via an informal network of servants, slaves, and free persons of all races who drank, socialized and fenced stolen goods. Some of these ties extended across long distances. Patience later engineered a move to Maine, "enticed by an Indian woman who was sold in those Parts," because of the promise of friendship and drinking. Still, her English "families"—her word for the various English households where she served—played central roles in her life. Both Patience and Joseph testified to the influence of religious training as well as the impact of their integration into Euro-American households and family life on their emotional development.

When her term expired, Patience celebrated, noting, "I thought myself happy that I had no Body to Command me."[21] As with Joseph Quasson her freedom was short-lived. Within a year Patience married an enslaved African whaler and agreed to become a slave or servant for life at his master's insistence. She became contractually bound to both her husband and her husband's master Elisha Thatcher in a perverse echo of the marriage vow, "until the end of his life, or as long as we both shall live."[22] Neither Patience's marriage to an African man nor her enslavement were unique events. Such marriages linked Indians enslaved in the wake of King Philip's War in the 1680s and 1690s to Africans in nearby Connecticut and Rhode Island, and more unions took place as the numbers of Africans in New England increased after 1700. The influx of enslaved Africans affected Indians in servitude and slavery in numerous ways beyond intermarriage, prompting adoption of new slave codes and tax laws restricting their rights and creating a push to bring New England law more in line with that of other slave societies on the issues of heritability of slavery and slave testimony in particular. Marriage to an African could become a pathway to lifetime servitude for free Indians and term servants and their biracial offspring, and women appear to have been particularly vulnerable to these machinations. Either through formal contracts, as in the case of Patience, or through extralegal means, masters gained control over the labor of free spouses and tried to assert ownership over the children of such mixed relationships in hundreds of other cases. Perhaps regretting her reversion to slavery, Patience quarreled with her husband, who was also often absent on long whaling voyages.

A few scholars are probing the notion that some Indians and Africans in New England might have chosen slave status as a means of protecting themselves and their children in certain situations, and that presentist ideas about personal freedom blind historians to other emotional possibilities. Early modern people might have valued other things—protection and clientage relationships with "masters," subsistence, proximity to family—more than they valued a meaningless "freedom."[23] My research suggests that free people entered into such contracts reluctantly or under duress, and that other Indians and Africans who married enslaved partners resisted permanent enslavement for themselves. Children and grandchildren of these unions brought freedom suits and otherwise challenged attempts to enslave them, although not always successfully. Trying to comprehend decisions like the one Patience made requires adopting the perspective of contemporaries who faced complicated gradations of power, freedom, and unfreedom that operated in places like colonial New England.

After her enslavement, Patience described a descent into alcoholism and escalating acts of violence and desperation very different from Quasson's more straightforward narrative of alcoholism, comeuppance, and repentance. In contrast, Patience's narrative is a litany of planned and executed acts that realized every paranoid fear of the slaveholding class (including arson, poison, and murder), not in response to particular wrongs but to the very condition of slavery. Patience may have suffered from mental illness and/or post-partum depression. She may have been a sociopath or simply a violent person. But it is also possible that as with Cassie in *Uncle Tom's Cabin* and the heroine of Toni Morrison's *Beloved* (both based on the historical figure of Kentucky slave Margaret Garner) the experience of enslavement literally drove Patience crazy. As with Garner, acts of real or imagined infanticide haunted her. Two of her three babies died under suspicious circumstances, and she twice (by her own claim) gave false confessions to infanticide. She may have imagined a pregnancy and infanticide in one of the latter cases.[24] After a jury acquitted Patience of murdering her own child her master temporarily rented her to another owner, Captain Dimmick, to cover court costs, "with my husband's consent"—possibly a kind of divorce proceeding from the husband who had been an instrument of her enslavement, but one that did not end her enslavement. Less than two years later she entered yet another household, the home of Joseph Bailey in Casco Bay, Maine. Patience claimed to have engineered this move herself in order to be closer to another enslaved Indian woman she knew—the second time she had exercised agency over her disposition if not her enslavement. Then Bailey apparently sold her again.

The crime that eventually sent Patience to the gallows was the murder of her new master's grandson and namesake, Benjamin Trot, whom she drowned in a well "tho' I seemed to love him, and he me." Consumed with anger and resentment toward her new master because of an unnamed incident, she considered poisoning him or burning the house, but soon decided to kill the child for whom she was a caregiver. Boston's account of the murder mirrors several true-life events in nearby colonies: accounts of Indian servants and slaves committing infanticide to escape penalties for fornication that would extend their terms of servitude or others, often teens themselves, accused of murdering the children they were supposed to care for. Anna Molatto, servant to John Easton of Newport, Rhode Island in 1737, for example, murdered the daughter of a neighbor by smothering her and pushing her down a well (circumstances very similar to Patience's crime). Diarist, justice, and legislator Samuel Sewall presided over several cases of Indians accused of child murder and infanticide in Cape Cod in the 1720s.[25] In Anna's case, the lengthy file contains three contradictory interrogations structured as a set of questions and answers. Anna had "run to tell my Family" about Alice Allen's disappearance, and initially denied being involved in any crime. Then, in a deposition dated March 30, Anna confessed to accidentally knocking the child into the well:

> Q: How long did Alice Allen leave you in the Kitchen before you discovered her being in the well
> Answer. I push'd her into the well by opening the Garden Gate.
> Q: How come you did not confess this before.
> A: I was afraid to tell thinking they would say I did it on purpose

One day later she admitted to unintentionally smothering Alice after the child witnessed Anna giving liquor to a visiting slave:

> A: … [She] said that she would tell my mistres whereupon I laid hold of her & clapp'd my hand on her mouth & she strugled & turn'd over & twisted as I had my hand on her mouth
> Q: the stir or speak after you had taken your hand from her mouth
> A: she did not speak after it & stirr'd but little
> Q: How came Alice in the well after you had done this
> A: I put her in the well

Court officials assumed the third was the true confession, but was it? Or had the interrogators projected on Anna their own stereotypes and fears that enslaved women might harbor violent impulses to kill Euro-American children under their care?

Reading these interrogations alongside Patience's narrative shows the difficulty of determining whether these women were guilty of the crimes they confessed to. Were Patience's claims of false confessions an attempt to absolve herself from guilt or a window into how servants and slaves might own to crimes under the pressure of questioning by officials? Were these merely violent crimes or acts of resistance to slavery? Was the death of Trot itself another accident that Patience pled guilty to and turned into a crime? Patience read Cotton Mather in gaol. She also delivered and nursed a baby and reluctantly surrendered up her living child, likely into servitude, prior to her own execution. A lifetime of struggle and sometimes violent resistance had not stopped the cycle of involuntary servitude. While in prison Patience told Joseph Moody that she resented God's power over the "Children of Men." Humans had little control over their disposition in life, and Patience (in servitude and slavery and in the penal system) had experienced even less control over what she could or could not do, but her life represented a struggle for agency and autonomy. Her searing narrative and Joseph Quasson's poignant tragedy inject emotion, passion, and uncertainty into stories of slavery in ways that elucidate and yet complicate more straightforward legal testimony.

Another genre, the conversion or missionary narrative, offers its own distinct insight into the Indian slave experience. Reverend Experience Mayhew of Martha's Vineyard published a series of Indian biographies under the title "Indian Converts" in 1727. Scholars have used Mayhew's source to assess Indian spirituality and cultural persistence, to debate the effectiveness of missionary activity, and to explore divisions within the New England church establishment on the eve of the Great Awakening, but Mayhew's "Indian Ministers," "Good Men," "Pious Children," and "Religious Women" included servants and at least one former slave.[26] James Spaniard was an anomaly in Mayhew's pantheon, married to a "Religious Woman" but himself an imperfect convert, yet Mayhew clearly found the man's story and personality compelling. He reported frequent conversations with James about the latter's traumatic past and "discontented" present.

Unlike Patience Boston and Joseph Quasson, James Spaniard told a story that involved warfare, kidnapping, and being trafficked over long distance in an abbreviated Middle Passage. Enslaved as a child in "the Spanish Indies"—a term that comprehended Mexico, Central America, Cuba, the lesser Antilles, Hispaniola and Florida—and brought to New England as a child, James pined for his former country and kinfolk, and expressed great anger about his ordeal. Despite Mayhew's attempts to find a silver lining by reminding the Indian man just how lucky he was to have been exposed to Christianity via his enslavement, James instead "laid much to Heart the unkind treatment he had met Withal, in being separated from all his Friends and Relations, and brought out of his Country into a strange Land, from whereof he never expected to return again."[27] Mayhew stressed the kindness of James' household, the generous master Benjamin Skiff of Chilmark who "never designed to keep him a Slave all his days," and the "good Instruction" the Indian boy received there, but James' persistent regret and anger over his brutal enslavement confounded the minister.

James managed to purchase his freedom after his master's death and to establish his own family household on Martha's Vineyard. He married a woman from the local Christian Indian community and dabbled with Christianity himself. But he also displayed what can only be described as alienation and trauma, a set of feelings that Mayhew captured with the term "discontent." To his death James remained barely able to communicate with his Aquinnah Wampanoag wife, "not being a complete Master of either the *English* or the *Indian* [Wampanoag] tongue."[28] They were both "Indians" in the generic sense, but theirs was an intercultural union just as much as any marriage across ethnic and cultural lines.[29] James' story matches up with other legal and newspaper evidence of the arrival of Spanish Indians in the 1680s through the 1720s: their greater tendency to run away (even to the extent of stealing ships for a return voyage home) and their more complicated and incomplete acculturation as compared to New England Indians in slavery.[30] This rebelliousness and lack of acculturation was one of the main reasons New England governments curtailed imports of Spanish and Carolina Indians. Yet his is also a relatively unique document, one that despite Mayhew's interventions testifies to the trauma the Atlantic/Caribbean slave trade caused for its Native victims.

In comparison with these biographical narratives, archival and legal narratives are a distinct genre, embedded in case files, following rules of legal argument, sometimes even printed forms, and occasionally a "Q & A" interrogation structure. Emotion is less central, although it can still be excited in the reader, and questions of religion are mostly absent. Legal files can be large but individual documents or stories are much shorter than typical print narratives. They often include multiple perspectives and testimonies from persons other than the Indian slave subject, who may only be on the edges of the central story. As with conversion and criminal narratives, in judicial documents we encounter the Indian subjects in crisis, at a point of criminal, debt, or other legal controversy.

What legal documents do provide in distinctive ways is information about the process of enslavement, notably the role of institutions and government officials and how important changes to popular and legal understandings of slavery occurred. Legal documents are useful in tracing the intricacies of racialization. They also shed light on culture, especially cultural persistence and social interactions among different races as well as the behavior of English masters and neighbors.

As a legal-subgenre, petitions most closely resemble first-person published narratives in that they sometimes involve an autobiographical arc. One example is the petition of an Indian man named Ben filed in Pennsylvania in 1693. Ben briefly recounted how he ended up in a condition of illegal enslavement. At the end of King Philip's War, Rhode Island towns held "dividences" of captives in which they gave Indian captives—many women and children unconnected to the fighting—to towns for sale or division among the inhabitants. The Providence Town Meeting sent some of its portion of captives in a ship under the command of Roger Williams' son, Providence Williams, to Newport for sale with the profits to be distributed back home. We know from Ben's account that Governor William Coddington purchased an infant boy, "a Native of their Majties. Colony of New England," whom he named Ben. Under Rhode Island law such captives were not to be slaves for life but rather were to be freed after a set, sliding term dependent on their age at sale that could extend to thirty years. When Coddington died, his will specified that Ben would receive his freedom in seven years. But his widow remarried and, with her new husband (now Ben's owner), Robert Eaves, took Ben to Pennsylvania. In the process, Ben's position changed from that of a servant with a finite, specified term to that of a slave. Ben petitioned the Pennsylvania Assembly for his freedom, noting that "yor. Pet[itione]r. Humbly conceives they can no longer detaine yor. Pet[itione]r. in their said possession but that hee is a Native Indian and by the will aforesaid a freeman." Ben claimed freedom on the basis of his origins—New England, not Florida, the Carolinas, or the Caribbean; his ethnicity—native Indian, not African or East Indian; and the legal contracts that should have assured his freedom but did not. He requested either his freedom or a new contract specifying his remaining obligation to Eaves.

Ben's case illustrates a shift toward natalism in arguments about Indian citizenship in the late seventeenth and early eighteenth century that helped undermine the legality of Native American enslavement in British imperial policy as well as in local colonial law. It also points to the many ways that would-be enslavers ignored colonial law to accomplish widespread conversion of Indian term servants into slaves.[31] What happened to Ben also happened to hundreds of other Indian children bound into what was supposed to be a term-limited service after King Philip's War. Transportation out of the region, the death of a master or mistress, and other changes in household were risk-factors in a term-servant being redefined in extra-legal ways by new owners as a slave. But even without these changes many of Ben's contemporaries who stayed in New England also experienced enslavement, despite laws to the contrary.

Freedom suits required significant social capital, and how Ben acquired so much as a young person taken far from his kin networks remains a mystery. A more complete case file or follow-up would help illuminate these connections. Ben was not literate; he made a diagonal mark on the petition in lieu of a signature. Someone—we do not know who—helped him prepare the petition and arrange a hearing of his case in Philadelphia. The outcome of the case is unclear, but it progressed far enough that Rhode Island officials assembled a file of papers relating to Ben's status. Evidence of social capital (in the sense of allies and friends in English-speaking communities), or at least complicated back stories,

are often present in Indian legal actions since framing petitions, challenging writs, and filing suits nearly always took significant experience,
legal expertise and knowledge of English. Other Indians managed to do
this, but sometimes at a devastating cost. A Rhode Island woman named
Betty Coyhees managed to quash a series of debt warrants pressed by
Christopher Champlin against her for technical reasons of language, but
a stray deposition by a neighbor revealed that she indented her two sons
to a third party to pay for legal advice. Coyhees' experience is a correc-
tive against assuming aid was altruistic, but elsewhere I see evidence of
Euro-Americans helping Indians make successful challenges to Indian
slavery in the eighteenth century and voting to free Indians in jury trials
because they viewed Indian slavery as illegitimate, a shift with consequences for all enslaved peoples.[32]

Another genre of legal evidence, the deposition, varied widely in
content and form across New England and among courts and justices.
Depositions help us map social interactions across class and ethnic lines,
in that they show who was near or in a place where a crime occurred,
or who had a relationship with the accused. Moreover, they reveal just
how intertwined Indian and English towns and households were. Some
of the best slave narratives found in legal testimony came not from the
enslaved person's own lips but from depositions of neighbors who, like
Experience Mayhew, returned, fascinated, again and again to "visit and
discourse" and to hear tales from Indian captives.

One such story was embedded in a freedom suit that a slave from
Plainfield named Elisha filed after running away from his Connecticut
master. When brought before the Justice's Court at Windham, Connecticut, Elisha announced that "he was freeborn and no Slave" and
refused to return to his purported owner, William Marsh. Elisha made
an argument similar to Ben's above: that his mother, Betty, had been
illegally enslaved in Rhode Island despite a ban on Indian slavery there,
and that he was thus free. Elisha had several strikes against him: he
was biracial (his father was African), and he was not clearly descended
from a New England Indian or any other group that could make a
claim to English or local birth citizenship. In fact, Marsh thought he
had scored a victory when he secured testimony from Thomas Power,
who had owned Betty, and from Edward Lillybridge of Rhode Island,
who had purchased her from William Crawford, a Newport trader.
Marsh claimed Betty was a Spanish Indian and therefore that Elisha
was a "Spanish Indian man servant or slave," and a "Negro Mulatto":
two categories for legal enslavement. Several New London neighbors
claimed long acquaintance with Betty and offered conflicting testimony, however, some saying she was a Spanish Indian and others that
she claimed to be Carolina born and a British subject, illegally enslaved, and therefore a free woman and mother to a son who should be
free. The latter clearly supported Elisha's suit. Regardless of how they

testified, these comments all also indicated how enmeshed Betty and Elisha were in their respective communities.[33] Marsh found to his chagrin, however, that fluid racial understandings in Connecticut, Elisha's local friendships, and rising revulsion toward all Indian enslavement made some of his best arguments moot when a local jury sided with Elisha regardless of where his mother was from.

The case's documents are rich with information about racialization, citizenship, and the grounds for freedom suits, but perhaps my favorite deposition provided deep biography on Betty in a kind of ghostwritten narrative. The ghostwriter was deponent and neighbor Thomas Williams. Williams frequented Power household, mostly to chat with Betty, who "was always forward in Talk." Betty had told him she came via ship from Carolina as a child but was in fact a Spanish Indian. Williams' deposition shifted from third person to first person while recounting her tale, a measure of how her gripping story enthralled him. Betty and her mother had retired to a fort (possibly a mission) while her father was away hunting, but it came under attack by English-backed Carolina Indians, whose guns soon overpowered the arrows of Betty's group. Her mother strapped the child to her back and attempted to swim to safety, but the attackers pursued:

[They] shot my Mother Thro the body and killed her and I swam yet but they Soon Took me and many others both old and young and when we Came to our fifth Nights Stand they Choped off the heads of the old people which they had taken and Saved the Young alive among which I was one and then we Set forward with our New Masters and traviled many days (I think to the best of my Remembrance Ten days or Twelve) Til we Cam to any white peoples settlement, being much pinched with famine being almost starved and then they would sale a boy or Girl for victuals at Last Arrived at Carolina where I was sold to a white man and Lived with him Some Time.

This man sold her to a New England vessel, whose captain in turn sold her to Lillybridge, the first of three English masters she served before Power.[34] Elisha's story was my primary target in investigating this file, but Betty's is the most well-developed capture narrative I encountered, and it came from a third party. The violence she witnessed and the many layers of human trafficking illustrated here help us better comprehend the parallels between the traumatic processes of enslavement in Africa and those in North America, as well as the "continental passage" of the regional slave trade. Williams' strong affective identification with Betty's story also reveals how relationships might upend the informal and dehumanizing networks of enforcement that made slavery possible in New England.

One final set of depositions shows how documents can themselves be the location of crucial changes in the status of the enslaved and in concepts of racialization, setting or challenging general precedents. In other words, depositions could be change agents that affected individuals as well as larger communities or legal systems. This case involved an eight-year-old boy named Pardon accused of burning a neighbor's mill in 1758.[35] Like Patience Boston, Pardon stood accused of one of the master class's worst nightmares: slave arson. Pardon's deposition and those of neighbors do not give us much biography. We know from other records that his mother, Sarah Ned, who lived in Dartmouth, Massachusetts, indentured him at around age six to farmer Job Almy in 1754.[36] The indenture was better than many because Sarah was present to insist that Almy provide Pardon with education, proper food, and a suit of clothes, and to prevent his future resale out of Rhode Island. Some Indian indentures, particularly those without a parent signatory, all but eliminated the master's obligations. But Almy quietly asserted ownership over Pardon as a slave.

The depositions tell us that Pardon took care of cattle and did chores, but also that he was afraid of Almy. We can guess that Almy planned to convert him to slavery because case documents, particularly motions and petitions that Almy and his agents originated, referred to Pardon as a "slave" despite the recent indenture contract that proved otherwise. Almy and several neighbors referred to him as a "Black Boy" and "Mallato boy" and so did the justice who took his first deposition. Court papers dropped the surname that linked him to his Indigenous mother. Pardon's final deposition, however, described him as an Indian, a crucial distinction in a colony where local Indians were not legally enslavable, but Africans were. At the very least this serves as evidence of how the expansion of African slavery and racialization in New England undermined the status of free and indentured Indians and biracial people.

Like Anna Mulatto, Pardon Ned gave several different depositions with varying narratives, but whereas each change increased Anna's culpability, the investigators in Pardon's case created a final version that established the boy's innocence. In the first, he admitted to burning Cook's mill. But in his final deposition, led by increasingly sympathetic questioners, Pardon contended that Almy had ordered the arson because of a feud and made him return twice to build up the fire and to move coals to various sites around the mill:

> Quest.: Where was you when you first saw the fire Near ye Mill
> Answer: I was a Going to turn ye Cows to pasture
> Q: where did you go after you turn'd ye Cows away
> A: home
> Q: what did you Do when you went home

A: I told my master I saw fire near ye Mill and went out of the Doors & he followed Me

Q: what Did you Master say to you

A: he told me to Go & put ye fire under ye Mill

Q: what Did you say to ye Master when he told you to put fire under ye Mill

A: I told him I wa[s]nt willing

Q: what Did your Master say to you then

A: he told me to Go & put ye fire under ye Mill or he would Whipp me—And I Went & put ye fire under that side of the Mill next to our house & was then a Going home & mett my Master & he asked Me Which side of ye Mill I Put ye fire & I told him that side Next to our house

Q: What Did your Master say to you then

A: he told me to take some More fire & put the other side & I Did

The court acquitted Pardon Ned and indicted Almy for the crime, eventually convicting him.

What's even more interesting about this case are the sideshow documents—the writs, the motions regarding evidence, and the appeals. Almy tried to convince the court to throw out Pardon's testimony, first because he was a minor, but later because he was an enslaved person of color. Allowing "a Negro or Mulatto ~~Slave~~ Apprentice about eight Years old and of No Education to be Sworn as a Witness against the Appell[an]t his Master," Almy fumed, was "altogether without precedent and against the laws of all Civilized Nations upon Earth."[37] Presumably, Almy was referring to the exclusion of slave testimony in other British slave societies. The appeal's language, with its references to "Negro" and "Slave" (the latter crossed out but still legible), strove to muddy the question of Pardon's true status and ethnicity.

Almy's legal strategy had larger significance, in that an attempt to exclude slave testimony could have created a precedent, one which court officials ultimately rejected. Even more extraordinarily, the Newport court freed Pardon from his indenture, a rare act on the part of officials who were very reluctant to interfere with indentures even in illegal and abusive situations. Pardon's case showed how depositions could be important not just on their face but as acts that confirmed the humanity of the deponents. The judges in this case also prevented Rhode Island's law of slavery from veering in even more oppressive directions. Legal institutions were central to enslavement in New England, but the enslaved sometimes won in court, and access to courts for people of color was a crucial differentiator between the region and other slaveholding areas. As in the case of Elisha, legal documents in the Pardon case provide a direct insight into the process and impact of racialization in the colonies, which is not always the case with African slave narratives, which often assume racial prejudice or point to other influences.[38] Both cases also reveal the legal foundations of antislavery, which in mid-eighteenth-century New England centered not on universal natural rights theory of the Age of Revolution but rather on an understanding of rights derived from imperial subjecthood and colonial legislation, natal origins, and from people of color's social embeddedness in their local communities.[39]

In categorizing these various documents as Indian slave narratives and in stressing their contributions to the canon, I argue for a broad definition of slave testimony that crosses boundaries and borderlands, not just of race, freedom, and slavery but of genre, a definition sensitive to the constraints and possibilities of each. Indian slave narratives come in many forms, and all have their value: first person as well as third person narration, print and manuscript, direct and indirect accounts. Read together they help provide a more complete historical portrait of slavery as contemporaries created it and experienced it, including slavery's hidden affective elements. These embedded biographies not only illuminate individual experience but allow historians to make arguments about the origins and evolution of Indian and African servitude and slavery more generally and to make comparisons across racial and regional lines, revealing variety in experience as well as common threads.

Notes

1 The probem of archival silence in slavery studies is well-established. One of the most articulate commentators on this question is Saidiya Hartman, whose relevant works include *Lose Your Mother: A Journey Along the Atlantic Slave Route* (New York: Farrar, Straus, and Giroux, 2007); *Scenes of Subjection: Terror, Slavery, and Self-Making in Nineteenth-Century America* (New York: Oxford University Press, 1997); and "Venus in Two Acts," *Small Axe* 12 (June 2008), 1–14. See also Marisa Fuentes, *Dispossessed Lives, Enslaved Women, Violence and the Archive* (Philadelphia: University of Pennsylvania Press, 2016).

2 A good introduction to literary scholarship on these issues is *Genius in Bondage: Literature of the Early Black Atlantic*, Vincent Carretta and Philip Gould, eds. (Lexington: University Press of Kentucky, 2001).

3 Samson Occom wrote a much-anthologized autobiography in 1792. It provides great insight into Indigenous life in the northeast, but his is not a slave narrative. For Occom see Kelly Wisecup, *Medical Encounters: Knowledge and Identity in Early American Literatures* (Amherst: University of Massachusetts Press, 2013. Andrew Lipman, *The Saltwater Frontier: Indians and the Contest for the American Coast* (New Haven: Yale University Press, 2015), uses Occom to consider issue of race and modernity in late eighteenth-century New England Indigenous communities. There is a New England-centric cast to many of the anthology texts on both slavery narratives and Native American literature for the early period, which tend to highlight Phillis Wheatley, Venture Smith, and Occom.

4 For thoughtful analyses of genre in slave narratives (including comparisons with the captivity narrative) see John Sekora, "Black Message/White Envelope: Genre, Authenticity, and Authority in the Antebellum Slave Narrative,"

Callaloo 32 (1987): 482–515; Kari J. Winter, *Subjects of Slavery, Agents of Change: Women and Power in Gothic Novels and Slave Narratives, 1790–1865* (Athens: University of Georgia Press, 1992); David Blight, *A Slave No More: Two Men Who Escaped to Freedom, Including Their Own Narratives of Emancipation* (New York: Houghton, Mifflin, Harcourt, 2007); Gordon Sayre, "Slave Narrative and Captivity Narrative: American Genres," in Paul Lauter, ed., *A Companion to American Literature and Culture* (West Sussex: Wiley-Blackwell, 2010), 172–191; Yolanda Pierce, "Reclaiming Bondage," in Audrey Fisch, ed., *The Cambridge Companion to the African-American Slavery Narrative* (New York: Cambridge University Press, 2007), 86–88.

5 Legal procedure and court structures varied across time and among the New England colonies. By 1730, Massachusetts, Connecticut, and Rhode Island maintained several layers of courts (Justices, County, Superior) with the colonial legislature also functioning as a final court of appeals. In the seventeenth century, courts might provide interpreters for non-English speaking Indians or even, in one capital case, an Indigenous jury, but such incidents were rare. Surviving testimony records are uniformly in English and subjects' understanding of the questions, proceedings, and implications of their testimony was limited in the early period, although Indians' legal knowledge and social capital increased over time. Depositions and the files associated with cases survive in far fewer numbers than the less-informative court docket books. Although fill-in-the-blank printed forms for warrants were in use in Rhode Island and Massachusetts by the 1720s, most testimonies took the form of handwritten documents created by Justices of the Peace or their deputies.

6 Vincent Carretta contends that slave narrative can include biography written by European and Euro-American observers, and in my own research I found that these intentional, putatively European-authored sources offer some unique perspectives on the experience of the enslaved and a sense of the Indigenous subject's individual narrative voice despite editorial presence of minister-authors. See Margaret Newell, *Brethren by Nature: New England Indians, Colonists, and the Origins of American Slavery* (Ithaca, NY: Cornell University Press, 2015).

7 Samuel Moody, *Summary Account of the Life and Death of Joseph Quasson, Indian...* (Boston, 1726); Samuel and Joseph Moody, *A Faithful Narrative of the Wicked Life and Remarkable Conversion of Patience Boston, Alias Samson...* (Boston, 1738); *Boston Gazette*, June 5, 1738. Some university catalogs list Patience Boston as the author of *Faithful Narrative*.

8 See, for example, Karen Haltunnen, "Early American Murder Narratives," in Richard Wightman Fox and T. J. Jackson Lears, eds., *The Power of Culture: Essays in in American History* (Chicago, IL: University of Chicago Press, 1993); Jodi Schor, "Reading Prisoners on the Scaffold: Literacy in an Era of Literary Spectacle," in Michele Lisle Tarter and Richard Bell, eds., *Buried Lives: Incarcerated in Early America* (Athens: University of Georgia Press, 2012); and Daniel E. Williams, "'Behold a Tragic Scene Strangely Changed into a Theater of Mercy': The Structure and Significance of Criminal Conversion Narratives in Early New England," *American Quarterly* 38 (Winter, 1986), 827–847.

9 Daniel A. Cohen, *Pillars of Salt, Monuments of Grace: New England Crime Literature and the Origins of American Popular Culture, 1674–1860* (New York: Oxford University Press, 1993).

10 For Indigenous enslavement and involuntary servitude in New England see Newell, *Brethren by Nature*, especially Chap. 9; David J. Silverman, "The Impact of Indentured Servitude on Southern New England Indian Society

and Culture, 1680–1810," *New England Quarterly* 74 (2001): 622–666; Ruth Herndon and Ella Sekatau, "Colonizing the Children: Indian Youngsters in Servitude in Early Rhode Island," in Colin Calloway and Neal Salisbury, eds., *Reinterpreting New England Indians and the Colonial Experience* (Boston: Colonial Society of Massachusetts, 2003), 137–173; John Sainsbury, "Indian Labor in Early Rhode Island," *New England Quarterly* 47 (1974): 378–393; and John Wood Sweet, *Bodies Politic: Negotiating Race in the American North, 1730–1830* (Philadelphia: University of Pennsylvania Press, 2003).

11 James Southerne's enormously popular 1695 play *Oroonoko*, based on the earlier novel by Aphra Behn, featured an enslaved African prince. Olaudah Equiano also claimed high status.

12 Delores Bird Carpenter, *Early Encounters: Native Americans and Europeans in New England from the Papers of W. Sears Nickerson* (East Lansing: Michigan State University Press, 1984), traces the Quasson family sachemate and their property in Monomoy. Thomas Doughton, "Twenty Years in Plymouth County," paper presented at a National Endowment for the Humanities program on slavery in New England, Harriet Beecher Stowe Center/University of Hartford, Hartford, CT, July 2007. Joseph's narrative appears in Samuel Moody, *Summary Account of the Life and Death of Joseph Quasson, Indian* (Boston, 1726), 3–7. "Sturgis" also appears as "Sturges" in contemporary records.

13 David T. Konig, ed., *Plymouth Court Records* (Wilmington, DE: Rowman & Littlefield Publishers, 1978), 255 and Charles Francis Swift, *History of Old Yarmouth* (Dennis, MA, 1884), 126–130.

14 Moody, *Life and Death of Joseph Quasson*, 2.

15 Newell, *Brethren by Nature*, 163–164.

16 Moody, *Life and Death of Joseph Quasson*, 3–4.

17 These included limited regional conflicts that erupted in the northeast at the end of King Philip's War, as well as wars with other global imperial theaters and combatants: King William's War, 1689–1697; the War of Spanish Succession/Queen Anne's War, 1702–1713; King George's War, 1744–1748/the War of Austrian Succession. Newell, *Brethren by Nature*, Chap. 8; Owen Stanwood, *The Empire Reformed: English America in the Age of the Glorious Revolution* (Philadelphia: University of Pennsylvania Press, 2011).

18 John Henry Clifford, ed., *The Acts and Resolves, Public and Private, of the Province of the Massachusetts Bay, Vol XI (1726–1729)* (Boston, MA: Wright & Potter, 1903), 32, 42, 63; Colin Calloway, *Dawnland Encounters: Indians and Europeans in Northern New England* (Hanover, NH: University Press of New England, 1991), 191–192; Richard R. Johnson, "The Search for a Usable Indian: An Aspect of the Defense of Colonial New England," *The Journal of American History* 64 (December 1977), 623–651.

19 See Samuel and Joseph Moody, *A Faithful Narrative of the Wicked Life and Remarkable Conversion of Patience Boston* (Boston, 1738); also reprinted and analyzed in Cohen, *Pillars of Salt, Monuments of Grace*, 72–74.

20 Moody, *Patience Boston*, 1–2.

21 Moody, *Patience Boston*, 3.

22 Moody, *Patience Boston*, 3. Patience does not name her husband's owner, but "Unrecorded Barnstable County Deeds," *The Mayflower Descendant* 16 (January 2014): 220, excerpts a land sale listing "nagro Boston" and Patience Boston his wife as "servants" of Thacher, but also as property owners who had conveyed property to a third party with Thacher's "concent." Massachusetts' 1705 anti-miscegenation laws simultaneously legalized slave marriage, and enslaved people did marry before Justices of the Peace

in Massachusetts, Connecticut and Rhode Island in the eighteenth century (marriage in New England was typically a civil ceremony), or formed unofficial but community-recognized unions that acquired some legal standing. Catherine Adams and Elizabeth H. Pleck, *Black Women in Colonial and Revolutionary New England* (New York: Oxford University Press, 2010), 104, 110–112; Newell, *Brethren by Nature*, 244.

23 Allega di Bonaventura, *For Adam's Sake: A Family Saga of Colonial New England* (New York: Liveright Publishing Corporation, 2013), ascribes these motivations to Adam, an enslaved man in Joshua Hempstead's household. Tera Hunter, *Bound in Wedlock: Slave and Free Black Marriage in the Nineteenth Century* (Cambridge, MA: Harvard University Press, 2017), discusses similar unions in a later period, while Gloria McCahon Whiting explores the purchase of enslaved spouses by freedmen of color in "Power, Patriarchy and Provision: African Families Negotiate Gender and Slavery in New England," *Journal of American History* 103 (December 2016): 583–605. Daniel Mandell's *Behind the Frontier: Indians in Eighteenth Century Eastern Massachusetts* (Lincoln: University of Nebraska Press, 1996) addresses interracial intermarriage and pays close attention to the economic activities of free Indian households.

24 The literature on African American infanticide is extensive, and cases involving Native American and mixed-race/African defendants share many features, including challenges of interpretation. Some scholars stress the role of Euro-American imagination in stereotyping actions of the enslaved, or see medical mis-diagnosis, post-partum depression or a desire to avoid punishment. Still others position infanticide as a form of slave resistance. Felicity Turner, "Narrating Infanticide: Constructing the Modern Gendered State in Nineteenth Century America" (Ph.D. Dissertation, Duke University, 2010); Todd Savitt, "Smothering and Overlaying of Virginia Slave Children: A Suggested Explanation," *Bulletin of the History of Medicine* 3 (1975): 400–404; Deborah Gray White, *"Ar'n't I a Woman?": Female Slaves in the Plantation South* (New York: W.W. Norton, 1985), 21–22, 84–89; and Daina Ramey Berry, *The Price for Their Pound of Flesh: The Value of the Enslaved, from Womb to Grave, in the Building of a Nation* (New York: Beacon Press, 2017), 77.

25 Moody, *Patience Boston*, 7. For Anna Molatto see Samuel Sewall and M. Halsey Thomas, *The Diary of Samuel Sewall*, vol. 2 (New York: Farrar, Straus and Giroux, 1973), 2 vols.,683–684, 691; also Sewall, *Samuel Sewall's Letter-Book*, vol. 1 (Boston: Massachusetts Historical Society Collections, 1886–88), 2 vols., 423; depositions of Anna Mulatto, March 30 and 31, 1737, Washington County Court of Common Pleas, in *Rex v. Anna Mulatto*, September 1737, Rhode Island Judicial Records Center (hereafter RIJRC).

26 For Experience Mayhew and his mission see David Silverman, *Faith and Boundaries* (New York: Cambridge University Press, 2005); James P. Ronda, "Generations of Faith: The Indians of Martha's Vineyard," *William and Mary Quarterly* 38 (July 1981): 369–394; and Laura Ann Liebman, 'Introduction,' in *Experience Mayhew's Indian Conversions: A Cultural Edition*, (Amherst, MA: University of Massachusetts Press, 2017).

27 Experience Mayhew, *Indian Converts: Or Some Account of the Lives and Dying Speeches of a Considerable Number of the Christianized Indians of Martha's Vineyard in New England* (London, 1727), 120.

28 Mayhew, *Indian Converts*, 120–122.

29 Ann Marie Plane, *Colonial Intimacies: Indian Marriage in New England* (Ithaca, NY: Cornell University Press, 1997), 143.

30 *The Acts and Resolves, Public and Private, of the Province of the Massa-chusetts Bay*, vol. 1 (Boston, MA: Wright & Potter, 1869), 634, 698; John Russell Bartlett, ed., *Records of the Colony of Rhode Island and Provi-dence Plantations in New England* (Providence: Knowles, Anthony & Co., 1857–1865), vol. 3, 482–483, vol. 4, 131, 185–186; *Boston News-Letter*, April 7–14, 1712; and Newell, *Brethren by Nature*, 323–328.

31 Petition of Ben Indian, September 1693, "Copies of Records of Warwick," Mss. 221, Box 1, Rhode Island Historical Society, Providence.

32 Newell, *Brethren by Nature*, 246–253.

33 Petition of William Marsh, October 1750, Connecticut State Archives Misc., 2:64a; Deposition of Sarah Longworthy, September 1750 and Deposition of William Dunlop, Connecticut State Archives, Misc., vol. 2, 69–70, 72–73.

34 Deposition of Thomas Williams, Connecticut State Archives, Misc., vol. 2, 71–71a-b.

35 "The Examination of a Black Boy who Lives with Job Almy of Little Comp-ton [k]no[w]ne by ye name of Perdon," September 1758, Newport General Sessions *Job Almy re: Pardon* file, and Newport Superior Court, March 1759, *Rex v. Almy* file, RIJRC.

36 "Pardon Ned Indenture," July 9, 1754 (copy in *Rex v. Almy*).

37 "Job Almys Reasons of Appeal to Honrd Court 1759," in *Rex v. Almy*; see also *Job Almy re Pardon* and Newport General Sessions of the Peace Minute Book 1746–1837, 94, 99, RIJRC.

38 Roxann Wheeler, *The Complexion of Race: Categories of Difference in Eighteenth-Century British Culture* (Philadelphia: University of Pennsylva-nia Press, 2000).

39 Newell, *Brethren by Nature*, 246–247.

6 "She Said Her Answers Contained the Truth"

Listening to and with Enslaved Witnesses in Eighteenth-Century New France

Brett Rushforth

In October 1750, a thirty-year-old enslaved Native American woman named Marie-Josephe, known as Manon, was accused of stealing a valuable silver fork and spoon from the home of her master, the Montreal notary Nicolas-Auguste Guillet de Chaumont. According to the complaint, Manon had become drunk with brandy stolen from her master's cellar, and, emboldened by the liquor, she had then stolen the silver utensils with the help of a French woman and a sixteen-year-old French servant. In one version of events, Manon had coaxed the key to the cellar from Jean-Baptiste Chicot, the credulous husband of Marguerite Charbonneau who served the notary's family as their *guardienne*. Claiming that she needed to fetch some brooms to do the cleaning, Manon allegedly entered the cellar from the house and then unlocked an outer door that opened onto the street, granting access to her accomplices. Once the complaint was submitted, court officials seized Manon and her suspected accessories and placed them in Montreal's royal prison to await trial.[1]

After two days of deposing other witnesses and assembling the facts of the case, an officer of the court led Manon to a special chamber in the prison where they subjected her to questioning, following procedures virtually indistinguishable from those observed with other defendants in New France, free or enslaved. Usually only vaguely aware of the charges facing them, defendants were asked a series of leading and sometimes deceptive questions designed to elicit a confession and identify other wrongdoers. Although having standing to testify in court could in some settings be a benefit and protection to enslaved people, it could also put them in real peril. Montreal's colonial justice system was no exception. Its court dossiers offer many examples of coerced testimony, threats by guilty masters worried about conviction, and reprisals for the few enslaved people who leveraged legal processes to their own advantage. In 1714, an enslaved Native man named Joseph, for example, when forced to testify against his master in a criminal smuggling case, faced a dual threat from colonial authorities and his fearful master. In 1725, an enslaved young Native woman named Marie-Joachim was threatened with death by her master and mistress prior to her testimony. Marguerite, an enslaved Native woman in Quebec, felt the wrath of her new master when she managed to sue for her freedom in 1740, maligned during the trial and then shipped to Martinique when her appeal ultimately failed.[2] This intentionally intimidating setting was especially fraught in Manon's case, as the man wronged by the theft was both her legal owner and an influential member of Montreal's administrative elite. He was also a contentious soul with a violent streak, accused, among other things, of assaulting the wife of a military officer. Only days before Manon's arrest he had appealed a failed lawsuit against a parish priest. More to the point, he had overseen the conviction and execution of an enslaved woman in this very court when Manon was a teenager.[3] Being forced to speak on the record against her master's interests while potentially implicating others offered Manon few rewards and many dangers. Despite the perilous terrain, however, court records show that she stood her ground under interrogation, denying any wrongdoing and offering alternative explanations for the key elements of the case against her.

Much of the record is quite bland and formulaic: "Asked: her name, age, status, and place of residence ... Asked: if she was not at the home of the said Vauquière Monday morning ... Asked: if she did not have a drink there ..." For the most part, Manon answered directly and offered little elaboration. "She said her name is Marie Manon, thirty years old, a slave living in this town of Montreal chez Monsieur Chaumont, a notary of this district." Yes, she had been at Vauquière's home. Yes, she had consumed some alcohol there. Yes, she had asked for the key to the cellar to fetch the brooms, but she returned the key immediately after getting them. And no, she had not opened any other door or stolen anything. Following standard courtroom procedure, at the end of Manon's interrogation the clerk read the transcript of her testimony back to her and asked her to confirm its validity. According to the clerk, Manon offered a rote assurance recited by virtually all witnesses in French colonial courtrooms: "she said her answers contained the truth."[4]

Her answers contained the truth. What are we to make of this routine declaration and the testimony it claims to validate? Accepting for the moment that Manon did, in fact, answer this way, her statement to the court could have meant three distinct things, all consistent with common usage in eighteenth-century French.[5] The first and most straightforward meaning is that her answers were completely true and honest, that her testimony was coterminous with the truth. In modern parlance this would mean that she had told the truth, the whole truth, and nothing but the truth, making this court dossier a full and faithful transcript of her actual words, a first-hand account from the mouth of an enslaved woman. In our desire to hear the voices of enslaved people—those whom slaveholders and their colonial supporters tried to silence—it is tempting to accept Manon's recorded declarations as the truth that the transcript assures us she offered, a rare but clear archival representation of Manon's own voice. There can be no doubt that echoes such as these are uncommon and thus highly prized. That Manon could testify in her own defense at all set her experience apart from many enslaved people in the early modern Atlantic world, particularly those bound in Britain's North American plantation colonies where enslaved people were either banned from testifying altogether or allowed to speak on the record only in the most exigent of circumstances.[6] That Manon's ostensibly verbatim testimony, brief as it is, survives in a Montreal archive is more remarkable still. Despite thousands of enslaved people living in New France between the 1660s and 1760s, and despite more than 6,000 of Montreal's court dossiers from the same period surviving intact, only about thirty trial records preserve first-hand testimonies of enslaved witnesses. Among the richest of these surviving dossiers, this 104-page court record offers tantalizing clues about Manon's daily routines—from coerced tasks performed for her master's benefit to chosen activities done for herself, from the invasive and effective "shared surveillance" of Montreal's compact urban environment to a few stolen moments of private conversation and camaraderie—indicating the complexity and variety of relationships that constituted any enslaved person's social world, whether in Canada, Carolina, or the Caribbean.

Rare as they are, these court transcripts remain the most detailed records available for illuminating the intimate lives and quotidian power struggles of enslaved individuals like Manon. Historians have understandably made extensive use of these documents. Tribunals investigating slave rebellions, Inquisition trials focused on West African religious practitioners, and everyday court testimonies like those offered by Manon and other enslaved witnesses in Montreal have all anchored rich reinterpretations of the social and cultural lives of enslaved individuals and communities. These words, though always coerced to one degree or another, offer the only glimpses available of what enslaved people valued, what they hoped for, what they fought to achieve.[7]

Yet the narrative language I have used here—Manon *said*, Manon *answered*, Manon *stood*—elides the many layers of selection, interpretation, and manipulation that intervened between Manon's act of speaking and a historian's act of reading, ordering, and narrating. The limitations of archival sources, from the voices they silence to the distortions they introduce, suggest caution to ensure that our deep commitment to animating, humanizing, and recovering the experiences of the enslaved has its own costs, its own analytical pitfalls. Even if Manon spoke the truth in this most literal sense, the clerk wrote only what he wrote and copied only what he copied. Archivists kept only what they kept, cataloged only what they cataloged. Due to the cumulative effect of these choices, the distance between what Manon said in October 1750 and what we read in the twenty-first century might be quite vast.

How to approach such records has thus been a topic of vigorous debate among historians for decades. Structured interrogations—whether conducted by the Inquisition, established courts, or ad hoc colonial tribunals—have been among the most valuable sources for uncovering three-dimensional experiences of marginalized historical actors, anchoring groundbreaking microhistories and community studies such as Emmanuel Le Roy Ladurie's *Montaillou*, Carlo Ginzburg's *The Cheese and the Worms*, and Natalie Zemon Davis's *The Return of Martin Guerre*. Where else, as Davis observes, could historians find evidence of what the most marginalized members of any community made of their world? Where else could we hope to find words (almost) directly from the mouths of those with the least social privilege, particularly those from oral cultures whose intergenerational memories were every bit as complex and powerful but left few traces in the documents we rely on to understand their lives and worldviews? A generation of historians depended on these sources to recenter most historical actors who had been eclipsed by a privileged minority of elite white men.[8]

Because they record moments of crisis and deviance, however, some have urged special caution when using trial records, arguing that they can just as easily distort our view of everyday life by refracting historical subjects through the lens of exceptional events. By their very nature such records overemphasize crime and deviance, for example, and there is a risk that enslaved testimony in the structured restraint of the courtroom bears little resemblance to the much more common negotiations of power that took place within households, farms, and plantations. Some insist that slaveholders and state officers conducting structured interrogations not only intentionally distorted, but also knowingly fabricated, the testimony of enslaved people to validate the anxieties of the powerful slaveholding elite. Recorded declarations like Manon's, in this view, tell us far more about the people producing the documents than about the enslaved whose words are ostensibly recorded in them.[9]

It is possible to take such cautions too far, retreating to the safety of cynicism to assert that we cannot ultimately know anything meaningful about the experiences of enslaved people, or any other marginalized people, whose voices tend to emerge only from exceptional circumstances through highly mediated texts. In the end, however, reflecting on archival silences is of little use without a corresponding willingness to risk error as we attempt to understand enslaved people's experiences and to approximate, to whatever degree possible, the range of choices available to them. Intuiting the intentions of a colonial functionary, about whom we know almost nothing, we map motivations onto his choices to distort, elide, or fabricate court records. To see archival silences, then, is an act of profound historical imagination at every step of the interpretive process. Surely enslaved people deserve imaginative reconsideration as much as the clerk or the archivist.

Then, too, as Carlo Ginzburg has argued, moments of deviation like Manon's trial can be especially useful for understanding more common norms and experiences. "Norms cannot foresee all possible anomalies," he insightfully noted, "but all anomalies—as anomalies—imply the norm."[10] In other words, by making clear what people found unexpected or disturbing, these documents reveal what people did expect, what they accepted as normal. Viewed this way, focusing on the extraordinary becomes a way of seeing the ordinary. To do this requires us, as Ann Laura Stoler has urged, to read "along the archival grain." Rather than trying to erase or think past the biases of the records we are interpreting, we are urged instead to think with these biases, to understand the work they do to shape what is and is not said, to see moments that they try to see and to recognize what they either could not or did not want to see.[11]

None of this supports a credulous acceptance of Manon's words as a straightforward record of "her voice," although at moments her words are certainly present. Her answers likely "contained the truth" in another, more limited, way, meaning that within the larger vessel of her testimony—the container—were some elements of the truth. Somewhere among all the things she said were kernels of what she considered accurate, statements that honestly represented her own subjective experience as an enslaved woman in eighteenth-century Montreal. This broader meaning invites our skepticism while allowing for the likely possibility that some of Manon's actual words, reporting her own sense of what was real, survive in the trial documents. It also allows us to consider Manon's relationship to the very paper that claims to preserve her words. We have no reason to doubt that, at the end of the interrogation, the clerk read Manon's testimony back to her as he claimed. This procedure was central to French confidence in the justice of their proceedings, so if only out of a sense of duty it is almost certain that the clerk followed procedure on this point. Although other records show that enslaved witnesses did sometimes correct testimony they viewed as inaccurate, whether Manon would have felt free to correct the clerk, whether his performance was itself an act of enforcement, a display of power—this *is* what you said, right?—remain open questions. But we can be confident that the paper we hold carries the very words Manon heard if not the very words she said. This knowledge allows us to eavesdrop on one moment in Manon's long struggle with those in power. If we cannot, with confidence, say that we can listen *to* this enslaved witness, we can certainly pause and listen *with* her. Reading her recorded testimony aloud, we can hear what she heard as the clerk read her words back to her. In a colonial society where paper carried so much power, from a bill of sale to a certificate of emancipation, she must have realized the importance of her words being so carefully recorded. And, perhaps most important, where there were omissions, distortions, or fabrications in the record, Manon experienced their production in real time. She knew from the very moment of the documents' creation how they did and did not reflect what she had said, what she had done, or who she was.[12]

Acts of imagination in historical representation are unavoidable, whether writing about slaves or anyone else, but even the most flawed documents reduce our possible interpretations by rendering some explanations implausible and some assertions false. The survival of Manon's testimony therefore "contains the truth" in a third eighteenth-century sense. In early modern French (as in twenty-first-century English) to contain could also mean to restrain or discipline: as "dikes and levees were built to contain rivers," or as a virtuous man contains his appetites "to abstain from forbidden passions of the flesh," according to the 1694 *Dictionnaire de l'Academie française*. Manon's testimony—especially when considered alongside surviving narratives from her enslaved contemporaries—narrows the range of possible interpretations and restrains our otherwise infinite imaginations. It limits what we can credibly claim to be true. As John Lewis Gaddis has written of historical documents, "The evidence of particular experience ... discipline[s] what we know from collective experience."[13]

Consider the question of Manon's defiance of authority by her alleged theft. Small acts of resistance by the enslaved offer inspiring evidence that enslaved people refused to assent to their confinement, fighting back in ways large and small to exact a cost from those who wished to control them. Recognizing the injustice of her confinement, we might be drawn to the poetic appeal of an enslaved woman snatching an actual silver spoon from the mouth of her oppressor, for example, but Manon denied the action and other witnesses confirmed her testimony so persuasively that the court acquitted her of all charges. Was her defiance of authority less profound—or her humanity less complex and compelling—for its mundane predictability? Should we emphasize her vulnerability and isolation (being accused in the first place, being jailed, having no family to turn to for support) or her connectedness (her friendships, her daily social interactions, her reliance on other witnesses to corroborate her story)?

One thing is certain: enslaved people in New France were embedded in dense webs of relationships with friends, lovers, neighbors, and relatives, with French servants working alongside them, with other enslaved people sharing their living spaces. These personal relationships clustered along the bottom rungs of the social ladder. Manon was closest with other enslaved women, servants, and those of low status. But when they spoke in concert with her, and she with them, it became difficult for a court to dismiss all of them as perjurers. This was doubly true when friendships crossed into the upper echelons of society. Manon had few chances to befriend high-status French colonists, but she had a well-established social circle: people she borrowed from, traded with, talked to, drank with, and, no doubt, also lied to, disappointed, and surprised. The notion that the trauma of slavery so thoroughly ravaged their sense of self that they could not form meaningful bonds might seem possible if not for hundreds of statements to the contrary—by the enslaved themselves and by those who interacted with them at all echelons of society. Their words and described actions *contain* what we consider to be the truth.

Court officials themselves acknowledged the many relationships formed by the enslaved when they composed a list of people they wanted to interrogate about Manon's activities. The lineup of witnesses, assembled by the court and the accusers rather than by Manon or her supporters, offers a sample of people known to have direct interaction with Manon, meaning that they could potentially provide first-hand testimony about her actions. To create the list Montreal's French elite conducted a hasty ethnography of a community they did not inhabit, charting interpersonal relations between enslaved people like Manon and other marginalized people in the community. They called soldiers, domestic servants, apprentices, and many others charged with conducting business on others' behalf, revealing the contours of a social world that powerful French colonists depended on as much as they mistrusted.

The list of Manon's associates is telling. Pierre Boisseau, a French servant working in the same household as Manon: eighteen years old. Françoise and Élisabeth Parent, daughters of a gunsmith: twenty and seventeen respectively. Jean-Marie Amiot, apprentice: sixteen. Marie Cluseau dite Loranger, domestic servant: sixteen. Manon was a thirty-year-old woman and yet much of her social circle consisted of French teenagers or very young adults: those temporarily bound in overlapping stations but who had every reason to expect to move on to various stages of respectability and independence. Such pathways were unavailable to Manon as an enslaved woman who would die in bondage, as a dependent, with no family or property of her own. It is quite likely that she had serial associations with waves of younger French laborers, servants, and soldiers, many of whom would have passed through rather than remaining within her orbit.

One notable exception to the youth of Manon's regular associates was her presumed accomplice, Marie-Josephe Croquelois dite Laviolette, the thirty-six-year-old wife of a wigmaker, who clearly spent a lot of time with Manon and was thus accused as an accomplice in the alleged theft. This suggests that there was a cost to middling colonists of forging bonds with the enslaved. Marie-Josephe's association, and seeming friendliness, with Manon made her a suspect and diminished the protections offered by her modest but still respectable social status. She might also have been suspected as a possible conduit for the resale of the stolen goods because of the commercial relationships that characterized her bourgeois household.[14]

Manon's relationships, confirmed by the request for these individuals to testify as much as by the testimonies they offered, contextualize and shape how we read some of Manon's experiences at trial. To take one example, during her interrogation Manon's complex sense of identity was reduced to a tidy category, captured on paper, read back to her by a man in authority, and affirmed by Manon herself. She knew, of course, that her identity was multi-faceted, that she filled many roles in her social world, that she could emphasize one element of her identity in some circumstances and another when the situation changed. From others' testimony we learn that she was a friend, a neighbor, a laborer, a joker, and possibly a lover. She was a woman, born to Native North American parents who had given her an Indigenous name and taught her their Indigenous language before she was captured. The court, however, was primarily interested in her legal identity as a slave. In that setting, it was her status—her *qualité* in French—that defined her. By asking the question about her status, requiring her response, reading her response back to her, and having her affirm her status again, they assured that the experience of testifying in court would, among other things, reinforce her understanding of where she fit into the social order, what category of person she was. What is your *qualité*? I am a slave. / You were asked to state your *qualité*, and you answered that you were a slave. Is that correct? Yes. / Belonging to whom? Belonging to Nicolas-Auguste Guillet de Chaumont. / You said that you belonged to Nicolas-Auguste Guillet de Chaumont. Is that correct? Yes. This tedious performance would have reinforced the ways that Manon's standing as an enslaved person categorized her at law and declared what she could and could not hope to become. Although all witnesses were asked to state their *qualité* when they testified, only the status of enslaved people rendered them the property of another. Some parts of the trial record merely identify Manon as "the panise [Native slave] of M. Guillet," erasing her name altogether and equating her identity with her *qualité*.

These reductive declarations notwithstanding, the court proceedings also featured a dozen witnesses with varying degrees of association with Manon, testifying in ways that demonstrated the full complexity of her social connectivity, something quite different from her legal status. During a period of witness confrontation, court officers read key sections of others' testimony and asked Manon to confirm or correct the information given. This protocol offers another opportunity to listen with Manon as the court clerk read her the testimony of friends like Marie-Josephe Croqueloit. It must have been heartening to hear what the court had recorded of Marie-Josephe's testimony: she affirmed that Manon had only come to her house to borrow a cauldron and tripod for doing laundry, which was the same justification Manon had offered at home. Marie-Josephe said nothing about a theft and nothing about Manon being intoxicated. After hearing the testimony of her friend, the court asked Manon if she wanted to contradict anything in it, to which she responded, "I have no reproach to offer against Marie-Josephe." This phrasing, although formulaic and commonplace, nevertheless offered enslaved witnesses opportunities to assess others and underscore supportive relationships. If the trial process had served to reinforce Manon's status as a slave, established procedures also afforded her a voice that many accused slaves were denied, and highlighted her embeddedness within a larger community of people who were often marginalized but still socially vital.

These networks also proved to be reliable sources of information for Manon in the early stages of the trial. In theory, she should not have known the full details of the charges against her or the key evidentiary contentions undergirding the case. But it became clear very early in Manon's interrogation that she had been fed information about the case and had even heard details of earlier testimony long before her opportunity to confront witnesses. One important claim against Manon was that she had become drunk by the end of the day, starting early with drinks at home, continuing her spree at the wigmaker's, and drinking throughout the day before pilfering the silver and passing out "dead drunk" in her quarters. Before any other details had been established, the first substantive question posed to Manon asked if she had been at the wigmaker's house the previous Monday morning.

> Asked: If she was not at the home of the said Vauquière Monday morning.
> Answered: That she had drunk a small cup of brandy that morning at home, and having gone to the home of the said Vauquière to see if she could put some laundry in the basin, she found the said Vauquière, his wife, and an old man who had another time been at Monsieur Noyan's, whose name she did not know, drinking a pot of wine.

Rather than simply answering the question, she added, unbidden, that she had had a drink of brandy that morning at home, and that she had gone to Vauquiere's place because she needed to wash some laundry. She listed three witnesses who would have seen her there. The court then asked if she had not had something to drink chez Vauquiere. Again, a simple yes or no question prompted an unnecessarily elaborate response. "She said that she drank three glasses of wine there and ate a piece of bread and a small piece of meat, and that she returned home *tout de suite*." Was her chattiness a form of sarcasm, offering a string of extraneous details as irrelevant to her as the one they were asking about? Was it a tactic to make her story more credible? Was she suggesting that drinking as part of a meal was commonplace and thus hardly evidence that she was a drunk? Was she indicating that she had spent enough time with the witnesses that they would undoubtedly remember her presence? Whatever her precise reasoning, she steered the interrogation toward conclusions that she believed would be better for her, something she could not do were she totally unaware of the charges or the prosecutor's strategy. She obviously knew that there had been allegations of drunkenness and wanted to shape the court's narrative about it. She also knew that these more socially elevated, and thus more presumptively reputable, witnesses could be highly valuable to her case, and her unsolicited testimony about their presence might have been an attempt to maneuver the court into calling on them to testify.

When the interrogator asked directly about a missing silver spoon and fork, even the staid tone of the court transcript fails to hide Manon's surprise and frustration. "Oh my god!" she blurted. "It wasn't me who took them ... and I don't know who might have taken them." Her flash of defiant anger, her choice to offer unsolicited details, her implicit charge that her French accusers were lying: As Sophie White has argued in this volume, these unscripted moments—"said, without being asked"—offer perhaps the clearest sense that we are hearing enslaved voices directly, despite many channels of interference.[15]

As the prosecutor seemed to narrow his sights on another likely thief, the teenaged servant Marie Cluseau dite Loranger, he attempted to corner Manon into accusing her associate of the theft. Manon had avoided questions about her drunkenness throughout her interrogation, deflecting the suggestion when she could. When they found an empty liquor bottle in her quarters, they asked if she had stolen the liquor on the day in question. She answered that "in her quarters [cabane] she only had a vinegar bottle and she wondered if they had mistaken it for a bottle of brandy." The next question shifted attention to Loranger, who had visited on the day of the theft. Manon answered that "she remembered well that the said Loranger was there." When asked "if the said Loranger and the respondent [Manon] were not together in the cellar," Manon shifted tactics, embracing the accusations of her own drunkenness to avoid accusing Loranger directly. Manon claimed, "that she had no memory of this, that she was too drunk and did not know what the said Loranger might have done in the house." Although Loranger was a servant and much younger than Manon, it could have been dangerous to point the finger in her direction. The strategy paid off, as the court ultimately absolved Manon, Loranger, and Marie-Josephe Croqueloit of the crime.

If there are moments like these that stand out for their spontaneity and inconsistency, some of the most important statements scarcely register. Alongside the questions asked, accusations leveled, surprising behaviors alleged, there was also a range of expected actions by enslaved Native women like Manon that witnesses mentioned only in passing, as if they were almost too obvious to note. These nonchalant statements, offered to explain someone's whereabouts or suggest a benign motive for one action or another, reveal the mundane reality that French colonists held people in slavery primarily for their labor. Manon purportedly stole the silver when she had gone to the cellar for brooms to do the cleaning. Jean-Baptiste Chicot, the man who gave her the keys, found this request so unremarkable that he thought nothing of it. Manon confirmed "that she had asked the said Chicot for the key to the cellar to fetch some brooms and when she had done that she had immediately returned the key to the said Chicot." This chore was so routine and expected for a domestic slave that no one could blame Chicot for complying with Manon's request. Manon also prepared, served, and cleaned up after meals, which explains her familiarity with—and known access to—the purloined silver. She knew the set well enough to notice, on the day of the theft, that it was "incomplete, because there had been eleven pieces, but she found only ten." She also cared for Guillet de Chaumont's children. On one trip to the cellar, for example, Manon testified "that the young children were with her," one of many chores she did while they were in her care, most of them mundane enough to warrant only passing mentions. The same could be said of washing clothes, retrieving water, picking up food at the market, returning tools, and many other domestic tasks performed by Manon and her fellow slaves. Sometimes mentions of Manon's labor took the form of an accusation, as when the court's original summary said she had gone to the Vauquieres' house "on the pretext of doing laundry," a pretext that, as either something Manon actually said or as a lie said about her, would have to reflect common practice to have any purpose. In what they take for granted, what they offer as background or context, how they plot the cadence of everyday life to situate other, more consequential, actions, judicial testimonies by enslaved people and those who interacted with them thus offer a remarkably complete portrait of the kinds of labor extracted from captive Native women, in particular, but also a host of temporarily bound laborers who interacted with them.

The persistence of enslaved voices, and the traces of their rich personal, social, and even legal personhood, do not demonstrate that slavery in New France was exceptional. Without plantation agriculture, without a Middle Passage, many have imagined slavery as a kinder, gentler institution in early Canada than elsewhere.[16] Many others have argued that urban slavery everywhere offered a degree of mobility and sociability unavailable to the enslaved living on plantations. A wave of recent scholarship has challenged both assumptions, however, showing that in many respects slaves living in urban settings were under more constant and varied scrutiny, facing a host of threats to their safety and survival. Slavery in New France exhibited the high mortality rates, sexual and other physical violence, and dislocations of slavery in other locations. Manon would die at the age of forty-one in a colony where French settlers routinely lived into their late sixties. But even her shortened life was much longer than the vast majority of enslaved Native people: of the nearly 800 slaves in the parish and hospital records of New France whose age at death was noted, fully three-quarters died by the age of twenty.[17]

In Canada as elsewhere, slaveholders and the colonial state apparatus that supported them built their system of power in part by structuring the production of records in ways that erased the enslaved and justified their continued oppression.[18] Manon's master, the notary Guillet de Chaumont, offers a revealing example. As a notary and *écrivain*, or official scrivener, for the crown and the *Compagnie des Indes*, his very job was to produce the documents that secured property, verified transactions, certified debts, facilitated trade and troop movements, and valued estates. His position of authority and public trust included occasional stints as an *assesseur*, or temporary judge, and in that capacity, he oversaw the judicial torture and execution of at least one enslaved woman in 1734, the infamous case of Marie-Josephe-Angélique, who was convicted for setting a fire that destroyed a substantial portion of Montreal. Guillet recorded details for a living, producing more than a thousand pages of surviving documents, and yet he left not a single word about Manon, a woman he coerced daily for at least eleven, and possibly as many as twenty-six, years.[19]

We know these details only because other sources hint at Guillet de Chaumont's long engagement with slavery and dependence on enslaved labor. When he retired as a notary, for example, moving from Montreal to the more rural parish of Terrebonne, he took Manon with him, compelling her to care for him and his family until her death in 1761—her final eleven years being reduced to two compact sentences in a Catholic parish registry. The Catholic church vacillated between silent complicity in and full-throated support for slavery in New France. Many priests and nuns held slaves, and some convents, hospitals, and other religious institutions relied on them for domestic work and other manual labor. Then, too, by concealing the identity of masters who fathered children with enslaved women, missionaries and parish priests facilitated the sexual violence that always attended slavery. Even as they recorded biographical details of enslaved individuals, they performed acts of violent erasure. Marie-Josephe, also called Manon, was born with another name, which was erased and replaced at her christening. By identifying her as a "panisse," or Native of the Panis nation, the priest reinforced a legal fiction designed to justify her bondage by categorizing her as a legitimate target of enslavement.[20] Yet for all their acts of annihilation, Catholic records are also essential for reconstructing the individual lives of the enslaved. Acts of erasure, in slavery and in colonialism generally, are often only visible when they are incomplete or accompanied by competing imperatives. These competing imperatives, from protecting the integrity of a judicial proceeding to demanding the payment of a debt, ensured that dozens of enslaved voices remain in the records of New

France. They also offer one of the rare moments when we can encounter the words enslaved people heard, including those that were attributed to them by those in power.

Manon's assertion that "her answers contained the truth"—bland legal boilerplate that appears at the end of every testimony in this trial and nearly all others in New France—thus invites us to examine some of the tensions within the project of writing about Atlantic slavery, and especially about the enslaved individuals who experienced the system's cruelties first hand. These tensions are often expressed as a series of binaries: devastating oppression vs. empowering resistance; the goal of historical recovery in service of the present versus a faithful retelling of the past on its own terms; the corrosive power of pain and the inspiring persistence of humanity. It was possible for Manon to be coerced and closely monitored on the one hand, and to have mobility and opportunities for social life on the other. The same court could give her standing to testify and classify her as another's property. She could both live a meaningful life and have the conditions created by her enslavement cut that life short.

Manon's story also lays bare another duality, one that historians are only now beginning to reckon with: that slavery in the early modern Atlantic world played essential roles in both Indigenous and African diasporic histories. Like nearly ninety percent of enslaved people in Montreal in the decades she was there, Manon was an Indigenous American rather than an African. Although by the mid-eighteenth century enslaved people of African descent vastly outnumbered enslaved Natives in most American colonies, the enslavement of Native people was far more prevalent than previously thought. As many as five million Indigenous slaves were held by Europeans over the first three centuries of colonization, and their enslavement laid both the legal and capital foundations of the early modern plantation complex. "Recent research," according to Margaret Newell, "has shown us that most enslaved persons in the Americas before 1700 were Indians; that Indians constituted a sizable proportion of the global slave population thereafter; and that Europeans enslaved Indians from Quebec to New Orleans, and from New England to the Carolinas." Intricately linked by laws and institutions, enslaved Africans and Amerindians also lived side-by-side, making the experiences of one group essential to understanding those of the other.[21]

To underscore the inseparability of Native and African slaveries, and of Indigenous and African diasporic legacies, we need to look no further than Manon and the man who claimed her as his property, Guillet de Chaumont. In his role as a royal official, he was appointed to a panel of judges that oversaw the trial, torture, and execution of the enslaved Luso-African woman named Marie-Josephe-Angélique. In April of 1734 a fire broke out in the home of Thérese de Couagne, Angélique's mistress. The flames spread quickly, consuming more than forty buildings that included the homes and warehouses of many of Montreal's leading

merchants. Because Angélique fled the scene she was immediately suspected as the source of the fire, and she quickly became the focus of
the town's rage. Arrested and imprisoned, Angélique faced a trial that
followed standard procedure in most respects, including a series of physical tortures designed to extract a confession and to get her to identify
any accomplices. Convinced that she was "well and duly proven guilty
of having set the fire," Guillet de Chaumont and his fellow judges made
individual sentencing recommendations. Guillet de Chaumont proposed
"that she make honorable amends with a torch in her hand, which will
be cut off in front of the cathedral of this town, and afterward that she
be thrown into the fire alive." Although the colony's Superior Council did not follow the sentencing recommendation—choosing instead
to have Angélique hanged, without severing her hands, with her body
burned after her death—the panel of judges, all slaveholders themselves,
sent a clear message to those who would challenge their authority.[22]

One of the key witnesses against Angélique was an enslaved Meskwaki
(Fox) teenager called Manon, who lived next door to Angélique. Manon's
testimony revealed a close relationship between the enslaved neighbors.
Trial testimony suggests that they interacted frequently and amicably, visiting each other and working together in town. They exchanged greetings
through the windows of their respective homes while they worked and
played games when they had moments at rest. In an almost maternal ges-
ture, Angélique once tickled Manon to cheer her up and make her laugh. Yet
Manon's testimony proved pivotal to Angélique's conviction. When Manon
rebuffed Angélique's efforts to cheer her up, according to Manon, Angélique
had said "she did not want to laugh. There's Madame de Francheville who
is laughing well with Madame Duvivier, she will not be in her home for
long and will not sleep there." Manon said that while she was turning meat
on a spit in her master's kitchen, she had seen Angélique scrutinizing the
roof where the fire would start later that day. When Manon heard someone
shout the alarm, she ran out of her master's house to see the fire and saw "that
the Negress [Angélique] was outside looking pallid and struggling to shout
'fire!'" When Manon's master, François de Berey, asked her if she knew
anything about the fire, she related these details to him, adding that Angélique "was right to say that her mistress would not sleep in her house."
Angry at this apparent betrayal, Angélique denounced her friend in the
confrontation stage of the trial, saying that Manon was "a deplorable liar
… an indigent and a wretch to speak such falsehoods." But with public
outrage trained on Angélique from the beginning, Manon chose to preserve her own safety by implicating her friend, an act she knew would lead
to Angélique's death.[23]

If the lives of Manon and Angélique were bound together by legal
status, daily routine, and what seems to have been a genuine friendship, their histories—like those of most enslaved Natives and Africans—
remain largely separate. Angélique's story has been widely told.

Historians, poets, and playwrights have produced dozens of interpretations, all of which have been embedded within broader histories of the African diaspora without accounting for the Indigenous context of her experience. Many of these accounts are remarkably insightful and often deeply moving. Afua Cooper, for example, placed Angélique's experiences into the context of the Atlantic slave trade, linking her conviction and execution to broader patterns of racialized violence against people of African descent by Portuguese, Dutch, English, and French colonizers in the eighteenth century. In an effort to reverse the "erasure of Black people and their history" from Canadian national narratives, Cooper uses Angélique's story to illustrate "how slavery instituted a new racial hierarchy based on Black subordination and White supremacy in the New World and Europe; and how the slave trade took Angélique to Montréal."[24] Many others have followed similar paths, building on the work of Robin Winks, whose 1971 book *The Blacks in Canada* traced the roots of modern Canadian racial inequality to the enslavement of African-descended people in New France.[25]

In one profoundly moving example, the playwright Lorena Gale drew on Angélique's trial records to imagine her intimate life as an enslaved woman, one among millions in a forced diaspora that links the early modern and modern worlds. Gale's play ends with a poetic invocation of the long history of racialized state violence against people of African descent. In Angélique's final moments, as she prepares to die, she glimpses the long shadow of her own terror. She breaks the fourth wall and turns to the audience:

> Look!
> The view is clear ...
> So clear from here.
> In the vista of tomorrow
> stretching out before,
> I can see this city ...
> swarming with ebony.
> There's me and me and me and me ...
> My brothers and my sisters!
> My brothers and my sisters ...
> Arrested for their difference.
> Their misery a silent scream,
> rising to crescendo
> and
> falling on deaf ears.[26]

Such acts of remembrance do important work by showing the depth of modern anti-Black racism in a country that tends to celebrate its role as a liberator of enslaved African Americans fleeing the United States in the nineteenth century, yet where racism still ensures that people of color are surveilled and incarcerated at far higher rates than others. As Kyle G. Brown has noted, "The United Nations has sounded the alarm on anti-black racism in Canada, stating that it can be traced back to slavery and its legacy."[27]

Because the political and personal stakes are so high, and because these examples offer models for linking the deeper past of slavery to present injustices, there are insights to be gained by connecting rather than disaggregating the legacies of slavery in New France, demonstrating the deeply imbricated pasts of Indigenous and African diasporic peoples. How can Indigenous voices enter vital conversations about the many legacies of colonial systems of slavery, dispossession, and racial inequality? How do we account for the fact that, in this historical context, most enslaved people—as much as ninety percent in some places—were Native North American rather than African captives?

The bridge between Angélique's arson case and Manon's theft trial suggests just some of the ways that these histories could be understood together. Not only were enslaved Native and African people living side-by-side as they experienced slavery in eighteenth-century Montreal, but they also had to navigate common household and state power structures erected to keep them in slavery, working and living for the benefit of others. The historical Angélique was thus one of only a handful of enslaved people of African descent in the city, and, before the late 1740s, the whole colony. Angélique's late master, François Poulin de Francheville, owned Native as well as African slaves. Manon's master, Guillet de Chaumont, was an agent of a global corporate quasi-state, the *Compagnie des Indes*, which made most of its profits from the stolen labor of African slaves. All New France's legal, commercial, and political dealings with slavery drew explicit comparisons between the two primary enslaved populations in the colony and the wider French Atlantic world.[28]

The archival practices of the state also recorded, silenced, and structured the words of Angélique and Manon in essentially identical ways, underscoring the value of considering them together. In New France, both women had standing to testify with none of the restrictions they would have faced in the French Caribbean or Louisiana, where variations of the Code Noir limited the conditions under which enslaved witnesses could testify and under which courts could consider their testimony. Yet both were considered property. Both appeared as part of complex social networks. Both had to confront those within their social circles who accused them of wrongdoing and thereby threatened their safety. And like Manon, Angélique had, at the end of her testimony, sworn that "her answers contained the truth." Angélique's emphatic denial of the crime for which she was executed remain for us to read today.[29] These imperfect archives, products of the colonial powers that oppressed these two women, contain the truth in complex and often contradictory ways: limiting how much of it we can know and shaping the limits of our imagination even as they allow us to listen to—and with—enslaved witnesses.

Even when basic factual questions remain elusive, the parameters of discovery can be revealing. Take one very basic question: was the Manon who testified against Angélique in 1734 the same person accused of stealing silver in 1750? There are many reasons to assume that she was. Her name (Marie, but called Manon) was common among the enslaved, but many other factors suggest the possibility. In 1734, Manon was said to be about fifteen years old, and in 1750 to be about thirty. Guillet de Chaumont, Manon's master in 1750, presided at Angélique's trial and had extensive interaction with her in that capacity. He was also connected with the young Manon's master, François de Berey, who lived on the same street and did business with Guillet de Chaumont. The two men both had connections to Terrebonne, the rural parish where the elder Manon died in Guillet de Chaumont's custody. There is no bill of sale or other record of transfer from de Berey to Guillet de Chaumont, but nor is there evidence of Berey holding this or another Manon in slavery after 1734 (although several enslaved people with other names appear in his records between then and 1751). Finally, because nearly all enslaved Native women in New France first entered the colony as children or teenagers, the elder Manon was almost certainly brought to Montreal between 1725 and 1735, when more captives were identified as Meskwaki than any other Native nation.[30]

One fragment from Angélique's court records does offer a clue, suggesting that perhaps the Manon from that case was not tried for theft fourteen years later. At the end of each deposition, witnesses were asked to sign the document they had heard read to them, attesting that they had seen and assented to its accuracy. When young Manon was asked to endorse the record of her first appearance, she said that she did not know how to write or sign. In a later appearance, she confessed that she did know how to write her name, explaining to the court that she misunderstood their previous request. "She explained to us," wrote the court reporter, "that if she did not want to sign her deposition from the interrogation, it was because she believed she was supposed to sign the name Sieur de Berey, which she does not know how to write." Categorized by the court as the property of Sieur de Berey, Manon believed—or claimed to believe—that she should identify herself in state records only in relation to him. Once she understood that she could sign her own name, she wrote it three times in a clear and careful, if simple, hand.[31] How Manon would have learned to write her name remains a topic of speculation. In many French colonial settings, Ursulines and other religious figures worked hard to instruct young women, including those of Native and African descent, although for the enslaved this instruction does not seem to have included literacy. Perhaps she was afforded such an opportunity or was taught by another young person who had learned in that way (Figures 6.1 and 6.2).[32]

In 1750, the elder Manon declared that she could not sign. This could signal that this was a different woman, or it could be that she simply did not wish to repeat an act that helped secure her friend's conviction,

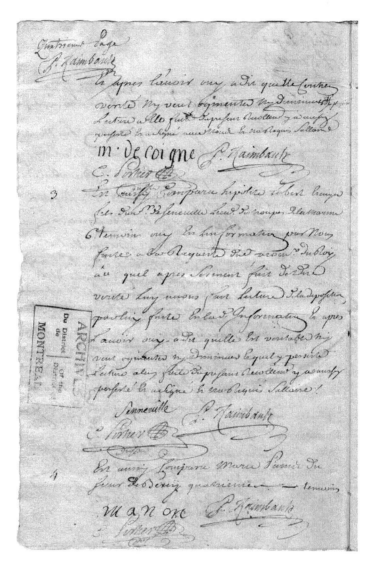

Figure 6.1 "Procès contre Marie-Josèphe-Angélique, née au Portugal, esclave noire de Thérèse de Couagne, veuve de Poulin de Francheville, et Claude Thibault, faux-saunier, accusés d'incendie criminel," April 11–June 21, 1734. Bibliothèque et Archives nationales du Québec, TL4, S1, D5547, fol. 103. Courtesy of Bibliothèque et Archives nationales du Québec. (CC BY-SA 4.0.)

Figure 6.2 "Procès contre Marie-Josèphe-Angélique, née au Portugal, esclave noire de Thérèse de Couagne, veuve de Poulin de Francheville, et Claude Thibault, faux-saunier, accusés d'incendie criminel," April 11–June 21, 1734. Bibliothèque et Archives nationales du Québec, TL4, S1, D5547, fol. 105. Courtesy of Bibliothèque et Archives nationales du Québec. (CC BY-SA 4.0.)

leading to her execution and postmortem burning. All other surviving evidence suggest that this was the same Manon, opening the possibility of imagining—if only uncertainly—the effects of racialized violence on those who escaped but witnessed its terror at a formative age. It also invites us to consider the possibility that some, if not many, of the archive's silences were chosen by enslaved people themselves to control the narrative available to those in power who wished to restrain them. The difficulty of answering this factual question indicates just some of the common ways that Native and African people were silenced and erased by historical records, but also how they could sometimes manipulate these processes to their own advantage.[33]

Such complex intersectional connections within historical slavery—both experiential and evidentiary—pose challenges to projects of historical recovery centered on modern descendant communities. They also offer opportunities for collaborative claims for redress. Because recovering the voices, identities, and lived experiences of the enslaved is about historical identity as much as it is about historical representation, enslaved voices remain fragmented, sounding in different registers and sought for different purposes. Will we diminish one narrative by recognizing its connections to others? For New France, and likely for most places in the Atlantic world, recognizing the intersections between African and Native slaveries can only underscore the ways that colonialism and white supremacy developed in tandem, and how slavery played a central role in these developments for Indigenous as well as African-descended peoples. As Octavia Pierre has written, "The rupture between the Québec government and First Nations, between the Québec government and black people, is still part of the very fabric of this society."[34] This present reality demands a historical narrative sensitive to all expressions of colonial violence and dispossession, hearing the voices of both Angélique and Manon as they speak across the centuries.

Notes

1 "Procès entre Marguerite Charbonneau, épouse de Jean-Baptiste Chicot, plaignante, et Marie-Manon, esclave panis de Guillet de Chaumont, Marie Decluseau dit Loranger, vivant chez son père à Lachenaie, et Marie-Josèphe Croquelois dit Laviolette, épouse de Nicolas Vauquière, perruquier, accusées de vol d'ustensiles en argent," Oct. 20–Nov. 30, 1750. Bibliothèque et Archives nationales du Québec, TL4, S1, D5547. For Guillet de Chaumont, see Michel Paquin, "Guillet de Chaumont, Nicolas-Auguste," in *Dictionary of Canadian Biography*, vol. 3 (Toronto: Univeristy of Toronto Press, 1974), www.biographi.ca/en/bio/guillet_de_chaumont_nicolas_auguste_3E.html.

2 For these trials and other instances of intimidation, see Brett Rushforth, *Bonds of Alliance: Indigenous and Atlantic Slaveries in New France* (Chapel Hill: University of North Carolina Press for the Omohundro Institute of Early American History and Culture, 2012), 299–367. For another recent interpretation of enslaved women in Montreal's judicial archives, see Dominique Deslandres, "Voix des esclaves autochtones et des esclavagistes: Un cas d'histoire intersectionnelle dans les archives judiciaires de la juridiction de Montréal," *Les cahiers des dix* 72 (2018), 145–175.

3 "Procès entre Jacques Bigot dit Lagiroflée, époux de Madeleine Dupont, sergent des troupes, plaignant, et Nicolas-Augustin Guillet de Chaumont,

accusé d'avoir frappé l'épouse du plaignant," Sept. 8, 1723, BAnQ, TL4, S1, D2967 and "Appel mis à néant de la sentence rendue en la Juridiction de Montréal, le 20 juin 1750, dans la cause entre maître Nicolas-Auguste Guillet Chaumont, notaire en la Juridiction de Montréal, contre Michel Gervais, prêtre, curé de la paroisse de Saint-Charles et Saint-Denis, près de la rivière Chambly," Oct. 12, 1750, BAnQ, TP1, S28, P20520. For Guillet de Chaumont's role in an enslaved woman's execution, see "Procès contre Marie-Josèphe-Angélique, née au Portugal, esclave noire de Thérèse de Couagne, veuve de Poulin de Francheville, et Claude Thibault, faux-saunier, accusés d'incendie criminel," Apr. 11–June 21, 1734, BAnQ, TL4, S1, D4136.

4 Testimony of Marie, dite Manon, Oct. 22, 1750, "Procès entre Marguerite Charbonneau ... et Marie-Manon," BAnQ, TL4, S1, D5547.

5 *Dictionnaire de l'Académie française* (Paris, 1694), s.v. "contenir." Project for American and French Research on the Treasury of the French Language (ARTFL), University of Chicago, *Dictionnaires d'autrefois*: https://artfl-project.uchicago.edu/content/dictionnaires-dautrefois.

6 For slaves and trials in mainland British North America and the early United States, see Philip J. Schwarz, *Twice Condemned: Slaves and the Criminal Laws of Virginia, 1705–1865* (Baton Rouge: Louisiana State University Press, 1988), 6–58; Thomas D. Morris, *Southern Slavery and the Law, 1619–1860* (Chapel Hill: University of North Carolina Press, 1996), 209–248; and Ariela Gross, *Double Character: Slavery and Mastery in the Antebellum Southern Courtroom* (Princeton, NJ: Princeton University Press, 2000). For the British Caribbean, see Natalie Zacek, "Voices and Silences: The Problem of Slave Testimony in the English West Indian Law Court," *Slavery and Abolition* 24, no. 3 (2003), 24–39. For two excellent studies of slave testimonies in the Spanish colonial world, see Michelle McKinley, *Fractional Freedoms: Slavery, Intimacy, and Legal Mobilization in Colonial Lima, 1600–1700* (Cambridge: Cambridge University Press, 2016) and Bianca Premo, *The Enlightenment on Trial: Ordinary Litigants and Colonialism in the Spanish Empire* (Oxford: Oxford University Press, 2017).

7 On the social lives of the enslaved, see Vincent Brown, "Social Death and Political Life in the Study of Slavery," *American Historical Review* 114 (December 2009), 1231–1249. For Inquisition records, see James Sweet, *Domingos Álvares: African Healing and the Intellectual History of the Atlantic World* (Chapel Hill: University of North Carolina Press, 2011). For court trials, see Sophie White, *Voices of the Enslaved: Love, Labor, and Longing in French Louisiana* (Chapel Hill: University of North Carolina Press for the Omohundro Institute of Early American History and Culture, 2019); McKinley, *Fractional Freedoms*; Premo, *Enlightenment on Trial*; and Rachel O'Toole, *Bound Lives: Africans, Indians, and the Making of Race in Colonial Peru* (Pittsburgh, PA: University of Pittsburgh Press, 2012). For slave rebellions, see Jason Sharples, "Discovering Slave Conspiracies: New Fears of Rebellion and Old Paradigms of Plotting in Seventeenth-Century Barbados," *American Historical Review* 120 (June 2015), 811–843; Brett Rushforth, "The Gaulet Uprising of 1710: Maroons, Rebels, and the Informal Exchange Economy of a Caribbean Sugar Island," *William and Mary Quarterly* 76 (January 2019), 75–110; and Emilia Viotti da Costa, *Crowns of Glory, Tears of Blood: The Demerara Slave Rebellion of 1823* (Oxford: Oxford University Press, 1997). For "shared surveillance" see Rushforth, *Bonds of Alliance*, 324.

8 Emmanuel Le Roy Ladurie, *Montaillou, village occitan de 1294 à 1324* (Paris: Gallimard, 1975); Ladurie, *Montaillou: Cathars and Catholics in a French Village, 1294–1324*, trans. Barbara Bray (London: The Scolar

Press, 1978); Carlo Ginzburg, *Il formaggio e i vermi* (Rome: Einaudi, 1976); Ginzburg, *The Cheese and the Worms: The Cosmos of a Sixteenth-Century Miller*, trans. John Tedeschi and Anne Tedeschi (Baltimore, MD: Johns Hopkins University Press, 1980); Natalie Zemon Davis, *The Return of Martin Guerre* (Cambridge: Cambridge University Press, 1983); Robert Finlay, "The Refashioning of Martin Guerre," *American Historical Review* 93 (June 1988), 553–571; and Davis, "On the Lame," *American Historical Review* 93 (June 1988), 572–603.

 9 Sharples, "Discovering Slave Conspiracies" and Michael P. Johnson, "Denmark Vesey and his Co-Conspirators," *William and Mary Quarterly* 58, no. 4 (October 2001), 915–976.

10 "A Peasant vs. the Inquisition: Cheese, Worms, and the Birth of Microhistory," CBC Radio Interview with Carlo Ginzburg, Mar. 21, 2017, www.cbc. ca/radio/ideas/a-peasant-vs-the-inquisition-cheese-worms-and-the-birth-of-micro-history-1.4034196.

11 Ann Laura Stoler, *Along the Archival Grain: Epistemic Anxieties and Colonial Common Sense* (Princeton, NJ: Princeton University Press, 2009). For a more skeptical view of these methods, see Fuentes, *Dispossessed Lives*; Laura Helton et al., "The Question of Recovery: An Introduction," *Social Text* 33, no. 4 (December 2015): 1–18; Greg L. Childs, "Secret and Spectral: Torture and Secrecy in the Archives of Slave Conspiracies," ibid., 35–57.

12 For the importance of paper, see Rebecca J. Scott and Jean Hébrard, *Freedom Papers: An Atlantic Odyssey in the Age of Emancipation* (Cambridge, MA: Harvard University Press, 2012); Ann Laura Stoler, "Colonial Archives and the Arts of Governance," *Archival Science* 2 (2002), 87–109; John Garrigus, *Before Haiti: Race and Citizenship in French Saint-Domingue* (New York: Palgrave Macmillan, 2006); and Sue Peabody, *Madeleine's Children: Family, Freedom, Secrets, and Lies in France's Indian Ocean Colonies* (Oxford: Oxford University Press, 2017).

13 John Lewis Gaddis, *The Landscape of History: How Historians Map the Past* (New York: Oxford University Press, 2002), 116.

14 For theft and resale in early modern court proceedings, including French North America, see Sophie White, "Slaves and Poor Whites' Informal Economies in an Atlantic Context," in Cécile Vidal, ed., *Louisiana: Crossroads of the Atlantic World* (Philadelphia: University of Pennsylvania Press, 2013), 89–102; Beverly Lemire, "The Theft of Clothes and Popular Consumerism in Early Modern England," *Journal of Social History* 24, 2 (1990), 255–276; and Rushforth, *Bonds of Alliance*, 320–324.

15 See also Sophie White, "'Said Without Being Asked': Slavery, Testimony, and Autobiography," in Sophie White and Trevor Burnard, eds., *Hearing Enslaved Voices: Africna and Indian Slave Testimony in British and French America, 1700–1848* (New York and London: Routledge, 2020), 17.

16 This interpretation is most fully expressed in Marcel Trudel, *L'esclavage au Canada français* (Quebec: Presses de l'Universite Laval, 1960).

17 Fuentes, *Dispossessed Lives*; Jorge Cañizares-Esguerra, Matt D. Childs, and James Disbury, eds., *The Black Urban Atlantic in the Age of the Slave Trade* (Philadelphia: University of Pennsylvania Press, 2013); Pepijn Brandon, Niklas Frykman, and Pernille Røge, "Free and Unfree Labor in Atlantic and Indian Ocean Port Cities (Seventeenth to Nineteenth Centuries)," *International Review of Social History* 64 , no. S27 (2019), 1–18; and Rushforth, *Bonds of Alliance*, Chap. 6 (p. 335 for mortality statistics).

18 Stephanie Smallwood, "The Politics of the Archive and History's Accountability to the Enslaved," *History of the Present* 6, no. 2 (Fall 2016), 117–132.

Marisa J. Fuentes, *Dispossessed Lives: Enslaved Women, Violence, and the Archive* (Philadelphia: University of Pennsylvania Press, 2016) and Saidiya Hardman, "Venus in Two Acts," *Small Axe* 26 (June 2008), 1–14.

19 "Procès contre Marie-Josèphe-Angélique, née au Portugal, esclave noire de Thérèse de Couagne, veuve de Poulin de Francheville, et Claude Thibault, faux-saunier, accusés d'incendie criminel," April 11–June 21, 1734, BAnQ, TL4, S1, D4136. For Guillet de Chaumont's notarial career, see "Nomination de Nicolas-Auguste Guillet de Chaumont, à titre de notaire royal de la Juridiction Royale de Montréal," Nov. 6, 1728, BAnQ, TL4, S1, D3496; Paquin, "Guillet de Chaumont"; and Pierre Georges Roy, *Inventaire des greffes des notaires du régime française* (Québec: R. Lefebvre, 1942–1976), 17 vols. The most complete treatment of Angélique's case is Afua Cooper, *The Hanging of Angélique: The Untold Story of Slavery and the Burning of Old Montréal* (Toronto: Harper Collins, 2006; Athens: University of Georgia Press, 2007).

20 Burial of Marie-Josephe, panisse, Feb. 21, 1761, Saint-Louis-de-Terrebonne. For a discussion of the term "panis" and its legal implications, see Rushforth, *Bonds of Alliance*, esp. chap. 3.

21 Andrés Resendez, *The Other Slavery: The Uncovered Story of Indian Enslavement in America* (Boston, MA: Houghton Mifflin Harcourt, 2016) and Margaret Newell, "The Forgotten Slaves," *Chronicle of Higher Education*, Dec. 11, 2016 (quote).

22 "Procès contre Marie-Josèphe-Angélique, née au Portugal, esclave noire de Thérèse de Couagne, veuve de Poulin de Francheville, et Claude Thibault, faux-saunier, accusés d'incendie criminel," April 11–June 21, 1734, BAnQ, TL4, S1, D4136. ["Je trouve L'accusée bien et duement atteinte et convaincû d'avoir mis le feu chez Mademoiselle francheville; pour reparation de quoi mon avis est qu'elle fasse amende honorable La torche au point que l'on lui Coupera devant la Cathedrale de cette ville, Et ensuitte Jetté au feu toute vive."]

23 "Procès contre Marie-Josèphe-Angélique."

24 Afua Cooper, *Hanging of Angélique*, 7, 9.

25 Robin Winks, *The Blacks in Canada: A History* (Montreal: McGill-Queen's University Press, 1971); Charaine Nelson, *Ebony Roots, Northern Soil: Perspectives on Blackness in Canada* (Newcastle upon Tyne: Cambridge Scholars, 2010); Nelson, *Legacies Denied: Unearthing the Visual Culture of Canadian Slavery* (Montreal: C.A. Nelson, 2013); and Kyle G. Brown, "Canada's Slavery Secret: The Whitewashing of 200 Years of Enslavement" and "Slavery's Long Shadow: The Impact of 200 Years of Enslavement in Canada," Canadian Broadcast Company Radio Documentary, June 28, 2018 and July 5, 2018, www.cbc.ca/radio/ideas/canada-s-slavery-secret-the-whitewashing-of-200-years-of-enslavement-1.4726313.

26 Gale, *Angélique*, 75. Courtesy of Playwrights Canada Press.

27 Brown, "Slavery's Long Shadow."

28 Rushforth, *Bonds of Alliance*, 299–367; Marcel Trudel, *Dictionnaire des esclaves et de leurs propriétaires au Canada français* (Québec: Hurtubise HMH, 1990), 400; and Paquin, "Guillet de Chaumont."

29 "Procés contre Angélique," fol. 78.

30 Paquin, "Guillet de Chaumont" and Trudel, *Dictionnaire des esclaves* s.v. Berey. Brett Rushforth, "Slavery, the Fox Wars, and the Limits of Alliance," *William and Mary Quarterly* 63, no. 1 (January 2006), 53–80.

31 "Procés contre Angélique," fols. 34 (no signature), and 103–105 (signatures).

32 Ann Little, *The Many Captivities of Esther Wheelwright* (New Haven, CT: Yale University Press, 2016), esp. 100–104; Emily Clark, *Masterless*

Mistresses: The New Orleans Ursulines and the Development of a New World Society, 1727–1834 (Chapel Hill: University of North Carolina Press, 2007), esp. 113–122; and Sophie White, *Wild Frenchmen and Frenchified Indians: Material Culture and Race Colonial Louisiana* (Philadelphia: University of Pennsylvania Press, 2012), esp. 150–151 and 162–163.

33 For an extended discussion of archival silences as a mode of enslaved resistance, see Brett Rushforth, "Gauolet Uprising of 1710," esp. 81–82 and 109–110.

34 ["La rupture entre l'État québécois et les Premières nations, entre l'État québécois et les personnes noires, fait toujours déjà partie du tissu même de cette société."] Octavia Pierre, "L'Égalité est un concept radical: Mise à mort de Pierre Coriolan," http://unconceptradical.tumblr.com/post/162446471378/mise-%C3%A0-mort-de-pierre-coriolan.

Section Three
African Americans

7 Ideologies of the Age of Revolution and Emancipation in Enslaved African Narratives

Aaron Spencer Fogleman

The number of published narratives produced by Africans caught in the transatlantic slave system is *much* larger than most scholars realize, and together they provide tremendous insight into Atlantic slavery from African perspectives. These incredible life stories depict a never-ending search by Africans to survive, improve their circumstances, and just live in a variety of ways, each depending on personal circumstances, desires, and environment. This essay investigates one of those ways, namely, whether and how Africans appropriated Enlightenment, revolutionary, and Christian ideals of liberty and equality, as well as Islamic ideas of reform (*jihād*), to improve their personal situation or end slavery altogether.[1]

Other historians have shown how enslaved African Americans and Africans appropriated revolutionary ideology unintended for them in their fight against slavery. Laurent Dubois, for example, criticizes recent scholars who deny the role of the Enlightenment to Black political and intellectual thought because, they argue, Enlightenment thinking was so racist and/or pro-slavery that they deny Blacks would accept it, in spite of its promotion of freedom. In fact, Dubois argues, they did appropriate ideas about liberty in the Enlightenment crafted in Europe and the Caribbean. The Enlightenment did not inspire Haitian rebels, but they did make good use of its ideals.[2] Robin Blackburn argues persuasively that revolutions from 1776 to 1825 were interconnected, with each helping to radicalize the next. The American Revolution declared popular sovereignty but then launched a white man's republic. The French Revolution initially ignored slavery but then struck at it because the patriotism of its Caribbean planters became suspect. Black Haitians took advantage of the turmoil and further radicalized the revolution.[3]

Janet Polasky develops this theme further, showing how Blacks became involved in a "call to liberty" throughout the Atlantic World. From 1776 to 1804 revolution "cascaded" through four continents. Historians frequently cite the example of a copy of the French Declaration of the Rights of Man found on the body of an ex-slave who fell in battle while defending Haiti from counterattacks, yet Haitians also explicitly expressed the desire during interviews to realize the ideals of the

Declaration and used that ideology to justify their actions, including winning independence in 1804. Polasky notes how the U.S. Revolution set thousands of ex-slaves into motion, including many who went to Sierra Leone. Upon arrival, they demanded the right to vote, representation in government, and property rights. Their promotion of women's suffrage put them on par with New Jersey, where women temporarily gained the right to vote. The Sierra Leone settlers struggled against white organizers and officials of the settlement, who denied them these rights. For this, William Wilberforce called the settlers Jacobins, a reflection of their radicalism.[4]

Recent historians have shown the trend in some Latin American revolutions as well. With so many slaves willing to fill his desperate need for soldiers and the support of Haiti so critical to success, Simón Bolívar found that he could no longer support the language of both liberty and slavery. Mexico too, freed its slaves with independence in 1829, by which time all other Spanish mainland colonies had done the same. The situation in Brazil and the Spanish Caribbean, where most Latin American slaves resided, was quite different. Creole elites in Brazil found a way to effect revolution and independence without war, which protected their slaves, and Spanish Caribbean colonists dared not revolt for fear of losing their slaves or worse, even though they held similar grievances against royal policies.[5]

Black appropriation of revolutionary ideology also occurred in the British realm, which scholars do not normally associate with "revolution." The thirteen North American colonies that successfully revolted from that realm affected the rest of the empire. Christopher Brown argues that the American Revolution directly influenced the British abolition movement, of which the radical Thomas Clarkson was an important leader.[6] Polasky agrees, arguing that antislavery efforts involving the British were part of the Age of Revolution. In addition to Sierra Leone, this included Olaudah Equiano's narrative, which Polasky calls a revolutionary document. Jamaican planters demonstrated the connection when they burned Wilberforce and Thomas Paine in effigy in 1793.[7] Clarkson and especially Wilberforce's connection to the Christian evangelical movement was especially important, but the key is that enslaved black people in the British Empire, the new United States, and elsewhere began converting and appropriating Christian ideals of liberty and equality to either improve their circumstances or challenge slavery altogether.[8]

Within the framework of the Age of Revolution, Emancipation, and Christianization in Protestant lands in the Atlantic World historians have addressed slaves and slavery in general but not specifically enslaved *Africans*: that is, those born in some form of relative freedom in Africa who were enslaved by Europeans and sought freedom once again, often telling their stories after having attained it. Paul Lovejoy argues that such people produced a different kind of "slave narrative," or what he calls "freedom narratives."[9] Robert Hanserd shows that by the late eighteenth century the desire or need for Africans to appropriate Enlightenment and revolutionary ideas to help them achieve freedom augmented or modified their ideas about freedom and resistance to slavery that they had brought from West Africa.[10] Lovejoy argues convincingly that we must consider the impact of the Muslim reform movement in West Africa (*jihād*) on the transatlantic slave trade in the Age of Revolution, to include the activities of members of the movement who were enslaved in the Americas.[11]

The expanded corpus of African narratives allows us to investigate whether and how individuals born in Africa and taken into the transatlantic slave trade appropriated ideas about liberty and equality from the Enlightenment, ongoing Atlantic revolutions, Christianity, and Islam to promote their own cause. To date, historians have not examined the impact of all these ideologies on appropriation or the interplay among them, in part because they have not stressed African perspectives enough. What does a thorough reading of the corpus of narratives reveal? Who or which of these Africans appropriated ideas regarding equality, liberty, or antislavery? How did they do it? Based on my reading of 221 narratives or life stories by Africans caught in the transatlantic slave trade, I argue that beginning with those produced in the 1770s many who were able to do so began appropriating Enlightenment, revolutionary, Christian, and/or Muslim ideals to condemn the transatlantic slave trade. Relatively few narratives were produced before the outset of the Age of Revolution, but in those that did appear Enlightenment ideals were absent, Christian ideology was either neutral toward or defended the transatlantic slave system, and criticism of the transatlantic slave system by Muslim reform ideology was vague and indirect. Beginning in the 1770s and continuing until the end of the slave trade in the 1860s and to some extent thereafter, however, the change was dramatic, as the overall number of published narratives increased and with that the number that appropriated the above ideologies to criticize transatlantic slavery. This suggests that, regardless of the intentions of their instigators, the events historians associate with the Age of Revolution (to include reform movements in West Africa) provided Africans victimized by the transatlantic slave system with another means of resistance that many actively seized upon.

There are limits to what these narratives or life stories in the Catalog can tell us, but the opportunities for new assessments and understandings based on African perspectives overshadow the limitations. With few exceptions, heavy editorial mediation is present in the final publications that we now read. Moreover, one might ask how reflective these 221 cases are of the experience of 12.5 million people who experienced the Middle Passage. But we should not dismiss these published life stories because they follow a rigid narrative posited by white abolitionists (or anyone else) because they do not. Instead, they reflect a diverse and changing set of life stories in conjunction with varied editorial interests. Many historians are familiar with the political and religious interests of editors, but less well known are scientific interests, especially in geography and linguistics. Throughout it all African voices are discernable. (In fact, those publications without this quality were excluded from the Catalog.) The voices of Maroons or members of confraternities in South America seeking to protect their precarious situations are discernable in the documents produced by colonial authorities trying to subdue or control them. Also discernable are the voices of people who, after years of victimization and displacement realized they could not return to their homelands, adopted a new religion (Christianity), and tried to spread its Gospel to Black people on both sides of the Atlantic. African voices are also present in the published articles about people enslaved in the Americas who, when approached by European scientists interested in detailed information about the geography of the West African hinterlands, recounted in stunning detail where and how they lived, often after years of enslavement in the Americas. The African voices collected in this Catalog provide invaluable information and stories of the kinds of things that could and did happen to individual men, women, and children that are far more diverse, complex, and rich in detail than most historians of slavery in the Americas have been willing to accept or investigate. These life stories tell us a lot more than previously realized by scholars and can help us get more, diverse African voices into our discussions of transatlantic slavery and Black life in the Atlantic World.

Obviously, little if any appropriation of revolutionary ideas occurred before the onset of the Age of Revolution in the 1770s, but my reading of the corpus of African narratives reveals that no one appropriated Christian ideals to critique slavery either. At the time this essay was prepared, the corpus of published narratives included fifteen produced before 1770, none of which appropriated Enlightenment, revolutionary, or Christian ideas to critique slavery. Although not published until recently, many of the narratives were produced in New Spain, where there was no tradition of publishing narratives by enslaved people. In these cases the narrators presented important aspects of their lives during legal proceedings that modern scholars have published. They describe individual struggles to escape slavery or gain and preserve individual freedom or that of a relatively small group. Maroons produced a number of narratives (and no doubt many more that have not yet been published). The earliest narrative in the collection is by Alsono de Illesca (Ecuador, 1586), who describes his efforts to preserve the autonomy of his Maroon community through diplomatic-military cooperation with colonial Spanish authorities against Native Americans in the region. He and two other Maroons named Anchico (*alias* Sebastián) and Francisco

Angola (Ecuador, 1634) revealed their personal stories of struggle and resistance in these documents, but they include no comments on slavery and freedom *per se*, nor were they given the opportunity to do so.

The narratives of enslaved Africans who converted to Christianity before the 1770s are filled with pain, sorrow, and triumph, but none of them employed Christian ideology to condemn slavery. The earliest narrative of an African who converted to Christianity is that of María de Huancavelica (Lima, 1666), who acquired her freedom and became a pious Christian. She did well financially and in her will revealed important details of her life story, including how she endeavored to free her own slaves and children in "Moorish lands." She did not condemn slavery, but her will was hardly the place to do so, had she so desired. Chicaba, *alias* Mother Sor Teresa Juliana de Santo Domingo (Salamanca, Spain, 1748), struggled with the sorrows of enslavement by Europeans, but she was taken to Spain, not America, where she embraced Christianity, lived as a nun in a convent, and was considered for sainthood, with no mention of a possible return to Africa. Her narrative was a hagiography, for which any critique of slavery, had she been so inclined, would not have been welcome. Magdalene Beulah Brockden (Bethlehem, Pennsylvania, c. 1755) was baptized by the Protestant Moravians in 1748. She never was emancipated, and her narrative describes above all how she embraced Christianity, with no criticism of even her own enslavement. Ukawsaw Gronniosaw, *alias* James Albert (Bath, 1770), embraced Christianity as well, in part as way to accept his enslaved status and improve himself without returning home, but without critiquing slavery or struggling on behalf of other slaves. One Christian convert, Jacobus Elisa Johannes Capitein, overtly defended slavery in his treatise published in Latin (Leiden, 1742), because he believed it necessary to do so in order to be allowed to complete his personal mission to spread the Gospel to Africans. Thus before the Age of Revolution and Emancipation, narratives by Africans in the corpus did not appropriate Christian ideals of liberty and equality to condemn slavery.

In fact, the pre-1770s narrative in the collection that came closest to critiquing the transatlantic slave system altogether was by the son of a Muslim imam, Ayuba Suleiman Diallo (*alias* Job ben Solomon), who was well-trained in Arabic. His narrative (London, 1734) describes how,

> In my good warm country all things are good, except the white people who live there, and come in flying houses [ships] to take away poor black prisoners from their mothers, their fathers, their sisters, and brothers, to kill them with hunger and filth, in the cellars of their flying houses, wherein if they do not die fast enough, and poor prisoners talk for bread and water, and want to feel the wind, and to see the Great Spirit, to complain to him, to tell him all, or to see the trees of his good warm country once more for the last time, the king

of the white people [the ship captain] orders the officer called Jack
to kill many of the black prisoners, with whips, with ropes, knives,
axes, and salt.

With the assistance of James Oglethorpe and others, who "discovered"
him in Maryland, Diallo became one of few enslaved Africans in the
corpus who returned home—not just to Africa but to his actual homeland in Fuuta Bondu, on the Senegal River.

Beginning in the 1770s, at the onset of the Age of Revolution and the
Age of Emancipation, the tone of the narratives in the corpus changed
quickly and significantly, and a number of them began to appropriate
revolutionary, Christian, and Muslim ideology to condemn the transatlantic slave system. Which of the enslaved Africans who produced
published narratives appropriated revolutionary or Christian ideology,
and which did not? Of those who did, how and why did they do so? A
total of 197 narratives were produced during the Age of Revolutions and
Emancipation, eighty-nine percent of the entire volume in the corpus. Of
these 121 had no opportunity to appropriate such ideology for reasons
explained below, while twenty-one did appropriate revolutionary and/or
Christian ideology to condemn slavery, and fifty-five did not.

The large number of narratives in the corpus (121) produced by people
during the Age of Revolution and Emancipation who had no opportunity to appropriate revolutionary or Christian ideology to condemn
slavery is, among other things, a stark reminder of how much mediation occurred in the production of these published African life stories.
Seventy-eight of the narratives appeared in scientific journals or books
in the first half of the nineteenth century, such as the *Journal des Voyages, découvertes et navigations modernes, ou, Archives géographiques
du XIXe siècle* (Paris, 1826), the *Bulletin de la Société de Géographie*
(Paris, 1848), Francis de Castelnau, *Renseignements sur l'Afrique Cen-
trale et sur une Nation d'Hommes a Queue qui s'y Trouverait, d'apres
le Rapport de Nègres du Soudan, Esclaves a Bahia* (Paris: Chez P.
Bertrand, 1851), and Sigismund Wilhelm Koelle, *Pollyglotta Africana*
(London: Church Missionary House, 1854). The authors of these works
interviewed enslaved Africans in the Americas primarily to query them
about details of the physical and cultural geography of the West African
interior. The interviews provide fascinating details of African voices—
not just those of their European editors, but most of the narratives end
at the point when the captives reached the African coast and were sold
to Euroamericans. Koelle interviewed people of all sorts in Sierra Leone, but he was so interested in their languages and the physical ge-
ographies of their homelands that he afforded them no opportunity to
express other views. Another example of enslaved Africans who produced published narratives but had no opportunity to condemn slavery
with revolutionary or Christian ideology are the thirty-seven captives

from the *Amistad* shipboard revolt, who were interviewed in 1840 in a Connecticut jail while awaiting trial. The African voices present in these narratives—despite the mediation of white abolitionists and others—are yet another testimony to the nature of resistance, but as recent arrivals from Africa, they had little or no opportunity to become Christian or discover and appropriate revolutionary ideology.[12]

The appropriation of both revolutionary and Christian ideology began in the 1770s and continued until the mid-nineteenth century, with Phillis Wheatley leading the way. Her case merits elaboration because, while she is well-known by scholars for her many literary contributions, until now it was not known that she was the first African-born person in the Atlantic World caught in the transatlantic slave trade who appropriated revolutionary ideals to condemn slavery. She did so in numerous publications, in which there was little mediation of her own consciously African voice.[13]

Although not published until Wheatley traveled to London with her owners in 1773, she began writing poetry earlier, including work that appropriated an ideology of liberty not intended for slaves. She was born ca. 1753 in West Africa, probably between modern Gambia and Ghana, and taken to Boston on a slave ship in 1761. Though enslaved, she received an education in English, classical literature (especially poetry), geography, history, and Latin, and she became a devout Christian. Wheatley began composing poetry in 1765 at age 12, and her first published work appeared in the *Newport Mercury* in 1767.[14] In 1768, at the height of the Townshend Duties protests, the fifteen-year-old Wheatley wrote a poem entitled "America." Like others, she described the Imperial Crisis in terms of a mother-child relationship, in which the mother (Britain) was a land of liberty losing its way. Wheatley gained strength from that tradition of liberty, writing, "Thy Power, O Liberty, makes strong the weak, And (wond'rous instinct) Ethiopians speak." Thus as an "Ethiopian" (African) Wheatley appropriated British traditions of liberty in order to support the American cause.[15]

In time the still youthful Wheatley developed from an enslaved African recognizing and supporting America's plight against the mother country to promoting emancipation in the name of Enlightenment and revolutionary ideals. When her owners took Wheatley to London in 1773 she wrote a poem to the Earl of Dartmouth that was published in her collection that year, contending that America had been wronged—enslaved by British tyranny:

> No more, *America*, in mournful strain
> Of wrongs, and grievance unredress'd complain,
> No longer shalt thou dread the iron chain,
> Which wanton *Tyranny* with lawless hand
> Had made, and with it meant t'enslave the land.

Wheatley went on to state the origins of her love of freedom: "I, young in life, by seeming cruel fate, Was snatch'd from *Afric's* fancy'd happy seat." Wheatley lost her freedom in Africa and did not want America to lose its liberty as she had.[16] Vincent Carretta persuasively argues that the Somerset case of 1772 and the new anti-slavery atmosphere it generated in England influenced her, yet by this point Wheatley associated herself not with British liberty but the American fight against the British for liberty.

Back in New England in 1774, in the midst of a rebellion about to become a war, Wheatley penned her famous lines to the Mohegan Christian clergyman Samson Occom, in which she declared that black people possessed natural rights, to include civil and religious liberty. This and her view that God had implanted a principle of freedom in all humans led her to compare slavery in her day to that of the Israelites in ancient Egypt, who had to be freed:

> [I] am greatly satisfied with your Reasons respecting the Negroes, and think highly reasonable what you offer in Vindication of their natural Rights ... Those that "invade" those rights most know that the divine light is chasing away darkness that "broods over the Land of Africa; and the Chaos which has reign'd so long, is converting into beautiful Order, and [r]eveals more and more clearly, the glorious Dispensation of civil and religious Liberty, which are so inseparably united, that there is little or no enjoyment of one without the other: Otherwise, perhaps, the Israelites had been less solicitous for their Freedom from Egyptian Slavery; I do not say they would have been contented without it, by no means, for in every human Breast, God has implanted a Principle, which we call Love of Freedom; it is impatient of Oppression, and pants for Deliverance; and by the Leave of our Modern Egyptians I will assert, that the same Principle lives in us. God grant Deliverance in his own Way and Time, and get him honor upon all those whose Avarice impels them to countenance and help forward the Calamities of their Fellow Creatures. This I desire not for their Hurt, but to convince them of the strange Absurdity of their Conduct whose Words and Actions are so diametrically opposite. How well the Cry for Liberty, and the reverse Disposition for the Exercise of oppressive Power over others agree—I humbly think it does not require the Penetration of a Philosopher to determine.[17]

Now in clear prose Wheatley appropriated revolutionary and Christian ideology to condemn slavery. In 1778, after the death of General David Wooster, Wheatley wrote a poem to his widow praising the Continental Army as an instrument of freedom and urged it to end slavery.[18]

Soon others in the new United States followed Wheatley by relating their stories as Africans taken into slavery while appropriating the cause for liberty in America for themselves and all enslaved Blacks, or at least those in the new republic. In 1779 a group of twenty enslaved Africans in Portsmouth, New Hampshire petitioned the legislature for their own freedom and that of all other slaves in the state. Led by the elected "king" of their African community in Portsmouth, a man named Nero Brewster, they declared that "the God of Nature gave them Life and Freedom, upon terms of the most perfect Equality with other men" and that "freedom is an inherent right of the human species." They then referenced how they had lost their freedom in Africa, when taken into the slave trade as defenseless children "thro' ignorance & brutish violence of their countrymen, and by sinister designs of others" who forced them "to drag on their lives in miserable servitude." Now seeing the winds of equality and freedom blowing in that land they declared, "we know we ought to be free agents! here, we feel the dignity of human nature! here, we feel the passions and desires of men, tho' check'd by the rod of slavery! here, we feel a just equality! here, we know that the God of Nature made us free!" They wanted the state of liberty they had experienced in Africa *restored*, and they linked their plight to the larger, ongoing struggle against tyranny and oppression in the new republic, proclaiming their desire to "regain our liberty and be rank'd in the class of free agents, and that the name of SLAVE may no more be heard in a land gloriously contending for the sweets of freedom." Perhaps an African-born woman named Belinda (*alias* Belinda Royall) in nearby Medford, Massachusetts heard them. She had labored fifty years for a wealthy Loyalist family forced to flee to England, and four years after the Portsmouth petition, she petitioned the Massachusetts legislature in 1783, associating her cause as an African-born slave struggling to regain her freedom with the patriot cause.[19]

Shortly after U.S. independence, the new trend by Africans to appropriate revolutionary ideology to attack slavery appeared in Britain with the published narrative of Quobna Ottobah Cugoano (*alias* John Stuart) in London (1787). He was taken in the slave trade to Grenada in 1770, when about thirteen years old. After two years of working in slave gangs in the West Indies, an English gentleman purchased Cugoano, took him to England in 1772, and provided for his education. The next year, in the wake of the Somerset decision and the uncertainty of its full meaning, Cugoano followed the advice of "good people," who told him to get baptized to prevent reenslavement. His two published treatises of 1787 condemned slavery within Africa and African participation in the transatlantic slave trade, as well as slavery in general. He universalized freedom and called for full, immediate emancipation. His comments on the recent war in America touched on the notion that revolutionary ideals did or should end slavery:

> ... since the last war, some mitigation of slavery has been obtained in some respective districts of America, though not in proportion to

their own vaunted claims of freedom; but it is to be hoped, that they will yet go on to make further and greater reformation.[20]

In other words, what happened in America was a noteworthy first step, but he hoped for much more so that their "vaunted claims for freedom" might be realized for everyone. By this time Cugoano was caught up in the growing British abolition movement, which was influenced significantly by the American Revolution.[21]

The next to appropriate revolutionary ideology was Jean-Baptiste Belley (1746–1805), who was born on the island of Gorée (in modern Senegal) and taken as a child in the slave trade to St. Domingue. He later purchased his freedom, and after the revolt began on Haiti in 1791 became an infantry captain, then brigade commander of the gendarmerie. Belley was wounded six times while fighting imperial forces attempting to defeat the revolution, and in 1793 he became the first black deputy to the French National Convention. Two years later he gave a speech in the Convention, responding to a planter who had called for the re-institution of slavery on the island. Belley passionately refuted the planter and defended emancipation, proclaiming that "I myself was born in Africa. Brought in childhood to a land of tyranny, through hard work and sweat I conquered a liberty that I have enjoyed honorably for thirty years, loving my country all the while." He added that Blacks had virtues of nature (not the vice of Europe) and were sensible, thankful beings "who have been brought back to life by the unexpected appearances of happiness and liberty ..." They resisted British conquest and "have become free and French have made a rampart with their bodies against the invasion and are bravely defending the rights of the republic." While Belley was strongly in favor of emancipation, he resisted independence (and thus Touissant Louverture) because he believed that being a part of the republic was the best way to defend against those who wished to reinstitute slavery in Haiti, namely the British, Spanish, white Haitian refugees in the United States, and reactionary forces in France itself. The republic promoted liberty—including that of former slaves, Belley believed in it, and used the ideals of the French Revolution to fight against slavery. Unfortunately, he agreed to cooperate with the LeClerc Expedition in 1802, not knowing that the French government planned to arrest him shortly after his return to Haiti, after which they deported Belley to an island off the coast of Brittany. In spite of this unhappy ending, it is noteworthy that in the maelstrom of revolution, slavery, emancipation, and war in the Atlantic World, Belley had proudly proclaimed his African background and willingness to adopt revolutionary ideology to achieve and defend emancipation.[22]

The appropriation of revolutionary ideals was more subtle in some of the narratives, such as that of Broteer (*alias* Venture Smith), but it was there. Broteer (ca. 1729–1805) was born in Dukandarra/Guinea, captured in war, and sold to Europeans, who took him on a slave ship first to Barbados and then Rhode Island, where he purchased his freedom in 1765. After some success as a businessman in Connecticut he began hiring, buying, and emancipating black workers. He did not fight in the war and did not mention it or other events of the American Revolution in his narrative (New London, CT, 1798), but he did condemn the hypocrisy and racism of Christians who cheated him in business, noting that "whatever it may be called in a christian land, would in my native country be branded a crime equal to crystalizing robbery. But Captain Hart was a *white gentleman*, and I a *poor African*, and therefore it was *all right, and good enough for the black dog*." Aged sixty-nine years, feeble, and almost blind he stated in 1798 that "my freedom is a privilege which nothing else can equal."[23]

When Boyrereau Brinch (*alias* Jeffrey Brace) appropriated revolutionary ideology, he attacked the paradox of slavery and freedom crystalizing in U.S. American society in the generation after independence. Born in the kingdom of Bow-woo in the middle Niger valley (modern Mali) in ca. 1742, Brinch was enslaved and taken to Barbados in 1759 and then Connecticut, where he joined the Continental Army during the Revolutionary War to reacquire his freedom and avenge the atrocities the British had committed on him and other enslaved people on Barbados. Still enslaved when enlisting, Brinch addressed the irony of his situation when narrating the story of his life in 1810, noting that "I also entered the banners of freedom. Alas! Poor African Slave, to liberate freemen, my tyrants," and "Thus was I, a slave, for five years fighting for liberty." In short, Brinch fought and lived through the Revolution, believed in its ideals, and used them to attack the paradox of slavery in a land of liberty.[24]

Four other narratives (Dick Eldridge and in his sons Dick, George, and Robin) describe their search for liberty in the Revolution (Providence, RI, 1838). With significant editorial mediation they describe the liberty for which they fought and the discrimination against them thereafter. While not as articulate and extensive as the criticisms by Brinch and others, theirs is nevertheless additional testimony to the desire of enslaved people born in Africa to take up a revolutionary cause to attack slavery.[25]

In addition to appropriating revolutionary ideals, some published narratives of African-born people began to appropriate Christian ideals of liberty, equality, and salvation to condemn slavery. Once again, Phillis Wheatley was the first to do so, although her use of Christian ideology was less overt than the revolutionary ideology she employed. Her 1774 letter to Rev. Samson Occom welcomed those who might spread "divine light" to chase away the darkness that "broods over the Land of Africa." She noted that civil and religious liberty were inseparably united: "In every human Breast God has implanted a Principle, which we call Love of Freedom; it is impatient of Oppression, and pants for Deliverance; and by the Leave of our Modern Egyptians I will assert, that the same Principle lives in us ..."[26]

Much more overt appropriation of Christian ideology is found in Cugoano's narrative (London, 1787), which described the entire Atlantic system of slavery and rigorously condemned it as a violent assault on Christian principles. Cugoano had become a part of the British abolition movement. He wrote that those "robbers of men, the kidnappers, ensnarers and slave-holders, who take away the common rights and privileges of others to support and enrich themselves... [work] ... opposite to every precept and injunction of the Divine Law, and contrary to that command which enjoins that *all men should love their neighbors as themselves*, and *that they should do unto others, as they would that men should do to them.*" Moreover, he rejected the view that Africans were fit for slavery, so slavery must have been willed by God, or that slavery must be acceptable, since it had always been there. The latter was true, but that didn't make it right, he wrote. Europeans might have built friendly alliances with Indians, but didn't. This was not Christian, but rather the work of *Antichrist*. While he praised the English and Christians for finally recognizing the evil of slavery and promoting liberty, he condemned the entire British, Spanish, and Portuguese systems of global empire, which only brought debt, idleness, war, and the decline of community at home. Cugoano believed that the British Royal Africa Company should tremble before God's pending vengeance because of the way they treated slaves, and he proposed days of mourning, fasting, and inquiry, as well as abolition, universal emancipation, a blockade of the African coast, and the closing of European forts serving as exchange points in the slave trade. He also proposed what they might do thereafter with freed slaves and a new Africa policy that included improving the situation in Sierra Leone, a well-meaning project that had not been done properly, he believed. Christianity, according to Cugoano, had been a part of the problem for a long time, and now it must be a part of the solution.[27]

Cugoano dramatically completed the reversal since Capitein regarding how published African narratives employed Christianity, and others contributed to the new trend, beginning with Olaudah Equiano (London, 1789). After escaping Atlantic slavery Equiano met Granville Sharp in England in 1774 and became interested in Christianity. In 1788, as part of the British abolition movement led by evangelical Christians, Equiano quoted the Bible when responding to a pro-slavery argument and condemned slavery as an affront to the "Universal and Almighty Legislator," as well as to civilization and religion. He argued for racial equality on a religious basis, noting that "God looks with equal good will on all his creatures, whether black or white ..." In the preface addressed to Parliament, Equiano wrote that slavery was against Christian religion, national liberal sentiments, humanity, freedom, arts and science, and the dignity of the human nation. He later noted that it also violated human rights.[28]

The narratives of Boyrereau Brinch (St. Albans, 1810) and John Jea (Portsea, UK, 1811) demonstrate how conversion to Christianity led Africans to use their new religion to condemn slavery. Brinch was baptized in 1805, over twenty years after reacquiring his freedom, and he told his tale five years later so people might see how enlightened Christians abused Africans and how that he, now Christian himself, old, blind, and poor, might find comfort by educating people on this point.[29] Jea was much more explicit in his appropriation of Christian ideology, describing Christian liberty and its antithesis. He was born in 1773 in Calabar (in modern Nigeria) and taken in the slave trade when very young with his family to New York, where he was badly treated. Against his master's wishes he was able to regain freedom in New York during the era of gradual emancipation that began during the American Revolution. Jea despised Christianity as the religion of slaveholders and wanted to kill them all, especially the local minister, but his views changed after his conversion, when he began preaching to black people and believed that his readers should be thankful they were not born in Africa, enslaved, and treated so badly. Instead, they were born in Britain, a land of freedom, with opportunities to know the true God. He thought something was terribly wrong with Americans and their religion, since they treated people so badly. *Britain* (not America) was the land of freedom, and he had a message for Americans:

> recollect that you possess much, much will be required; and, unless you improve your advantages, you had better be a slave in any dark part of the world, than a neglecter of the gospel in this highly favored land [Britain]; recollect also that even here you might be a slave of the most awful description; a slave to your passions, a slave to the world, a slave to sin, a slave to Satan, a slave of hell, and, unless you are made free by Christ, through the means of the gospel, you will remain in captivity, tied and bound in chains of your sin, till at last you will be bound by hand and foot, and cast into outer darkness, there shall be weeping and gnashing of teeth forever.

Thus, Jea's narrative describes a life trajectory of someone enslaved by Christians who condemned their religion to someone who accepted Christianity and used it to attack slavery.[30]

William Rainsford's published letter (London, 1835) to Richard R. Madden, a doctor in the Royal Geographical Society, co-signed by Gorah Condran (*alias* Benjamin Cochrane), Benjemin [*sic*] Larten, and Abu Bakr Al-Siddiq (*alias* Edward Doulan), warns of pending divine judgment because of slavery. Rainsford was Mandinke, born in Sancran and brought up as a learned warrior. The slave ship carrying him was intercepted by the British, who took everyone to Jamaica. Written in the wake of emancipation in the British empire, but still during the Apprenticeship, Rainsford warned that at Judgment Day all will stand before God, as their good and evil deeds are considered. Good and bad souls would cry out. Nations would be judged. God ordained rich and poor, but the rich were not to oppress the poor, and God would bless those who promoted justice and punish those who had not.[31]

Not unlike the relationship of Christianity and slavery in this era, the impact of reformist Islam (jihād) was complicated and contradictory, but it was there.[32] While Diallo's narrative (London, 1734) provides some indirect critique of slavery—more than other narratives of the period—narratives by Muslims from the 1820s to the 1850s, at the height of the Age of Revolution, Emancipation and jihād, include severe and explicit condemnations of the transatlantic slave system based on religious principles. All were from people learned in Arabic and influenced by jihād.

Some of the jihād-influenced narratives came from people who had converted to Christianity just before publishing their life stories. Ibrahim Abd ar-Rahman (*alias* Abduhl Rahhahman) produced the first (New York, 1828). He was a native of Timbuktu, a grandson of its "king" and the son of a warrior. Ar-Rahaman himself became a cavalryman, was captured in battle, sold to an English slave ship at the mouth of the Gambia River, and taken first to St. Domingue, then New Orleans, and finally up the Mississippi River to Natchez in about 1789. Years later, after meeting a surgeon whom he had once befriended in Sierra Leone, an effort led by the doctor began to free ar-Rahaman and his family that lasted nearly three decades. Ar-Rahaman wished to go to Liberia and assist in the struggle against the slave trade. After being baptized in 1827 he announced that he wanted to introduce Christianity and civilization in Africa, including Timbuktu. Ar-Rahaman's high position and Islamic education placed him squarely in the jihād movement, which helps to explain his desire to go to Liberia and fight against the slave trade, although his own experiences of the realities of the Middle Passage and slavery in America also must have motivated him, as they did so many others. His conversion to Christianity began earlier, but the final step (baptism) and his desire to spread the Gospel in Liberia and elsewhere in West Africa coincided with a fund-raising campaign to free his family and take them back to Africa. This does not necessarily mean that his conversion was insincere, but it is clear that his position, education, and religion before enslavement likely influenced his expressed desire. His condemnation of the transatlantic slave trade with Christians based on his Muslim beliefs must be inferred—he does not explicitly state this in his narrative, but under these circumstances it would not have been wise for him to do so.[33]

Born in the city of Djougou (in present-day Bénin) in ca. 1824, Ma-hommah Gardo Baquaqua (Detroit, 1854) knew Arabic as a second language. He was captured in war and sent to Brazil in 1845. Later sold to a ship captain, he was taken to Haiti and freed. By 1849 he became Christian and was in New York to raise money for a Christian African settlement project. Although exposed to revolutionary ideals in the United States and Haiti, what influenced him most were ideals of Christian liberty, which he best expressed when attaching the poem "Prayer of the Oppressed" by James Whitefield to his narrative. The poem called on Jehovah to end the oppression of "Afric's" sons and daughters. Baquaqua told his story for publication in Ypsilanti, Michigan.

Other Muslims did not convert, and their religion influenced their resistance against slavery, which included criticism of Christianity. They were most prominent in Bahia during the Malês revolt of 1835 but were also present in dozens of smaller revolts and conspiracies leading up to it and in Cuba.[34] A few other individuals cooperated with white abolitionists to critique slavery. José Maria Rufino, for example, was taken to Brazil and years after achieving his freedom was arrested for involvement in a slave conspiracy: Authorities feared that he secretly taught Arabic to slaves to promote an uprising. Rufino's life story, revealed in a police report and newspaper article (Recife, 1853), indicates that his goals were to promote freedom and Islam in Brazil. He had passed up an opportunity to go to Sierra Leone when his ship was captured by the British. When he did go later it was to learn Islam and Arabic and then return to Brazil.[35] Samba Makumba (*alias* Simon Boissere) was a Muslim from Fuuta Toro. Captured in warfare and sent on a slave ship to Trinidad in ca. 1797, he later purchased his freedom and became a devout Muslim imam with a large following of other Mandinkes. The community pooled their resources to purchase and free other Mandinkes from slave ships in Trinidad and surrounding islands. When interviewed by a U.S. Quaker in 1841 he was shocked to hear that Christians in that country enslaved other Christians.[36] Mohammedu Siseï was born in the village of Nyáni-Marú on the Gambia River. He grew up reading the Koran and writing in Arabic, was captured during warfare, and sold to a French slave ship that was intercepted at sea by the British and taken to Antigua. He served in a British grenadier company from 1811 to 1825 and later became a member of the Mandingo (Mandinke) Society of Mohammedans, which rescued their Muslim brothers from newly arriving slave ships by paying ransoms for them.[37] It was these enslaved Africans in the Americas who most explicitly employed Muslim ideals to critique the transatlantic slave trade. In some cases, such as with Rufino and perhaps Siseï, their cooperation with editors might be viewed as an act of resistance, as it allowed them to use Muslim ideas to critique transatlantic slavery through publication. In any event, their critique was so powerful that it captured the attention of both authorities desiring to protect the Atlantic slave system and white abolitionists desiring to end it.

While evidence from the Catalog that enslaved Africans in the Americas appropriated Enlightenment, revolutionary, Christian, or Muslim ideals to critique transatlantic slavery is significant, if not striking, it should be noted that for a number of reasons, many in the Catalog who had the opportunity to appropriate this ideology in their narratives did not. Some found other means to resist, for example Muhammed Ali ibn Said (*alias* Nicholas Said). Said did not overtly use such rhetoric in his published life story (Memphis, 1873), but his actions spoke louder than words when he fought in the Union Army during the U.S. Civil War and assisted with Reconstruction in the South thereafter. James Bradley (New York, 1834) found freedom, equality, and salvation in Christianity, but did not attack slavery for violating Christian ideals. As noted, a very small number like Capitein (Leiden, 1742) employed Christian ideology to defend slavery. Also, while Samuel Ajayi Crowther (London, 1837) and Joseph Wright (London, 1841) embraced and promoted Christianity as missionaries in West Africa as part of the British abolitionist-colonization effort, they did not overtly use Christian ideology to attack slavery because the slave owners they worked against were not Christian. Their task was to spread the Gospel, and that was what they wrote about (in addition to their personal lives before enslavement and later as Christians).[38]

The large number of life stories in the Catalog include a wide variety of scenarios and episodes that demonstrate the breadth and depth of exploitation in transatlantic slavery and how people trapped within it lived and told their stories in ways that need not or did not involve appropriation of the above ideologies. Those who appropriated Enlightenment, revolutionary, or Christian ideals implicitly gave up on the notion of ever returning to their homelands, since such ideology would do them little good there. But some Africans who produced narratives in the Catalog, like the seventeen men and women from Lagos who were taken to Cuba and returned decades later in the 1850s via Britain (London, 1854), tried very hard to return to their homes and families, even after decades in the Americas. They did not appropriate this ideology because it would do them no good when they returned home.[39] Finally, a number of published life stories appearing in the late nineteenth and twentieth centuries, after the Age of Emancipation, emphasize remembrance of slavery, rather than overtly condemning it, although their condemnation is certainly implicit.

While African appropriation of Enlightenment, revolutionary, Christian, and Muslim ideology to critique transatlantic slavery did not become important until the outset of the Age of Revolution, thereafter it became a powerful critique. Until this time, Africans in the Catalog who became Christian tended to defend slavery, but beginning in the

1770s and continuing throughout the Age of Emancipation, African use of Christian ideology to critique slavery became intertwined with revolutionary ideology to condemn Atlantic slavery. Further, African use of Muslim ideology to condemn transatlantic slavery coincided with jihād in West Africa that crescendoed at the same time and ought to be considered as part of the Age of Revolution, since it had such an impact on transatlantic slavery.

The narratives in the Catalog allow greater use of African perspectives in the study of transatlantic slavery and with that provide greater insight into the experiences and dilemmas of Blacks throughout the Atlantic World during the Age of Revolutions and Emancipation. Those who appropriated Enlightenment, revolutionary, and Christian ideology to critique transatlantic slavery made their choices (such as they were) to embrace these aspects of society in the Americas to improve their lot, rather than trying to return to Africa, which was impractical for most. They appropriated these ideologies for their own causes in their own way in spite of resistance from white people who also promoted revolutionary and/or Christian ideologies of freedom and equality, but excluded slaves and free Blacks. In part because of their African birth and loss of freedom before being sold into the transatlantic slave trade, the Africans who produced the narratives in the Catalog found effective ways to promote their own freedom. The commitment to abolition meant that they had to give up the goal of returning to their homelands in Africa, even for those who returned to the continent in one of the colonization projects. In doing so they argued for an African ethnic identity and connections across boundaries. This was less the case for the small number of Muslims who did not convert to Christianity and committed to continuing aspects of reform in America that they had learned and practiced in West Africa. They only worked to free other enslaved Muslims, yet their actions and continued beliefs did present an implicit critique of Christianity for tolerating the enslavement of other Christians.

The African narratives in the Catalog provide significant potential for deepening our understanding of the impact of revolution on slavery from Black perspectives. This includes a better understanding of the role of Africans in accepting revolutionary ideology. A consideration of the impact of jihād further complicates these matters, yet improves our understanding of how the Black Atlantic functioned during the Age of Revolution and Emancipation by showing how ideological, political, and cultural views of people from Africa shaped transatlantic events. Many people recognized the hypocrisy in the revolutionary ideology developing in lands where slavery was prominent and took it upon themselves to apply its full meaning. This had the dual impact of both furthering an African ethnic identity, yet distancing themselves from their homelands in Africa. As the calls for liberty and equality cascaded throughout the Americas and Europe, people experienced different treatment even after their emancipation. They called themselves "Africans" and "Afric" in their publications to point out this problem and solicit sympathy and support, but in some ways embracing radical ideology of liberty and equality meant turning their backs on their homelands in Africa: Achieving emancipation and equality in Europe or the Americas meant nothing if one returned to the homeland. The families, villages, religion, and political states there simply would not have recognized it. The solution for some was to carry the banner of liberty and often Christianity to the new colonies of Sierra Leone, Liberia, and Aguda. The Catalog contains numerous narratives of people who went to these colonies, especially Sierra Leone, often involuntarily after their slave ship was intercepted by a British patrol. But this too represented a tragic displacement and interruption of their lives, and it was quite rare that anyone was able to return to their actual homeland. Thus appropriation, regardless of whether one participated in a colonization project, reflected a dramatic approach for which there was no turning back.

Notes

1 Research for this essay is based on the experiences of 221 people born in Africa and taken into the transatlantic slave trade who produced a life story that was published. See Aaron Spencer Fogleman and Keith Arbour, "A Catalog of Published Narratives by Africans Enslaved in the Transatlantic Slave Trade, 1586–1936," in preparation. Reference in parenthesis in the text to place and date of each narrative or life story refer to when and where the original narrative was produced, although it may not have been published until much later.

2 Laurent Dubois, "An Enslaved Enlightenment: Rethinking the Intellectual History of the French Atlantic," in D'Maris Coffman, Adrian Leonard, and William O'Reilly (eds.), *The Atlantic World* (London: Routledge, 2015), 127–241.

3 Robin Blackburn, "Haiti, Slavery, and the Age of Democratic Revolution," *William and Mary Quarterly*, 63:4 (October 2006), 643–674. Blackburn elaborates on these points in *The American Crucible: Slavery, Emancipation and Human Rights* (London: Verso, 2013).

4 Janet Polasky, *Revolution without Borders: The Call to Liberty in the Atlantic World* (New Haven, CT: Yale University Press, 2015).

5 Chris Schmidt-Nowara, *Slavery, Freedom, and Abolition in Latin America and the Atlantic World* (Albuquerque: University of New Mexico Press, 2011), especially 90–119.

6 Christopher Leslie Brown, *Moral Capital: Foundations of British Abolitionism* (Chapel Hill: University of North Carolina Press, 2006).

7 Polasky, *Revolution without Borders*.

8 Jon F. Sensbach, *Rebecca's Revival: Creating Black Christianity in the Atlantic World* (Cambridge, MA: Harvard University Press, 2005) and Sylvia R. Frey and Betty Wood, *Come Shouting to Zion: African American Protestantism in the American South and British Caribbean to 1830* (Chapel Hill: University of North Carolina Press, 1998).

9 Paul E. Lovejoy, "'Freedom Narratives' of Transatlantic Slavery," *Slavery & Abolition*, 32:1 (March 2011), 91–107.

10 Robert Hanserd, *Identity, Spirit and Freedom in the Atlantic World: The Gold Coast and the African Diaspora* (New York: Routledge, 2019).

11 Paul E. Lovejoy, *Jihād in West Africa during the Age of Revolutions* (Athens: Ohio University Press, 2016).

12 Another example includes the brief narrative of an anonymous woman discovered on her death bed (Antigua, 1826).

13 Note that owners assisted with her education, Christian and otherwise, but they were Loyalists, so little influence on her ideas about liberty and slavery and the American cause.

14 Phillis Wheatley, *Complete Writings*, edited by Vincent Carretta (New York: Penguin Books, 2001), xiii–xv.

15 Wheatley, "America," *Complete Writings*, 75–78. The quotation is from p. 75.

16 Wheatley, "To the Right Honourable William, Earl of Dartmouth, His Majesty's Principal Secretary of State for North-America, &c." (1773), in *Complete Writings*, 39–40.

17 Wheatley to Rev. Samson Occom, 11 February 1774, *Connecticut Gazette*, 11 March 1774, in *Complete Writings*, 152–153.

18 In Wheatley to Mary Wooster, (Boston, 15 July 1778), *Complete Writings*, 92–94.

19 "Petition of Nero Brewster et al., natives of Africa, now forcibly detained in slavery..." to the Council and House of Representatives of New Hampshire," 12 November 1779, printed in *The New-Hampshire Gazette*, vol. 24, 1233 (15 July 1780), and "The Petition of Belinda an Affrican [sic]," to the Senate and House of Representatives of the Commonwealth of Massachusetts," 14 February 1783, printed in *The Massachusetts Sun*, 29 May 1783.

20 See the edition of Cugoano's narrative in Vincent Carretta (ed.), *Quobna Ottobah Cugoano: Thoughts and Sentiments on the Evil of Slavery and Other Writings* (New York: Penguin Books, 1999), 126, 146 and 155–156. The quotation is from 146.

21 See Brown, *Moral Capital*. Seymour Drescher strongly disagrees in *Abolition: A History of Slavery and Antislavery* (Cambridge: Cambridge University Press, 2009).

22 My interpretation of Belley is based upon Jean Baptiste Belley, *Le Bout d'Oreille des Colons ou Le Système de l'Hôtel de Massiac, mis au jour par Gouli. Belley, Depute noir de Saint-Domingue, à ses collegues* (Paris, 1794), parts of which are translated in "The True Colors of the Planters, or the System of the Hotel Massiac, Exposed by Gouli," in Laurent Dubois and John D. Garrigus (eds.), *Slave Revolution in the Caribbean, 1789–1804: A Brief History with Documents*, 2nd ed. (Boston, MA: Bedford and St. Martin's, 2017), 137–139; *Lettre Écrite de New Yorck par les deputés de Sainte-Domingue, A leurs Commettans* (New York: French National Convention, 1793); *Lettre de Belley, député à la Convention nationale, à ses frères* (Paris: Imprimerie de Pain, 1793); Belley, *de Saint-Domingue Représentant due Peuple, à ses collègues*. 6 fructidor l'an 2e (Paris: Imprimerie Nationale, 1794); and three manuscripts available online: Belley, Déclaration d'âge et de mariage des représentants de Saint-Domingue à la Convention nationale. 22 August 1795; Situation de fortune de Jean-Baptiste Belley, représentant de Saint-Domingue à la Convention nationale, 2 October 1795; and Instructions au vice-admiral Decrès, ministre de la Marine et des colonies, à donner au général en chef capitaine général Leclerc. Chapitre III Instructions politiques intérieures, relatives aux Noirs et à leur chef. Minutes. 9 brumaire an X/31 octobre 1801, 32, Centre historique des Archives nationales (Paris) website, Histoire-image.org, images C 352/1837/3/p. 16, C 353/1838/10/p. 43, and AF/IV/863/21 p. 32. The quotations are from Dubois and Garribus, *Slave Revolution in the Caribbean*.

23 James Brewer Stewart (ed.), *Venture Smith and the Business of Slavery and Freedom* (Amherst: University of Massachusetts Press, 2010) contains the full text of Broteer's narrative. The quotations are from 26.

24 Jeffery Brace, *The Blind African Slave*, edited by Kari J. Winter (Madison: University of Wisconsin Press, 2004), 159, 166.

25 See *Memoirs of Elleanor Eldridge*, edited by Frances H. Green (Providence, RI: B.T. Albro-Printer, 1838), 12–21.

26 Wheatley to Occom, 11 March 1774.

27 Cugoano, *Thoughts and Sentiments on the Evil of Slavery*, 146–147, 151, 156, 161–179.

28 Olaudah Equiano, *The Interesting Narrative of the Life of Olaudah Equiano, Written by Himself, with Related Documents*, edited by Robert J. Allison, 2nd edition (Boston, MA: Bedford and St. Martin's Press, 2007), 41, 61,166–182, and 215–218.

29 Brace, *The Blind African Slave*, 178–182.

30 *The Life, History, and Unparalleled Suffering of John Jea, The African Preacher. Compiled and Written by Himself*, reprinted in *Pioneers of the Black Atlantic: Five Slave Narratives from the Enlightenment, 1772–1815*, edited by Henry Louis Gates, Jr., and William L. Andrews (Washington, DC: Civitas Counterpoint, 1998), 367–439. The quotation is from 373.

31 William Rainsford, Benjamin Cochrane, Benjemin Larten, and Edward Doulan to Dr. Madden, 2 October 1834, published in R.R. Madden, *A Twelvemonth's Residence in the West Indies*, vol. II (London and Philadelphia, 1835), 2 vols., 138–141.

32 See Lovejoy, *Jihād in West Africa* on this point.

33 For the original narrative see *A Statement with Regard to the Moorish Prince, Abduhl Rahhahman*, edited by T.H. [Thomas Hopkins] Gallaudet (New York: Daniel Fanshaw, 1828) and Ralph R. Gurley (ed.), "Abduhl Rahahaman: The Unfortunate Moorish Prince," *The African Repository and Colonial Journal* (May 1828), 77–81. For more on ar-Rahaman see Allan D. Austin, *African Muslims in Antebellum America: Transatlantic Spiritual Struggles* (New York: Routledge, 1997), 65–83, and especially Terry Alford, *Prince among Slaves* (New York: Harcourt Brace Jovanovich, 1977). Gurley's article includes a translation of ar-Rahaman's original Arabic autobiography, also reprinted by Austin (80–82).

34 See Lovejoy, *Jihād in West Africa* on this point.

35 Rufino in Habeeb Akande, *Illuminating the Blackness: Blacks and African Muslims in Brazil* (London: Rabbah Publishers, 2016), 239–243.

36 In George Truman, John Jackson, and Thomas B. Longstreth, *Narrative of a Visit to the West Indies, in 1840 and 1841* (Philadelphia, PA: Merrihew and Thompson Printers, 1844), 108–112.

37 John Washington, "Some Account of Mohammedu-Siseï, a Mandingo, of Nyáni-Marú on the Gambia," *Journal of the Royal Geographical Society of London*, 8 (1838), 448–454. See also the illustrated broadside "The Lives of Two Ashantee, Coast of Guinea, Slaves, Who Were Sold in Rio Grand" (Portsmouth, UK: s.n., 1840).

38 Here the reprints of Samuel Ajayi Crowther of Oyo (edited by J. F. Ade Ajayi), 289–316, and Joseph Wright of the Egba (edited by Philip D. Curtin), 317–333, both in Philip D. Curtin, *Africa Remembered: Narratives by West Africans from the Era of the Slave Trade* (Madison: University of Wisconsin Press, 1967).

39 See the seventeen narratives in "Cuban Slaves in England," *The Anti-Slavery Reporter*, ser. 3, 2 (1854), 234–239.

8 Slave Voice and the Legal Archive

The Case of Freedom Suits before the Paris Admiralty Court

Miranda Spieler

In eighteenth-century France, the Seven Years' War proved an imperial cataclysm that changed the tone of the country. Gangland violence, perhaps the work of ex-soldiers, gripped the city. The army patrolled the streets for deserters, whom they found in drag, wearing their uniforms inside out, carousing with street walkers. The paramilitary wing of the Farmers General, which controlled royal trade monopolies, raided illegal tobacco-choppers and snuff-makers in a style resembling modern drug busts. Police inspectors wielding orders from the king seized noblemen back from Louisburg, Montreal, Chandalore and Wandiwash, on whom the Crown heaped blame for the disaster.[1]

The city also became a gathering point for imperial people, including slaves of African, Indian and Malagasy descent. The soldiers, royal officials, and employees of the Indies Company who streamed into the capital during and in the immediate aftermath of the war often came accompanied with several enslaved domestics.[2] Other people of color, enslaved or free, reached France and eventually Paris without masters due to wartime displacement. British ships delivered war captives from the shrinking French empire, including people of all colors, to French Atlantic ports during the 1750s and 1760s. In 1759, the *Mary*, the *Samuel*, and the *Saint John* left Senegal for Calais with 230 passengers whom the English expelled from Gorée when seizing the trading post. The inclusion of a substantial number of people of African descent on these ships is suggested by the general lack of surnames on the passenger rolls. Aboard the *Samuel*, for instance, were passengers who included Domino, Prêt à boire (Ready to Drink), Barbe (Beard), Abraham, Baptiste, Barnard, Raphael, Abraham, la Pipe, Diagnaque (derived from the Wolof surname Diagne), Augustin, Point Libbe (a bowdlerization of *point libre* or "not free"), Marmiton (soup pot), and Souvenir. Passengers from the *Mary* included Bernard, Rustique, Balthazar, Chiron, Bazel, Crespin, and Claude.[3]

What little we know about the life of Jacques Ledoux, a West Indian sailor, at least reveals how much the Seven Years' War changed the community of slaves and former slaves living in the French capital. The scarce facts that have come down to us about Ledoux's life come from records of the Paris court of admiralty, a court endowed by the monarchy with special jurisdiction over slaves and other people of color who lived in the city. On 5 May 1762, Ledoux checked in with the clerk of that court, headquartered at the city's Palace of Justice (Palais de Justice) to report his name, birthplace (Martinique), and the state of his soul (newly baptized). He claimed to have entered the country through Brest in 1759 aboard a frigate captained by Boisy [probably Doisy] in the squadron of the Marquis de Bompar. He gave the name and address of his employer. Ledoux was a servant of a Polish grandee—the Prince Blazinski. He lived in the Hôtel de Nassau, near the Louvre and the stock market. Amidst this abundance of detail, Ledoux did not explain why he sailed with the troops.

Two years later, on 14 September 1764, Jacques Ledoux returned to the admiralty, anxiously. He "fear[ed] being bothered because his nation." (The word race is never used in the records of this court to describe a person's descent.) He asked the court to confirm his freedom "seeing that he was never a slave, that he was born free, as he declared." At the time that Ledoux made this declaration, a shipping merchant from Martinique, newly arrived in Paris, was hunting for a slave called Hippolyte, whom he believed to be Ledoux. A tradeswoman in Saint Pierre, Martinique had hired the merchant to recover her slave. The supposed owner of Ledoux claimed to have sent him to sea on a privateering ship at the beginning of the war. Hippolyte—or Ledoux—escaped to Saint Domingue and thence to France. He married Anne Couachy Diaquoy, a literate freed woman from Saint Domingue whom he met either in the colony or in Paris. In 1764, two weeks after Ledoux's second petition to the admiralty, he and his wife settled with the shipping merchant who hunted him down. In a notarial contract dated 28 September 1764, the merchant gave Ledoux his liberty in exchange for 2,000 livres.[4]

People like Ledoux and his wife comprised a tiny fraction of the city's population. They were also a conspicuous group in certain areas and social groups in Paris. For the eighteenth century, historians estimate the number of people of color, enslaved or free, to lie between 5,000 and 15,000 for the whole kingdom. About ninety percent of those people lived in the capital. When pictured in relation to the city's vast population (500,000–600,000), one might imagine that slaves and freed people comprised a nearly invisible minority. This does not capture the oddity of their predicament. Whether you spotted slaves in eighteenth-century Paris depended on where you went and whom you knew. Nearly all slaves in the kingdom lived in about six Parisian neighborhoods: Saint Eustache, the Marais, Saint Roch, and the Faubourg de la Madeleine on the right bank; Saint Sulpice and the Faubourg de Saint Germain des

Près on the left bank. These were the wealthiest parts of town, home to the wealthiest people in the country. The geographical concentration of slaves in a handful of the city's parishes helps to account for the otherwise baffling hysteria of Crown officials in the late eighteenth century about the dangerous ubiquity of black people. Most of the black people lived near the officials.[5]

At the conclusion of this essay I will return to the case of Ledoux to reflect on the broader significance of his case. For now, however, let us consider the court from which he sought assistance. In Old Regime Paris, the city's court of admiralty was the only legal forum to which slaves could appeal for their freedom. The admiralty's jurisdiction over slaves began with two royal decrees, of 1716 and 1738, concerned with slaves who sojourned in domestic France.[6] The first of these decrees required that masters obtain permission from colonial governors for slaves to accompany them. These permissions needed to be registered with courts of admiralty both in the colonies and at their port of arrival in metropolitan France. After registration, slaves were allowed to stay in France for three years. The 1738 declaration concerning slaves in France toughened the rules. According to this new law, no slave could marry in France and no master could free his slaves there, except by testament. According to the 1716 law, slaves who were unregistered were supposed to become free. According to the 1738 law, the Crown was supposed to confiscate unregistered slaves for the profit of the state. In addition, the 1738 text was a veritable expulsion order. It required that all slaves in the country be returned to the colonies within a year.[7]

That Parlement failed to register either of these laws might be taken as a sign of precocious abolitionism on the part of Parisian jurists. But the city's courts recognized slaves as a form of legitimate property for the whole of the eighteenth century.[8] At stake was not the immorality of slavery but the legal character of the domestic state. Judges sought to keep colonial laws from being explicitly recognized and applied in France. The first article of the 1716 law—repeated in the 1738 version—referred to the Code Noir, the colonial slave code. In a literal sense, the 1716 and 1738 royal decrees incorporated colonial law into domestic law.

Neither this ban on manumissions nor the confiscation of slaves by the Crown seemed to matter in Paris. Yet the 1738 law was not quite a dead letter. It took effect, to a limited extent, in plain sight of Parlement, and with the involvement of lawyers licensed by that court. The 1738 law required masters to register slaves with the so-called *table de marbre*—clerk of the admiralty—on their arrival in Paris. The Paris court duly opened new log books in 1739. In practice this meant that slave owners and their lawyers registered slaves in the Palais de Justice, which housed both the admiralty and the Parlement the very court that refused to enact the 1738 law.[9]

The admiralty's slave registration system fell apart during the Seven Years' War. The old laws had sought to limit the sojourns of slaves in metropolitan France to three years. Before the war, masters extended those sojourns by renewing their slaves' registration before the admiralty clerk. In an era of prolonged war, three-year stints became impossible. The renewal protocol became absurd. Practically no one could leave the country

The collapse of the registration system provoked attempts by admiralty administrators to assert control over enslaved people in France while redefining the scope of the admiralty's authority. From 1738 until the war, the purpose of the registration system was to safeguard colonial property in the form of people. In April 1762, however, the admiralty devised a new registration system that applied to free people of color as well as slaves. What began as a procedure defined by a person's legal status became a racial measure. The new text enjoined "all people under the jurisdiction of the admiralty of Paris...who have negroes or mulattos in their service, of either sex, to make a declaration in person or through a representative or face the consequences." The decree went on to require all people of color to register, whether or not they were domestics.[10] Jacques Ledoux's original petition was a direct consequence of this new decree.

The collapse of the old registration system during the war left people of color in Paris to enjoy what freedoms the city offered without needing to prove who they were. The 1762 ordinance required all of those people to produce their bona fides. The decree also forced masters to decide, and spell out, whether their domestics were persons or things. In requiring the registration of all people of color in the city, the decree assured that they would learn, if they did not know already, about the admiralty's special role in defining their status. The 1762 ordinance created an explosion of freedom stories by posing the question *Who are you?* to which all those narratives were a reply. People scurried to prove their status, fearing that their freedom would soon disappear.

As the war drew to a close, the Paris court of admiralty became a space of experimentation. The people behind the experiments included masters, lawyers, slaves and people who moved in the orbit of slaves (like Anne Diaquoy, Ledoux's literate wife). The shared purpose of these experiments was to bestow liberty on slaves by methods that defied the laws of domestic France and of the colonies.

To understand those experiments, this paper focuses on petitions in which slaves asked the Paris court of admiralty to confirm their freedom. The petitions I discuss here cover the period of the Seven Years' Year and its immediate aftermath (1756–1765). To sharpen my reading of these sources, I have identified four kinds of freedom stories that structure the content of these documents. Some petitions include only one of these stories; sometimes multiple freedom stories appear in the same petition.

1   According to the first story type, people sought to have their freedom recognized without supplying any supporting documents. They had no written proof of their manumission. Instead they recounted their lives as free men to the court. They did so in the hope of obtaining official-looking papers.

2   According to a second story model, slaves asked the admiralty court to register, and thus to confer legitimacy on, documents granting freedom to slaves. These documents came in many forms. They ranged from informal notes on scraps of paper to notarial contracts. According to eighteenth-century statute, when it came to freeing slaves, all forms of freedom papers had the same status in France, with the exception of testaments. It was supposed to be illegal for living masters to free their slaves inside the kingdom.

3   The third and fourth types of freedom story were confrontational. These narratives figured in legal cases against slave masters. Stories of the third type were tales about personal endangerment. Petitioners warned of their imminent sale in France. Or they described plans to deport them from the kingdom. The people who awaited removal expected to be resold in the colonies. In recounting these problems, slaves and their lawyers asked to be recognized as free on a variety of grounds—often as victims of injustice.

4   The fourth story type was more conventionally legal than the others. It was the only freedom story type in which petitioners embedded their demands in an explicit language of rights. In this narrative, which has already received considerable attention by historians, slaves lay claim to freedom by invoking a French legal maxim of purported medieval origin: France was supposed to be the soil of liberty. To set foot there meant instantaneous deliverance. Petitioners did not identify themselves as slaves in free-soil petitions to the court of admiralty. Instead they asked the court to recognize and protect their prior freedom, which was supposed to date from the moment they stepped into the country.

Few of the slaves who sought freedom before the admiralty court could read and write. To what degree did they participate in the drafting of these petitions? There can never be a precise or uniform reply to this question and yet the question cannot be wished away. We cannot even begin to consider the contributions by people of color to these documents before grappling with the scope of the interpretive challenge posed by these sources. To begin with, the voice of slaves did not require their direct or even indirect participation. The danger of mistaking a petition written on behalf of a slave for a document dictated by a slave is amply shown by the 1755 freedom suit by the slave Corinne. On 2 October 1755, two months after the admiralty court declared her free and awarded her back wages, Corinne, *négresse de nation*, petitioned the admiralty to ask that "the laws of the realm be executed and that she be declared free...and that the defendants be sentenced to return the clothes and linen she used and to pay her a sum of 500 pounds for wages." At the time of the drafting of this petition, and for months— since August 1755—the voice of Corinne in legal documents had been the work of her lawyer Collet. Corinne and other slaves from the same Parisian household were then locked in a Le Havre prison.[11]

Slaves did not necessarily instigate their own legal battles for freedom let alone craft their own legal strategies. In a 1765 letter to the Parisian police, Claude-Denis Ronseray, who was an admiralty judge in Saint Domingue, described local attempts to liberate his wife's teenage chamber maid. "[T]he first step taken by this slave was the work of a scribe named Gravel who is stationed in the hotel of the Company of the Indies, Rue Neuve des Petits Champs, who presented himself to the procureur du roi (prosecutor at admiralty court) and also told Monsieur Bigot, secretary to the Lord Admiral."[12]

It is still clear that the petitioners shaped the content of these documents. Nearly all slave petitions were the work of a single *procureur*, Pierre-Etienne Regnaud—later known as Regnaud de Paris. We know from police records that the people who sought Regnaud's assistance gave his house on the Rue des Singes in the Marais as their permanent address and may even have lodged there. There was nothing impersonal or merely opportunistic about his engagement with slaves seeking liberty.[13] Pierre-Etienne Regnaud is remembered as a royalist eccentric during the 1790s. What linked the early and later life of Regnaud was his persistent, antiquarian reverence for the old French constitution, whose key elements were the free-soil maxim, salic law, and the sacredness of the king.[14] Indeed, the free-soil maxim, for those who believed in its antiquity, was supposed to be a decree of medieval kings.

Regnaud might have satisfied his clients' demands by producing identical petitions. Everyone, in principle, might have demanded liberty in the name of the free-soil doctrine. But they did not. While the petitions he created on behalf of slaves were often formulaic, those texts were not identical. Regnaud's petitions followed different story models and incorporated personal anecdotes. We can surmise that his clients helped to choose the basic narrative or template of their stories by furnishing Regnaud with details about their experiences.

Jacques Ledoux supplied no proof of his free status to the admiralty either in 1762, at the time of his original petition, or two years later. His statements to the admiralty clerk conform to the first type of story, in which petitioners declared themselves to be free without manumission papers or written documents of any kind to prove their status. Here the court furnished freedom papers to people on the basis of unsupported claims and hence converted tales, true or not, into legal facts.

This sort of freedom story did not exist before the Seven Years' War. Usually, though not always, these narratives chronicled wartime mis- adventures involving defeat, capture, and daring escape. Never before or since had it been possible for a person of color to obtain freedom papers in exchange for his autobiography. In July 1763, a man called Jean-Baptiste, born in Guadeloupe, was the first to seek freedom papers in Paris by this method. Captured while fighting to defend Martinique, he was sent to England "whence he escaped through cunning along with ten Frenchmen."[15]

The success of Jean-Baptiste in obtaining freedom papers emboldened other soldiers from the Antilles to follow his example later that year. In October 1763, a Martiniquan called André Bordenave wrote to the Paris court of admiralty in October 1763 because "he had been advised" by persons unknown "to affirm his liberty." He claimed to be a free-born man who volunteered as a soldier when the English laid siege to the island. Captured, sent to England, Bordenave had "the good fortune to save himself and went to France, having the intention of returning to America." But he needed a document attesting to his freedom to make the journey.[16] A version of the Jean-Baptiste/Bordenave story recurred in the later petition of Louis, a Creole from Guadeloupe, who petitioned the court in December 1763 for a document certifying his status as a free man. "Despite being naturally free, he fears being bothered about this in France." After joining the negro troops in the defense of Guadeloupe, he was sent to England as a captive. He became the valet of an English colo- nel. He followed the colonel to Germany. Captured by the French, Louis wound up "as a prisoner in a French hospital." The colonel disappeared. The petition by Louis did not mention the name of the colonel he served or the place of his arrest and detention; nor did he explain what it meant to be naturally free.[17]

The effort by slaves (or former slaves) to become rights-bearing Frenchmen on the strength of stories about their unwritten freedom was a novelty of the war; but soldiers were not the only people who sought papers on these grounds. Cahitanne, a baptized man from Bombay, pe- titioned the court in 1763. He then enjoyed de facto liberty. The Count of Breteuil took him from Pondicherry to Paris in 1758. Soon thereaf- ter, Cahitanne became the paid servant of the Marquis de Breteuil, the count's brother. He approached the court because "the petitioner fears being troubled in this right."[18] The next year, a Creole woman from Port-au-Prince called Marie-Veronique petitioned the court to recognize her status as a free woman. Born on a plantation near Port au Prince belonging to the Duval family, she claimed to have been free at the time she left the colony in 1748. Her master died during the voyage to France.

She served Madame Duval, who soon remarried, until the woman's death in 1761. Marie-Veronique had since found work in Paris as a cook. As these examples from the 1760s suggest, domestics who arrived in France before the war later petitioned the admiralty out of concern for their status. These stories suggest that the multiplication of freedom petitions to the admiralty in Paris during these years resulted from a general fear by non-white domestics that the freedom they enjoyed in France would soon disappear.

Three years after the admiralty confirmed Jean-Baptiste's freedom, a merchant in Martinique, Sieur de la Prise-Héligon, claimed him as a slave. Héligon asked the navy to arrange for Jean-Baptiste's forcible return to the colony. He said nothing of Jean-Baptiste's military service. In this new version of events, Jean-Baptiste left Martinique involuntarily. Héligon and another white merchant accused a grenadier, Boullonnière de Poussy, of secreting slaves out of the colony. Documents about this controversy— and the men's resulting deportation from France—make it possible to grasp important features of these cases that would otherwise elude us.[19]

Slaves who fought the British in the French Antilles imagined themselves to be free because they had borne arms for France. A Martiniquan slave called Hyacinthe, who wound up in Caen, told the city's admiralty court in December 1762 that, "believing himself free after taking up the island's defense," he had been captured by the enemy and "embarked on an English vessel called *The Three Sisters*" that delivered him to Port Louis. Jean-Baptiste's employer in Paris, the Vicomte d'Oudenarde, even claimed to have seen a note from the Minister of the Navy granting freedom to his valet.

Antillean soldiers had every reason to believe in the authenticity of their freedom. According to the articles of capitulation for Guadeloupe of 1 May 1759, "It will be permitted for the inhabitants to give freedom to the negroes to whom they promised it for defending the island" on condition "that [the freed people] leave the island" (art 20).[20] The articles of capitulation for Martinique from 1763 proclaimed that "slaves freed during the siege, or to whom freedom was promised, are reputed and declared free and will enjoy that status peacefully" without their being obliged to leave the colony (art. 19).[21] In both places, "black and mulatto prisoners who are free, and were taken during the conquest, will be treated as such and returned with the other prisoners to continue to enjoy their liberty" (art. 9 in both) with the provision in Martinique that "all blacks taken prisoner with their arms in hand [i.e. not having surrendered] will be presumed slaves." There is no reason to credit the story of Héligon over that of his slave, Jean-Baptiste; he provided no evidence—other than whiteness—to support his claim. But the word of white people easily overruled whatever recognition the Paris admiralty court gave to former slaves and freeborn black people. After the war, Héligon's claims to Jean-Baptiste and to a second slave in Paris were expressions of disavowal—breaches of the promise made to island men at the surrender of both islands.

The discovery and removal of Jean-Baptiste, the former soldier, reveals a remarkable degree of cooperation across the Atlantic. The slave removal system that allowed the police and navy to remit Jean-Baptiste back to his master in Martinique worked efficiently because the French kingdom was becoming an imperial state, a legal and administrative whole divided by an ocean.

The experience of Guadeloupean and Martiniquan soldiers helps us to understand the role of the colonial war in generating this particular model of freedom story. Men from Martinique and Guadeloupe sought to obtain recognition as free men from the admiralty because of pledges made to them by planters and officials. It was the war that lured enslaved people in those colonies to fight for France in exchange for the promise of freedom. It was a promise that planters and the Navy chose to forget.

In December 1762, the notary Fournel—a man with slave-trading connections—recorded the manumission of several Martiniquan children of mixed descent.[22] The slaves included Marianne (fille Monique), age nineteenth, Camille (fille Monique), age fifteen, Philippe, age twenty (fils Monique), and Pierre-Charles (fils Martonne), age twelve.[23] All the children belonged to two masters, both colonial administrators, who fled or got deported from the island.

On colonial soil, masters could only free their slaves—whether by testament or by a manumission contract—with the assent of colonial governors. In the event of non-compliance, slaves were supposed to be seized by the state. According to the 1738 Declaration of the King, slaves in domestic France could not be manumitted except by testament. It was supposed to be harder to free a slave in France than in the colonies.

The freeing of slaves before notaries on domestic soil, which flouted the 1738 rules, predated the Seven Years' War.[24] In Paris, the war, nonetheless, played an important role in normalizing this practice. The capture of Martinique and the loss of colonies including Senegal increased the number of masters arriving with slaves to Paris. In drawing imperial people to the capital, the war led the freeing of slaves before Paris notaries to become commonplace.

The admiralty did not apply any legal restrictions, or touchstone of authenticity, to the freedom papers it registered. The documents did not need to be notarized. They could be little notes scratched out by masters (or supposed masters). In April 1759, the first time that anyone presented this sort of thing to the court of admiralty, even the bearer of the note, Jean-François (or rather his lawyer) seemed skeptical about whether a slave could get freedom papers using so dubious and informal a document.[25]

The admiralty authenticated *billets de liberté* of all sorts, ranging from formal contracts to the jottings of missing masters. A Creole from

Mauritius, Louis Patté, managed to register a note freeing an unspecified person (this was a conveniently transferrable document), as in: "I certify that the bearer of this note is a negro born on the Ile de France who served me faithfully all the time I was in India. I give him liberty, which he has promised will make him even more attached to me."[26]

Because of the repetitive character of these petitions from the 1760s, it would be easy to mistake the registration of freedom papers for a bureaucratic routine. Yet there are no instances of this practice before the mid-eighteenth century. In 1754, a Martiniquan planter called Louis-Robert-Giraud de Crésol registered an act of manumission for his slave, François Durand. According to that document, Crésol gave freedom to his slave conditionally and in the future so long as the man, a trained pastry chef, completed three years of service to Antoine La Valette, the Reverend Superior of the Jesuits.[27] The Paris court of admiralty did not register any other notarial documents freeing slaves until the Seven Years' War. By the end of the eighteenth century, however, the registration of freedom papers became routine, as was the processing fee. One slave master, when freeing his slave Almanzor in 1781, gestured toward "that which is customary for the ratification of his liberty."[28] He left the slave to pay the fee himself.

This practice of registration would seem to have extended from a common function of the admiralty court that had nothing to do with slaves. Merchants in the age of sail looked to admiralty courts in port cities to register *pièces*—important legal, commercial or personal texts—on the eve of ocean crossings. Thus, for instance, on 31 August 1761, the Longuemare brothers, a merchant house, explained to the Lieutenant-General of the admiralty in Le Havre that they would soon be dispatching "different bills and IOUs pertaining to merchandise they had sold in Saint Domingue" aboard a vessel bound for the colony; since these "might be mislaid or even lost definitively during the crossing" they wanted them registered with the clerk of the court.[29] The Paris admiralty court, unlike other admiralty courts, did not have a coast or a port to oversee. It did not register important documents on the eve of perilous journeys (at least not in a literal sense). Instead, by registering documents like *billets de liberté* or notarized manumission contracts, the court conferred legitimacy on what were otherwise legally inconsequential documents.

What is revealed by all of these cases is the crucial role played by the Seven Years' War in standardizing new procedures for the manumission of slaves in Paris. Those procedures afforded masters more latitude in freeing slaves than the government allowed them on colonial soil. The use of these notarial documents and *billets de liberté* in Paris suggest that the war shaped new and enduring legal practices in the capital.

Petitions to the admiralty on behalf of slaves resembled one another in basic form. They were all written in the first person. The texts seemed to channel the voices of slaves, whoever wrote them and however they came about. When enslaved litigants sought authority from the admiralty court to sue masters in Paris, their petitions also spoke in the same mood of foreboding.

Petitioners who challenged the right of masters to own them warned the court about an imminent threat to their wellbeing. The danger took one of two forms: either a slave described his master's plan to sell him in France. Or he divulged a plot to deport him and sell him in the colonies. The same petitions might also dramatize the iniquity of slave owners in Paris by recalling (where possible) prior instances of a slave's sale in and around the capital.

The small number of slaves who lived in Paris were comparatively free to exit the confines of their masters' households. Paris was not a place where the sale of humans loomed as a prominent feature of daily life. As domestics, they had an identity within their masters' households and a close personal relationship to masters. For such people, the prospect of sale, resale, or just forcible return to the colonies did not augur a merely distasteful change in living conditions. At stake was their transformation into commodities.

The anthropologist Igor Kopytoff describes the experience of enslavement as "de-socialization, dehumanization and de-individualization."[30] If we take these admiralty documents at their word, they describe the predicament of people who lived on the edge of personhood. Petitions of this sort were letters about people on the brink that sought to prevent the transformation of people into things.

Should we take these petitions about sale and removal seriously? Or were these alarming portents part of a legal strategy? By the time of the Seven Years' War, all Crown officials would have assented—at least in public—to the notion that selling slaves in France was taboo. Was it illegal? The Paris Parlement refused in 1716 and 1738 to enact royal decrees relating to slaves who sojourned in France. Both of these statutes banned traffic in slaves on domestic soil. These documents were the only formal legal texts that forbade the sale of slaves in the kingdom.

In a technical sense, through Parlement's refusal to enact the royal decrees of 1716 and 1738, Paris became the one place in the country where people could traffic in slaves with impunity. But statutes are not everything. Unanimity of principle developed among Crown officials by the mid-eighteenth century. Earlier, in 1711, a scandal had erupted at Dinan when the port jailer sold the slave of a paroled English merchant to an Irish officer.[31] Navy officials voiced dismay. But they did not describe the sale of the Englishman's slave as a violation of the ban on slave sales in France. They focused their attention elsewhere. They reproached the jailer for despoiling a prisoner of war.

The condemnation of slave sales by Crown officials became more explicit in later years. In 1747, the Maréchal de Saxe—bastard prince and war hero—took steps to create a new troupe of personal guardians. He wanted to encircle himself with richly upholstered brown people. He preferred heathens. His recruiters scoured the kingdom in search of able-bodied colored men. On learning that twelve slaves were jailed (for safe-keeping) in Bayonne, he wrote to Maurepas, minister of the navy. He hoped to buy them for his troupe. In an otherwise fawning letter, Maurepas refused: "The Council of Maritime Prize [Conseil des prises] ordered that these Negroes be sent to the islands to be given to shipowners whose corsairs captured them." The Council of Maritime Prize intended sea rovers and their wealthy sponsors to profit from these Africans, who were war booty. But "there [could not] be any slave sold inside the realm."[32]

Louis-Jean-Marie de Bourbon, Duc de Penthièvre, Admiral of France, was the titular head of Council of Maritime Prize, to which Maurepas also belonged. (It is worth signaling that Penthièvre became Admiral of France at the age of eight, at his father's death, and would have been twenty-one at the time of the council's 1747 decision about slaves in Bayonne.) As Maurepas indicated, the council prescribed the overseas sale of African captives while preventing their sale in France. A similar moral outlook guided new legislation by the Paris admiralty fifteen years later. The 1762 ordinance, crafted by the admiralty's chief attorney, did not condemn slavery; the text merely denounced the frequency with which Parisians bought and sold slaves in the capital. Paris had become an emporium for human flesh. "France, and above all the capital, is now a public market where men are sold to the highest bidder; there is no bourgeois, no worker, who lacks his own negro." Such auctions (which probably never happened) were supposed to insinuate slavery into France, destroy ancient liberty, and corrupt the blood and spirit of Frenchmen. This 1762 ordinance both forbade the sale of slaves in Paris while requiring that all people of color register with the admiralty.

Did the slaves who expressed fear of removal and resale truly face those dangers? The repetitiveness of petitions might lead one to picture warnings by slaves about their future resale or vanishing as an empty formula. Yet the dangers noted in these petitions were for the most part real. The Paris police together with the Department of the Navy helped planters to whisk enslaved domestics out of Paris. Slaves who petitioned for freedom before the admiralty court were arrested, locked in prisons, and shunted to ports pending removal overseas. Antoine de Sartine, who did a lengthy stint as lieutenant general of police in Paris (1759–1774) before becoming the Minister of the Navy, described the Crown's handling of Parisian freedom suits in a memorandum of August 1777 to the royal *Conseil des Dépêches*: "The old king [Louis XV] always prevented those judgments or interfered with their effect by causing orders to be dispatched [e.g., *lettres de cachet*] to the secretary of state charged with the department of the Navy so as to arrest and return to the colonies negroes who fled or demanded their liberty."[33]

Slaves who wound up in Paris during the Seven Years' War feared the return of peace. With the end of war came a return to normal maritime travel between France and the colonies. In 1760, woman called Isabel-Flore (or Sara) told the court that her mistress planned to have her arrested and returned to Pondicherry "as soon as the war permits."[34] Soon she disappeared. A 1765 passenger list for the *Adour*, an Indies Company ship, indicates that Isabel Flore was sent back to Pondicherry in 1765 without her mistress.[35]

Isabel Flore had been living in France for less than a year when she petitioned the court. But even longtime residents of France experienced the end of the war as a moment of endangerment. In 1762, Séraphine-Bertrand, age twenty-four, *mulâtresse*, instigated a freedom suit against her owners, Gabriel Dubois-Jourdain and his wife, Marie-Félicité de Belloy, who came from Martiniquan planter families. Séraphine traveled to France from Martinique ten years earlier with Madame Hallet, her master's cousin. After home schooling in the rudiments of religion, Séraphine spent two years (1755–1757) in a vocational training camp for orphans inside Salpetrière, a Parisian compound for derelict females. In 1762, Gabriel Dubois-Jourdain told the admiralty that he had always meant "to send this *mulâtresse* back or take her back himself for the purpose of educating the negro youth on his plantation." At the war's end, she awaited removal to a colony she had not seen for thirteen years. Her petition warned the admiralty that "her person would not be secure if she remained in the home of her masters."[36]

If Séraphine was the chambermaid of Monsieur and Madame Gabriel Dubois-Jourdain, she spent her teenage years inside a vast Wunderkammer—the private house museum of Séraphine's mistress. A servant in the Dubois-Jourdain household moved among, and possibly dusted, jars and cases that contained, for instance, a child skeleton with two heads, a bird with four wings, the sculpture of a winged phallus from ancient Greece, and "the hair of a white negro." Yet it was not the house, but the prospect of vanishing from the house, that inspired this petition.[37]

Some petitions in this archive focus on racial injustice. It was easy for unscrupulous people to enslave free people because of the way they looked. A petition by the slave Anne-Philippe/Hector claimed that he came from to France from Africa as a young boy with a one-time director of the Indies Company at Galam. At the death of his master, Anne-Philippe/Hector became the domestic of Claude Roques, a Parisian banker. In 1764, Hector complained that Roques "could have no right to his person, yet wishes to take advantage of his being *noir de nation*, and wants to embark him to the colonies and sell him as a slave."[38]

Ann-Philippe Hector's petition drew attention to a chronic feature of black experience. Other male slaves who sought liberty in the 1760s gestured to wartime chaos and displacement when they described toppling into servitude because of their skin color. A Malagasy youngster, Constant Olivier Joseph, age thirteen, complained in 1764 that he had arrived in France as the free servant of a soldier in the Regiment of Mont-morency and then entered the service of the Comtesse de Frémicourt, "who claims to hold him as a slave." The next year, another Malagasy calling himself Hazan or Azat made the same complaint about another officer who "wants to send him to America as his slave." Petitbois, the alleged master of Constant Olivier Joseph, was a second lieutenant in the escadre d'Aché, which fought in India. Coutanceau, the alleged mas-ter of Hazan/Azat, was the name of a prominent soldier in India. Both officers would have been more likely to acquire Malagasy slaves than Malagasy free domestics in the French East Indies.[39]

Petitions on behalf of Africans, Indians, and Malagasies were usually about thresholds in a double sense. These documents harked back to the original moment of a person's enslavement and warned of his future return to nothingness. Slave petitions to the admiralty aimed to pre-vent people from reverting to the status of commodities. On the other hand, the petitions drew attention to slaves' prior identity as free people, described their past experience of losing their freedom, and demanded liberty in the name of the people they were before.

The fact of being born free recurs often in these petitions. In several cases, Indian slaves claimed liberty as their birthright, as non-Africans. In 1764, Louis Aisbaignan, a self-described "mulatto of Balibar," pe-titioned for freedom, "not being of a servile nation, as the blacks of Guinea can be."[40] Yet Africans, too, described liberty as their original condition and birthright. The African Joseph Pellement was "born of a free father and mother, obliged to serve in a war of his nation."[41] The Malagasy man called Favory "was taken as a slave at the age of five" to Mauritius.[42] Celestin, son of Emée, noted that his "family enjoys a certain reputation" in Cape Verde, where he became a war captive at the age of five. Sold to the English, he was intercepted by the French at sea and, he wound up in Martinique. In 1762 he was the Parisian domes-tic of the colony's ex-Governor de la Touche. Petitions by men during the era of the Seven Years' War described the enslavement of free-born young people by wartime misadventures. In a twist, that was also the life story of most Africans who wound up by the millions on slave ships in the eighteenth century.

Séraphine was a Creole mixed person from Martinique. In contrast to the Africans, Malagasies, and the Indians, she had never been free. On what grounds could Séraphine's lawyer contest the right of the Dubois-Jourdain family to own her? Séraphine's petition invoked "the constant maxim that all slaves who enter France are free."

Lawyers in the eighteenth century who represented slaves drew at-tention to the free-soil maxim, a doctrine of purported antiquity, yet inscribed in no body of law, by which slaves were supposed to become free by merely setting foot in France. The free-soil maxim was a legal doctrine because lawyers and judges called it one. The measure of its authenticity was its use. The maxim was said to originate with medieval decrees that banned serfdom in the kingdom. A skeptical investigation of those sources by an eighteenth-century monk revealed, alas, that no such thing occurred. Medieval decrees empowered serfs to testify and urged lords to accept fair payment from serfs who wanted to buy their freedom. Centuries after the publication of those decrees, lords continued to manumit serfs in Parisian courts while serfdom retained the force of law in the kingdom.[43]

In the work of historians, the free-soil principle has inadvertently diminished the richness of slave petitions to the admiralty by overshadowing all other claims to freedom that appear in this corpus of documents. To the extent that scholars have written about these petitions, they have done so by focusing uniquely on invocations of the free-soil maxim. Yet there is danger in reducing slave petitions to a tale about the lawyerly revival of an ancient French idea. This reading of slave petitions gives central importance to Parisian men of the law and recasts these petitions as pendants of the French Enlightenment. The stories about freedom found in these petitions become expressions of the French legal tradition. In consequence, the slaves and freed people mentioned in these petitions—who seem to speak in these sources—become more or less irrelevant to the content of the documents. They become mouthpieces, or passive beneficiaries, of someone else's rights culture.

A close reading of slave petitions to the admiralty makes it possible to correct for this over-emphasis on metropolitan law. By returning to these sources, it becomes evident that enslaved people fashioned their own version of the free-soil maxim, which differed in essential ways from the doctrine put forward by French lawyers. This alternative form of the free-soil doctrine was anticolonial and abolitionist. As such, it anticipated notions of imperial citizenship that later surfaced both during the French Revolution and the nineteenth century.

Until the Seven Years' War, masters who registered slaves had no reason to fear losing them. They avoided lawsuits by submitting to expensive formalities. As the Seven Years' War drew to a close, however, the scrupulous compliance of masters to these requirements stopped mattering. Lawyers for slaves began demanding freedom for their clients simply by virtue of the free-soil maxim. In late 1762, the Paris court of admiralty began freeing slaves even when their masters had followed the rules.

The free-soil maxim had precisely the opposite of its intended effect. The people who invoked this doctrine against their masters tended to disappear. Take, for instance, Jean-Baptiste Petitjean, who belonged to Jacques-Barthelemy Gruel a slave-trading magnate. In December 1762, Petitjean fled as his master prepared his postwar return to Saint Domingue. Petitjean petitioned for liberty. The court declared Petitjean free and awarded him back wages. Gruel appealed the decision.

On 1 February 1763, one day after Gruel lost his appeal, "We Pierre Chenon, royal councilor and commissioner at Chatelet in Paris, transported ourselves with Sieur Buhot, Inspector of the Police, to the Rue du Bout du Monde, to a house occupied downstairs by the cobbler Sacré, and went upstairs to the first floor, to the room of Marie-Anne-Gauthier, laundress, where we found Jean-Baptiste called Petitjean, age 30, native of Saint Domingue, belonging to Sieur Barthelemy-Jacques Gruel....Mister Buhot arrested this negro in execution of the orders with which he is charged and conducted him to his destination." The destination was Le Havre, where Petitjean would await "the first ship leaving for Saint Domingue."[44]

Documents about Petitjean's freedom suit furnish almost no information about him. When the free-soil maxim became central to slave petitions, the life stories of litigants dropped out of those documents. Why should petitions recount their lives if the mere fact of their presence sufficed for a legal ruling? It did not matter whether you had been kidnapped, captured at sea, stolen while a baby, or lured into slavery as a wandering valet. The point was not who you used to be but where you were living.

Despite the formulaic and even anti-biographical character of these petitions, we should not be too quick to dismiss them. They reveal more than they seem to. There is evidence that slaves subtly reshaped the free-soil maxim. A 1710 tract by an Indies Company employee describes habits of mind among slaves on the Isle of Bourbon (now Réunion) that more or less anticipate the content of every petition for freedom in the admiralty archive—while predating those petitions by at least thirty years. Slaves born on the Isle of Bourbon "say that their mother and father were truly slaves, but that they, being born in France, where there are no slaves, should rightfully be free." Indian slaves "say that they are the issue of a free mother and father; and that if they are slaves, it is because they were stolen and tricked, and sold without their consent. And so say the others."[45]

If we think of the free-soil doctrine as an inherited language—something that slaves absorbed from the master class—then it is clear they altered that language, making it more subversive and distinctly their own. Beginning in January 1763 a new version of the maxim began circulating in slave petitions to the admiralty, which harked back to the remarks of Creole slaves earlier in the century. No longer did people claim freedom by virtue of setting foot in metropolitan France. Now slaves demanded freedom as native-born subjects of land governed by France. In late 1762 and during the winter and spring 1763, litigants including Jean-Louis, Jacques Médor, Charles-Auguste, Charles-Marie Conty, and François Annibal all invoked the same, slightly altered version of the maxim to demand freedom *vu qu'il n'y a point d'esclaves en France et que le suppliant est né sous la domination française*. The Creole slave

Jean-Baptiste Petitjean, whom his master arrested and deported to Saint Domingue, was among the first people to invoke this new version of the maxim.

The new version of the free-soil maxim hinged on an entirely new principle of colonial governance. At stake was the idea that colonial soil should be governed according to the same public law—constitutional law—as European territory; and that the people who lived there, with respect to their status, should be governed as any other French subjects. At the time that slaves made these demands, no lawyer in the country would have argued that the children of Africans and Indians, who were born on French islands at two or even six months journey from Nantes, had a birthright to liberty as natural subjects of the French king.

The notion that colonies counted as French soil, and that domestic French law should apply there, later became a prominent feature of revolutionary constitutional law; after slavery returned under Napoleon, the same vision of legal uniformity resurfaced in the writings of nineteenth-century abolitionists—notably Victor Schoelcher. But the idea of a trans-oceanic state under a single law, with freedom as its maxim, did not originate with Parisian lawyers. It began as the doctrine of Creole slaves in the empire.

The free-soil doctrine had a further significance to the legal claims of slaves after the Seven Years' War. All story models that I have described in this essay—whether these involved new sorts of freedom papers, new legal procedures, picaresque autobiographies, portents of slave sale, or appeals to the famous maxim—occurred simultaneously. These stories did not merely coincide but in a sense created and reinforced one another. It became possible to produce hitherto illegal documents (or no documents) to the court of admiralty to prove one's freedom at more or less the same instant that the admiralty court began declaring people free for simply being in the country.

Let me conclude by reflecting on the relationship between French slave petitions and narratives by former slaves that circulated in eighteenth- and nineteenth-century North America and England. The differences are striking, with respect to both form and content. French and Anglophone texts developed from dissimilar institutions and political contexts. They were distinct in form, worldview, and intended purpose. Anglophone freedom stories appear in published texts. French freedom stories are drawn from unpublished petitions in a legal archive. French admiralty petitions were legal instruments that aimed to establish the petitioners' freedom in the future. Anglophone texts were elements of abolitionist propaganda that sought to end slavery in general.

In spite of many glaring points of unlikeness, these texts need to be seen for what they share. Ultimately, French and Anglophone texts can be read as diverse expressions of a single truth, which transcended national histories and affected all slaves and people of color who lived or circulated through modern slave societies in the Caribbean, East Indies, and the Americas. Historians tend to describe slave emancipation as a linear and forward-moving process, full of crescendi, energized by sacrifice and struggle. These French and English texts give the lie to that narrative. Re-enslavement was common. Freedom was a fragile and tenuous condition. French freedom petitions and Anglo-American slave narratives both recount the picaresque vulnerability of free people of color to the loss of their liberty. Leaving the town or island of your bondage felt like deliverance. But slave owners—or people pretending to be them—had a long reach. What all of these texts teach us is that the route between slavery and freedom ran in both directions and that people frequently moved back and forth.[46]

The case of Jacques Ledoux illustrates this general truth with particular poignancy. Ledoux obtained freedom papers from the admiralty on at least three occasions during his stint in France. He presented himself as a freeborn man to the admiralty in 1762. Two years later, in September 1764, Ledoux returned to the admiralty; he sought protection from the maneuvers of a Martiniquan tradeswoman, Marie-Therese Tridon, who claimed to own him. Days later, Jacques Ledoux and his wife paid 2,000 livres to a Martiniquan merchant who was empowered to act on Tridon's behalf. In exchange for that sum, according to their notarial contract, Ledoux got his freedom and could keep the money he earned during the war as a privateer. In the end, however, the payment did not matter. Just after Ledoux's wife bought his freedom, he disappeared.

The case of Ledoux is particularly suited to drawing connections between French and English texts. His experiences during and after the Seven Years' War bear a striking resemblance to events recounted in *The Interesting Narrative of the Life of Olaudah Equiano, or Gustavus Vassa* (1789), the most famous published slave narrative of the eighteenth century.[47] The book is full of clues about the circumstances of Ledoux's vanishing. Consider Gustavus Vassa's 1761 abduction and sale by his master while docked in England. The same master describes stealing from Vassa as a legal right. "[He] said that if my prize money had been 10,000 pounds he had a right to it all and would have taken it." Vassa later recounts the capture of a freeborn sailor from Saint Kitts. Despite the notoriety of the man's freedom among the crew and papers he held, it sufficed that a white captain lay claim to him for the man to be hauled away, unbeknownst to his wife and child. To these details one might add that Vassa, at the time of his kidnapping from England in 1761, believed himself free not only because of verbal reassurances but also because "I have served him...for many years and he has taken all my wages and prize money...I have been baptized...by the laws of England no man has a right to sell me."

On the basis of Vassa's account, it is tempting to surmise that the merchant, Pichaud de Pavillon, who gave Ledoux his freedom, took his money and arranged for his kidnapping soon afterward. Based on the conduct of other masters and supposed masters in this period, there is no reason to think that Pichaud would feel bound by the contract he signed. Moreover, based on the patterns of treachery that Equiano recounts, it also seems likely that Pichaud took more than the 2,000 livres mentioned in the contract.

Gustavus Vassa's book helps us to picture the world that Ledoux inhabited—into which he disappeared. But the point of reading fragments about this obscure French sailor against Vassa's *Interesting Narrative* is not to fill gaps. The act of juxtaposing these texts reveals how much we lose without written narratives—and what it means to be someone who cannot tell his story.

How do we know that Ledoux vanished? In May 1780, Anne Diaquoy asked a civil court in Paris for permission to wield legal powers that would otherwise belong to her husband, Jacques Ledoux. To acquire the legal powers of Ledoux, she needed to prove that her husband was not there. Proof came in the form of a notarial document, drafted that month, in which two men of color attested to the mystery of Ledoux's fate and whereabouts. One of those men would have been nine years old, living somewhere in Saint Domingue, at the time Ledoux vanished. On the strength of that document, the court declared Ledoux to be *absent*.[48]

To be *absent* in Old Regime France was a distinctive legal status. It did not mean you were out of town. It did not mean you were dead. "The absent person is not merely a non-present person whose existence is not in doubt … a deeper analysis of the situation reveals that the *absent* … is a person engaged in a distant adventure whose return, whose existence even, seems uncertain."[49] To be absent meant living at unknown coordinates as a speculative being who might or might not exist. In the law, an absent person dangles in a permanent state of uncertainty. He lives outside time and space. He cannot die. What defined Ledoux, from a legal perspective, was his exclusion from all events and whereabouts as a man without a story.

Notes

1 These observations summarize the contents of the following Y-series cartons: Y-10885A and Y15647B (*patrouilles* 1762–1763), Y-15460 (*Affaire du Canada*), Y10884B (tobacco sting), Y15463A (*Affaire de l'Inde*). On tobacco see Michael Kwass *Contraband: Louis Mandrin and the Making of a Global Underground* (Cambridge, MA: Harvard University Press, 2014). On the Seven Years' War in the West Indies, see Trevor Burnard and John Garrigus, *The Plantation Machine, Atlantic Capitalism in French Saint-Domingue and British Jamaica* (Philadelphia: University of Pennsylvania Press, 2016), 82–100; on scapegoating and scandal, see F. Bosher "The French Government's Motives in the Affaire Du Canada, 1761–1763," *The English Historical Review* 96, no. 378 (1981): 59–78; for India, see Eoghan Ó. Hannracháin, "Lally, the Régime's Scapegoat," *Journal of the Galway Archaeological and*

Historical Society 56 (2004): 75–84; and Danna, Agmon, *A Colonial Affair: Commerce, Conversion, and Scandal in French India* (Ithaca, NY: Cornell University Press, 2017), 143–162.

2 On the French Indies Company, see René Estienne, *Les Compagnies des Indes* (Paris: Gallimard and Ministère des armées, 2017); Philippe Haudrère, *La Compagnie française des Indes au XVIIIe siècle (1719–1795)* (Paris: Les Indes Savantes, 2005); idem, "Les Officiers des vaisseaux de la compagnie des Indes" *Histoire, Économie et Société* 16, no. 1 (1997), 117–124; Albert Girard, "La Réorganisation de La compagnie des Indes (1719–1723)," *Revue d'histoire moderne & contemporaine* 11, no. 1 (1908): 5–34; and *Revue d'histoire moderne & contemporaine* 11, no. 3 (1908): 177–197.

3 See "État des prisonniers de guerre faits sur l'Isle de Gorée" for these ships in Marine F^{2}83, AN. On life in Senegal during this period, with details on personnel at the French settlement, see Marie-Hélène Knight-Baylac, "La Vie à Gorée de 1677 à 1789," *Outre-Mers: Revue d'histoire* 57 (1970): 377–420; Abdoulaye Bathily, *Les Portes de l'or: le royaume de Galam (Sénégal) de l'ère musulmane au temps des négriers–VIIIe-XVIIIe siècles* (Paris: L'Harmattan, 1989); Barry Boubacar, *La Sénégambie du XVe Au XIXe siècle: traite négrière, islam, et conquête coloniale* (Paris: L'Harmattan, 1988); André Delcourt, *La France et les établissements français au Sénégal entre 1713 et 1763: la Compagnie des Indes et le Sénégal* (Dakar: Cahors, 1952); Léonce Jore, *Les établissements français sur la côte occidentale d'Afrique de 1758 À 1809* (Paris: Maisonneuve & Larose, 1965); Hilary Jones, *The Métis of Senegal, Urban Life and Politics in French West Africa* (Bloomington: Indiana University Press, 2013); and Jean-Bernard Lacroix, *Les Français au Sénégal au temps de la compagnie des Indes* (Vincennes, IN: Service historique de la Marine, 1986). On wartime captivity, see Alain Cabatou, "Gens de mer, guerre et prison: la captivité des gens de mer au XVIIIe siècle," *Revue d'histoire moderne et contemporaine* 28, no. 2 (April–June 1981): 246–267 and Renaud Morieux, "French Prisoners of War: Conflicts of Honour and Social Inversions in England 1744–1783," *The Historical Journal* 56, no. 1 (March 2013): 55–88.

4 Declaration of 5 May 1762, quatrième registre, Z-1d-139; petition of 14 Sept. 1764 in Z-1d-132, both from the Archives Nationales (Paris) [hereafter AN]; notarial contract of 28 Sept. 1764, MC/ET/XXIV/794—from the notary Damien-Louis Dupont. Diaquoy's belongings were seized at her death as a consequence of her dying intestate with no direct heirs. On Ledoux, see also Pierre Bardin, "La Population noir dans le Paris du XVIIIe siècle," *Généalogie et histoire de la Caraïbe*, Bulletin 242 (2010), 6–7. For the freedom contract, see Affranchissement et obligation Jeanne-Thérèse Tridon et Hypolite, MC/ET/XXIV/794, AN.

5 Pierre Boulle, *Race et esclavage dans la France de l'Ancien Régime* (Paris: Perrin, 2007) and Erick Noël, *Être noir en France au XVIIIe siècle* (Paris: Tallandier, 2006).

6 Sue Peabody, *"There Are No Slaves in France": The Political Culture of Race and Slavery in the Ancien Regime* (New York: Oxford University Press, 1996); idem, with Keila Grinberg, "Free Soil in the Atlantic World: the Generation and Circulation of an Atlantic Legal Principle," *Free Soil in the Atlantic World*, eds., Sue Peabody and Keila Grinberg (New York: Routledge, 2015), 1–11; on the nineteenth century, see Peabody, "La question raciale et le 'sol libre de France': l'affaire Furcy," *Annales, Histoire, Sciences Sociales* 64 no. 6 (2009): 1305–1334; Peabody, *Madeleine's Children: Family, Freedom, Secrets and Lies in France's Indian Ocean Colonies* (New York:

Oxford University Press, 2017); See also Dwain C. Pruitt, "The Opposition of the Law to the Law: Race, Slavery, and the Law in Nantes, 1715–1778," *French Historical Studies* 30, no. 2 (2007): 147–174; and Marcel Koufinkana, *Les Esclaves noirs en France sous l'Ancien Régime (XVI–XVIIIe siècles)* (Paris: L'Harmattan, 2008).

7 Édit du roy donné à Paris au mois d'octobre 1716, concernant les esclaves nègres des colonies, http://pudl.princeton.edu/objects/hh63sx27b#page/1/ mode/2up; Déclaration du roi concernant les esclaves nègres des colonies qui interprète l'Édit du mois d'Octobre 1716, donne à Versailles le 15 décembre 1738, http://staraco.univ-nantes.fr/fr/ressources/documents/d% C3%A9claration-du-roy-1738.

8 Chambon, *Le commerce de l'Amérique par Marseille, ou, Explication des lettres-patentes du roi, portant règlement pour le commerce qui se fait de Marseillle aux isles françoise de l'Amérique, données au mois de février 1719*, vol. 2 (Avignon, 1764), 225. http://gallica.bnf.fr/ark:/12148/ bpt6k1041911g/f253.image.

9 Premier registre pour la déclaration des nègres, in Z-1d-139, AN (Paris).

10 Ordonnance de l'amirauté de France, 31 March–5 April 1762 (Paris: Imprimerie d'Houry, 1762).

11 On Corinne, see MS 11941, Arch. Bastille; and Z-1d-129, AN, Paris.

12 On Hélène, see MS 12245, Arch. Bastille; and *Mémoire pour Monseigneur Claude-Dénis de Ronseray* (1765), ANOM COL 357.

13 See the file of Narcisse (1765), MS 12252, Arch. Bastille; and that of François (1765), MS 10748, ibid.

14 Pierre Etienne Regnaud, *Adieux aux députés de la première législature ou réflexions sur leur départ* (Paris, 1791); *Lettre à Monsieur de Fontenai sur la fidélité due au souverain* (1792); *Défense pour Louis XVI suivie d'un discours sur la loi salique* (Paris, 1814); *Discours sur l'antique gouvernement de la monarchie française et sur la sagesse des rois qui l'ont fondé* (Paris, 1798); and *Discours sur les beautés de Virgile, prononcé le 23 aout 1810, suivi d'une lettre adressé au petit-fils d'un ancien magistrat pour prouver la nécessité de garder la fidélité due à la famille des Bourbons* (Paris, 1815).

15 Petition of Jean-Baptiste, 27 July 1763, in Z-1d-132, AN.

16 "Il est conseillé de constater sa liberté." Petition by André Bordenave, nègre libre de la Martinique, 21 November 1763, Z-1d-132, AN.

17 Petition of Louis, 3 December 1763, Z-1d-132, AN.

18 Petition of Cahitanne, 31 August 1763, Z-1d-132, AN.

19 See Colonies C8b/12, no.103, ANOM (Aix-en-Provence).

20 Art. 20 of Capitulation de l'Ile Guadeloupe (1 May 1759,) in Martin Durand-Molard, *Code de la Martinique–Nouvelle édition*, vol. 2 (Saint-Pierre, 1807–1814), 60.

21 Capitulation de l'Isle Martinique (13 February 1762), ibid, 113.

22 Fournel notarized a slave-trading contract involving the syndic of the company of the Indies, Colabau, maître des requêtes, Michau de Monteran, and several secretaries du roi See MC/ET/LIX/268 (3 May 1761).

23 For these acts before Fournel see ET/LIX/273.

24 A 1751 survey of Parisian notarial documents turned up the following instances of this practice: MC/ET/V/462 (23 September 1751); MC/ET/ XVII/797 (8 April 1751); and MC/ET/CXII/705/A (19 August 1751).

25 Petition of Jean-François, former slave of Jean-Marie de Partenay (deceased), 2 April 1759, Z-1d-131, AN.

26 Admiralty session of 20 April 1763, Z-1d-132, AN.

27 Petition of Louis-Robert Giraud de Crésol, 24 June 1754, Z-1d-129, AN.

28 Letter freeing Almanzor, signed by Maupin, 17 November 1781, Z-1d-138, AN.
29 Archives départementales Seine-Maritime, 212 BP 262.
30 Igor Kopytoff, "Cultural Biography of Things: Commoditization as Process," in *The Social Life of Things*, ed., Arjun Appadurai (Cambridge: Cambridge University Press, 1986), 64–95.
31 Lempereur to M. de Ponant, 8 August 1711, Marine B3/195, AN.
32 André Corvisier, "Les Soldats noirs du Maréchal de Saxe: le problème des Antillais et Africains sous les armes en France au XVIIIe siècle," *Outre-Mers: Revue d'histoire* 55 (1968): 367–413.
33 Recueil des Pièces relatives à la législation sur la police des noirs (1778), FR 13357, Salle des Manuscrits, Bibliothèque nationale.
34 For Isabel Flore du Rozel (dit Sarah), see documents of 10 September 1760 and 17 December 1716, Z-1d-131.
35 She embarked from Lorient on 2 Feb. 1765 and disembarked in Pondicherry six months later, on 2 August 1765. See Rôle de l'Adour, 2 P 40-II.12, 1765–1766. www.memoiredeshommes.sga.defense.gouv.fr/fr/_depot_mdh/_depot_images/INDES/SHDLORIENT/TABLESPDF/ROLE2P40-II.12.PDF.
36 Petition of Séraphine Bertrand, 22 December 1762, Z-Id-132; for the declaration of 2 June 176 Dubois-Jourdain, see cinquième registre, 10 May 1762, Z-1d-139. Gabriel de Boisjourdain made this statement as a response to a legal judgment of the admiralty on 9 April 1762. The only extant trial-related documents date from December of that year.
37 Pierre Rémy, *Catalogue raisonné des curiosités qui composoient le cabinet de feu Madame Dubois-Jourdain* (Paris: Chez Didot, 1766).
38 Petition of Anne-Philippe dit Hector, 26 October 1764, Z-1d-132; see also his one-page file in the Archives de la Bastille (MS 12445) which contains a letter of 7 June 1765 from the Duc of Choiseul demanding his arrest and removal to the port of Le Havre.
39 Petition by Constant-Olivier Joseph, 16 May 1764, Z-1d-132; petition by Hazan/Azat, 26 November 1765, Z-1d-132, AN. On the slave trade to the East Indies, see Robert Bousquet, *Les Esclaves et Leurs Maîtres à Bourbon (La Réunion) au temps de la Compagnie des Indes 1665–1767*, vol. 1 (self-published, online edition, www.reunion-esclavage-traite-noirs-negmarron.com/spip.php?rubrique2); on the importance of Malagasy slavery to the culture of the eighteenth-century French East Indies, see Pier M. Larson, *Ocean of Letters: Language and Creolization in an Indian Ocean Diaspora* (New York: Cambridge University Press, 2009); on child slaves from Madagascar from the late eighteenth-century forward, see Gwen Campbell, "Children and Bondage in Imperial Madagascar , ca 1792–1898," in *Child Slaves in the Modern World*, ed., Gwyn Campbell (Athens: Ohio University Press, 2011), 37–63.
40 Petition of Louis Aisbignon dit Thrace, documents of 5 September 1764 and 1 March 1765, Z-1d-132, AN.
41 Petition of Joseph Pellement, 25 July 1765, Z-1d-132, AN.
42 Petition of Favory, 29 May 1765, Z-1d-133, AN.
43 Mémoire touchant l'affranchissement des esclaves par le Sieur Chevalier Delarue, religieux à Saint-Germain des Prés (1716), COL C6/5, ANOM, Aix-en-Provence.
44 On Petitjean, see MS 12193, Arch. Bastille. In admiralty papers, see declaration by Barthélemy-Jacques Gruel, 5 May 1762, Z-1d-139, AN. On Gruel's activities as a slave trader, see Bertrand Guillet, *La Marie-Séraphique: navire négrier* (Nantes: Musée d'histoire de Nantes, 2009).

45 Antoine Boucher, "Mémoire d'Antoine Boucher sur l'île de Bourbon," *Recueil trimestriel de documents inédits pour servir à l'histoire des Mascareignes françaises*, 9ᵉ année, no. 4 (January–March 1941): 279–355.

46 On slave narrative, see Christian Dahl, "Unfreedom and the Crises of Witnessing, a Republican Perspective on the African American Slave Narratives," in *To be Unfree: Republicanism and Unfreedom in History, Literature, and Philosophy*, eds., Christian Dahl and T. A. Nexö (Bielefeld: Transcript Verlag, 2014), 213–228; Pier M. Larson, "Horrid Journeying: Narratives of Enslavement and the Global African Diaspora," *Journal of World History* 19, no. 4 (2008): 431–464; Nolan Bennett, "To Narrate and Denounce: Frederick Douglass and the Politics of Personal Narrative," *Political Theory* 44, no. 2 (2016): 240–264; and Natalie Zemon Davis, "Decentering History: Local Stories and Cultural Crossings in a Global World," *History and Theory* 50, no. 2 (2011): 188–202.

47 Werner Sollors, ed., *The Interesting Narrative of the Life of Olaudah Equiano, or Gustavus Vassa, the African, Written by Himself* [1789], Norton Critical Editions (New York: W.W. Norton and Company, 2001). In this essay, I follow the African historian Paul Lovejoy's counsel that we refer to the author of *The Interesting Narrative* as Gustavus Vassa and not by the African name that appears in the title of *The Interesting Narrative*; according to Lovejoy, he never used Equiano in life. Lovejoy, nonetheless, rejects the suggestion that Vassa was born in the New World and insists on his African birth. See Paul E. Lovejoy, "Olaudah Equiano or Gustavus Vassa: What's in a Name?" In *Igbo in the Atlantic World: African origins and diasporic destinations*, eds., Toyin Falola and Raphael Chijioke Njoku (Bloomington: Indiana University Press, 2016), 199–217. Of Vassa's perhaps imaginary African past, see Vincent Caretta, *Equiano, the African: Biography of a Self-Made Man* (New York: Penguin Books, 2006). On Vassa's wartime experience, see Shaun Regan, "Olaudah Equiano and the Seven Years' War: Slavery, Service, and the Sea," in *The Culture of the Seven Years' War*, eds., Shaun Regan and Frans De Bruyn (Toronto: University of Toronto Press, 2014), 235–256.

48 Autorisation Diaquoy, Femme Ledoux, 12 May 1780, Minutes (1780), Parc Civil, Châtelet de Paris, Y/5069/A, AN.

49 Denis Roughol Valdeyron, *Recherche sur l'absence en droit français: travaux et recherches de la Faculté du Droit et des Sciences économiques de Paris* (Paris: PUF, 1970), 9.

9 "I Know I Have to Work"

The Moral Economy of Labor among Enslaved Women in Berbice, 1819–1834

Trevor Burnard

Not long ago, when we wrote about slaves, we imagined them to be male. A pioneering book on slave demography in Jamaica published in 1977 was titled *Searching for the Invisible Man* without much worry about how gendered such a title was.[1] Succeeding decades saw gender become a more significant category of historical analysis in the historiography of West Indian slavery.[2] This chapter is a modest contribution to this welcome development of writing about slavery with due attention to women and to gender. It provides empirical information on the lives of enslaved women living in the British West Indian colony of Berbice. This colony was, from 1831, a part of the larger colony of British Guiana, on the northeastern littoral of South America.[3] It relies on an extraordinarily rich set of sources that allows us to hear the enslaved speak—the Fiscals' Records as preserved in the National Archives in London—for the years between 1819 and the early 1830s. These were years when British officials believed that slavery was capable of being ameliorated (or improved without being terminated) through legislative fiat and imperial will. It was only after 1831 that Britons started to concentrate on immediate emancipation, achieved in 1834.[4]

Hearing West Indian slaves speak is very difficult.[5] Most were illiterate and left no written records. All were poor, without the means to make their voices heard, let alone count, within an imperial society increasingly concerned with countering the immorality of slavery while not destroying British Caribbean prosperity.[6] If we pay close attention to what these sources say, how they said it and the context in which they made complaints, then in the rare cases where slave voices are heard we can catch a glimpse of what James C. Scott calls the "private transcript" of the views of the oppressed.[7] We might, if we listen hard enough, start to hear what enslaved persons said to each other when their masters were not around or when representatives of the state did not monitor or judge their words. Laura, for example, was aggrieved in 1823 that she was not allowed the liberty to take her child "at her breast" to the field where she could "nurse her child in a proper manner." She was righteously indignant about the injuries done to her when she was punished for leaving the field to attend to her very young child. She declared that "she brought this child with great pain into life, it being of a weak constitution," meaning that the child "requires of course maternal attendance; and she is not allowed to provide fully for the same." Laura was successful in her claim, the Fiscal declaring that he "on all occasions recommends every possible lenity and accommodation be shown to women in a state of pregnancy or nursing children."[8]

The Fiscal's records of Berbice, 1819–1834, were records created by official authorities as part of a governmental judicial process.[9] They are deficient in many ways and need to be interpreted with care, bearing in mind that ultimately, as Mary Turner asserts, the principal role of the Fiscal (and after 1826, the Protector of Slaves), was to "mediate conflict in the best interest of slave property owners, sparing the manager legal prosecution and reinforcing where possible the attorney's authority."[10] Turner tends to think that the Fiscal, himself a slave owner and member of the planting class, was particularly biased toward masters and against slaves. Nevertheless, it is clear, not least from the hostility that many planters evinced toward the Fiscal, that the Fiscal was, by the standards of white men in authority in the Caribbean, at least prepared to hear slaves' complaints with some degree of impartiality. As she concedes, "the slaves' right to lay grievances before a high-ranking, salaried official legitimized and, arguably, gave added value to their estate-based struggles."[11]

In short, the Fiscal's records, used with care, provide a rich and close to unparalleled source of evidence about the contours of slave experience in a late developing British plantation society. They give us a good guide to the moral economy of enslaved people: what they considered their rights; what they thought they owed their owners in terms of work and respect; what they thought owners in turn were duty-bound to give them; and what actions they thought so egregious that they would walk long distances to put forward their concerns to the Fiscal. This set of records gives us a rare entrée into the world of enslaved people in Berbice in the second and third decades of the nineteenth century. It introduces us to their hopes and fears, and to the constraints and opportunities that they faced.[12]

Plantation work was not gender-neutral. Although planters quickly overcame European prejudices about the inappropriateness of forcing women to do hard physical labor (concepts like 'the gentler sex' had little relevance in the plantation economy), they never took the next step, which was to consider women suitable for all roles on the plantation, including being drivers or tradespeople.[13] Consequently, the clear majority of women worked as ordinary field hands, with only a small number of women being domestics or nurses. Field work was very onerous and female field hands were subjected to an incredibly harsh and health-destroying work regime.[14] Their gender gave them little respite. Indeed, they were probably worked even harder than were men. Certainly, little gender differentiation existed in the most burdensome areas of agricultural work. On sugar and cotton plantations, women were employed in heavy field tasks, including the onerous, monotonous and dangerous tasks of planting, manuring, harvesting and processing, as well as unskilled jobs around sugar mills. Planters had little reason to deviate from the practice of putting most women to work in the field. The feminization of field labor, which was particularly pronounced in the last decades of West Indian slavery, advanced rather than retarded productivity rates on a plantation. Bridget Brereton concludes that "as the sugar regime consolidated its grip, women slaves found that most of their time and energy was absorbed in gang labor, to the detriment of their health, their fertility and their opportunities to gain status and income from non-plantation work."[15]

What did slaves want when they came before the Fiscal? Planters were suspicious of their intentions. They thought that slaves were overly solicitous of their rights and that they used the complaint process in front of the Fiscal or Protector in a calculating fashion, shaming managers or overseers they thought disagreeable or harsh. Alexander McDonnell, an experienced manager in Demerara, argued both points in a book written in 1824 intended to defend planters against abolitionist attacks from William Wilberforce. McDonnell insisted that "no class of persons are more alive to their own rights than the slave population of this country." He believed that they brought complaints to the Fiscal for the most trivial reasons, with most "only brought forward by some of the ignorant of the slaves, who have been urged on by the more artful and vicious, for the purpose of forwarding their own private designs." Those designs included getting rid of masters they did not like and undermining the order of slave communities from within.[16]

McDonnell was right about the reasoning behind why slaves brought issues that bothered them to the Fiscal or Protector, even if he was not correct about slave motivations and intentions. He thought they complained incessantly about trivial matters and went to the Fiscal whenever they felt aggrieved, meaning that managers were forced continuously to defend their actions. Enslaved people, however, do not seem to have thought their grievances trivial. McDonnell thought slaves owed masters blind obedience and assumed that masters knew it was in their material interests to treat slaves properly. Enslaved people were not so trusting. They accepted certain realities about enslavement—one suspects mainly because they had little choice but to agree. Those realities included the rights of owners to own them and to force them to do work for them. But they believed that slavery was not a question of blind obedience to masters. They saw slavery as a reciprocal relationship, albeit one in which enslaved people had few significant weapons and where masters held most of the trump cards. Masters may have seen enslaved people as slaves; slaves saw themselves more as peasants, with rights and obligations resulting from their condition.

West Indian slaves, as Sidney Mintz and Douglas Hall argued in a seminal essay over half a century ago, were petty producers wedded to an ideology of protopeasant capitalist accumulation. They were intensely conservative in outlook; more concerned about hanging onto what they had rather than trying to enact visionary schemes of improvement that had little chance of success.[17] Moreover, like many workers in protoindustrial settings, including the members of the English working class whose mores E.P. Thompson memorably chronicled over fifty years ago, enslaved people believed that there was a moral economy of slavery. In that moral economy, workers and masters had rights, duties and reciprocal obligations that amounted to an unwritten contract, an invisible text that made clear what each side could expect from the other. Slaves were insistent, as McDonnell intuited, on being able to go to court when they were aggrieved because they saw the Fiscal not as their friend (as McDonnell thought they saw him) but as the closest thing that existed in Berbice society to an independent regulator who could enforce through law the moral economy of work and society that they believed in.[18] The British state shared slaves' views, at least after the establishment of the Office of Protector of Slaves in 1826. The Protector's role was to show enslaved people "a firm conviction among them that their rights will be strenuously defended, and their just complaints promptly addressed" so that they would become "accustomed to looking to the Law for security" and encouraged to "value the relation in which they stood to the State." The new office was instituted soon after the Demerara revolt of 1823, precisely because managers could not be trusted to hold to their side of the bargain in offering protection for slave "rights."[19]

Emilia Viotti da Costa provides a concise and beautiful summary of what slaves felt they were entitled to in the moral economy of slavery in Berbice and Demerara-Essequibo. She notes that "slaves expected to perform a 'reasonable amount of work,' to be defined according to customary rules and adjusted to the strength and competence of individual workers." They believed they should get food and clothing, have some access to both land and free time and to be assisted when ill or old. Women had special expectations, including the right to nurse their children and to be able to look after them when ill. Men expected that their control over womenfolk be recognized. All these expectations, da Costa argues, were part of the "public transcript" of slavery, using the phrase made popular by James C. Scott. Da Costa concludes, in phrases akin to the biblical injunction of do unto others as one would have done unto oneself, "all slaves should perform according to their abilities and all should be provided according to their needs. And whenever this norm was violated and the implicit 'contract' broken, they felt entitled to protest." She also noted that there was probably a "hidden transcript," such as a desire for freedom, and the ability to form and determine the conduct of families, that enslaved people did not admit in public but which was part of what they believed was "their right to live according to their own rules of decency and respect." Occasionally, the "hidden transcript" became the "public transcript" when rules changed. After 1825, for example, the British government decreed that women were not to be flogged. Enslaved people quickly started complaining to the Fiscal when women were flogged after that date.[20]

Slaves were worked very hard, especially after the end of the slave trade when labor exploitation intensified. The primary reason for the hard driving of enslaved people was due to the management structure of Berbice plantations, in which owners were absent and managers were under contract. Managers were rewarded by getting commissions of between two and ten percent of an estate's production and thus had every incentive to make short-term decisions to accelerate production at almost any cost. Consequently, they were relentless in their demands on slaves and severe in their punishments, confident that if profits from plantations remained high that their employers would turn a blind eye to any managerial indiscretions. The result was that enslaved women faced almost intolerable work demands. Whenever they were finished with one job, they were required to do another. If planters had no work for slaves, they rented them out to other planters who needed labor. Enslaved women rented for hire did not have the privileges of resident enslaved people but had all the obligations. Managers, determined to increase productivity and hence profitability by any means possible to maximize their own as well as their employers' income, were convinced that enslaved people were lazy and recalcitrant. They often claimed that enslaved people just pretended that they could not complete the tasks they were given, that they deliberately slowed down when annoyed at being asked to do anything, and were careless in how they did their tasks and in how they cared for plantation property. As McDonnell whined, "If slaves are curtailed in the least, either by mistake or design, of the time allowed them for breakfast or dinner, or made to work at improper hours, or punished on trivial occasions, they do not fail to make complaint of it, and are redressed accordingly." McDonnell was certain that the Fiscal was overly solicitous of slave rights and that the office itself was a tool of ignorant abolitionism, determined to undermine planter authority.[21]

Few enslaved women would have agreed with McDonnell, as they knew that the Fiscal and then the Protector of Slaves seldom supported them in their concerns against managers who imposed unreasonable demands. Complaints against managers were a large proportion of the enslaved women's irritations. Enslaved women often came to the Fiscal specifically to complain about hard driving managers whom they thought exploited them and who violated common understandings of what managers could demand and what enslaved people could be expected to do.

A good example of this was a complaint from November 17, 1823 from ten female slaves belonging to the plantation De Resolutie. Felice, "speaking for the rest," outlined the issues at hand, which was that the manager was overworking them and was going back on an understanding the women had with their owner, the governor of Berbice. She claimed that when her master purchased them he gave them a "tax," or task, which was to weed and cleanse one-hundred trees, and that "with this [they] were satisfied." Ziemine testified that they had great relations with their master, noting she "is content and happy when her master comes, who talks and laughs with me." But, Felice argued, the manager of De Resolutie "says this is no work," and that he would not give the slaves task work but instead made them each look after three rows of trees (180 trees in total) which was more work than they could do in the ordinary working week. Felice claimed that "[they] are made to do it on Sunday" against regulations and were locked up in the stocks when they complained.

Ziemine amplified these statements. She argued, in a statement that was probably intended to appeal to a Fiscal who saw himself on the same level as the governor, that "the governor is too good, he minds us as if we were children." The manager, Ziemine claimed, was cruel and calculating, deciding that "he cannot flog us, because that can be seen, but he will punish us with work" and that he will work pregnant women as hard as anyone else on the plantation because "he does not come to mind children." Consequently, the women complaining were forced to work harder than was allowed, knowing that if they left the field when the bell was rung but with rows of trees unfinished, that they would be punished. There is no notation as to whether this complaint was accepted or not, but the women's comments are evidence of how managers were prepared to disobey colony legislation and their master's commands to maximize production.[22]

A more chilling case was that of Roosje from Plantation L'Esperance, who complained to the Fiscal on 10 June 1819 that she had been worked when pregnant. She was ordered to sort coffee beans in the logie and when she argued that she could not stoop to sort she was directed to pick coffee on her knees. Because her tally was low, the driver, Sondag, was sent to whip her "with the whip doubled," which was a means of increasing the pain of a flogging. Sondag commented that Roosje was heavily pregnant but the manager commanded him to flog her "till the blood flies out." He confirmed that these were the words used by the manager. Roosje felt ill after the flogging but when examined by a doctor the next day was declared fit to work. On the Sunday evening, five months pregnant, she miscarried. It was a painful process and the midwife had to rip the child from her. Roosje noted that "the child was dead, one eye was out, the arm broken, and a stripe visible over its head." These injuries could only have occurred, she argued, because the whip had been used, illegally, in a doubled form. J.H. Enhuys, the plantation doctor, attended Roosje but, Roosje claimed, was very insensitive, not seeing what Roosje called the "child: who was buried by the assistance of female slaves." In his evidence, Enhuys confirmed his insensitivity, remarking that "many women miscarry from not taking exercise, and contracting lazy habits." He felt Roosje was one such lazy slave, Hearing of Roosje's child's death, he enquired about "the afterbirth" and was re-assured it had been dealt with. In this case, the injustice done to Roosje was clear enough that the Fiscal ordered that the complaint should be heard in the court of criminal justice—a court that allowed white people to be fined for misdemeanors.[23]

The centrality of work to the experience of enslaved women and the extent to which disputes over work formed the basis of argument on estates is seen in the punishment records of the colony. In 1827–1828, women were punished 3,173 times in the colony, of which 1,756 punishments (55.3 percent) were for "bad work." Another 161 punishments were for "refusing to work," 148 were for "disobedience," 258 for insolence or insubordination and ninety-four were for "absenting from work." In sum, 2,417 punishments (76.2 percent of all offences) were work related. In a four-month period in 1830–1831, similar patterns pertained, with 855 of 1,406 offences (60.8 percent) being for deficiencies connected to work. Men, of course, were just as likely as women to be punished for poor work or "idleness or laziness" (and much more likely to be punished for "neglect of duty"). The one area where women were punished more often than men was in the category "not coming to work on time" where 106 received punishments to fifty-eight men. The same ratio of women punished for coming to work late also occurred in 1832 when 279 women received punishment for this offense, compared to 108 men.[24] One suspects that the reason so many women could not get to work on time was that they had other duties associated with their roles as wives and mothers which made it hard to meet work demands. John Lean estimates that sixty-one percent of complaints to the Fiscal were about work. Perhaps just as unsurprisingly, managers were even more concerned about how enslaved people worked than were slaves. In 1827–1828, 76.9 percent of all punishments of both men and women were for managerial dissatisfaction for how men and women did their work.[25]

One reason for the differences in percentage between enslaved people complaining about work and managers punishing for work related issues was that the Fiscal was noticeably unreceptive to slave work complaints. When they complained about not being given their allotted allowances of food or sought redress for their quarters, and most especially with interference in their private economic activity, the Fiscal often granted them their requests. In some cases managerial interference constituted the grounds of the complaint, such as the case of Rossetta on plantation

Beerenstein who complained that though the manager, Mr. Deussen, kept "a considerable quantity of stock" he did not allow the slaves to do so, "killing whatever he finds."[26] Conversely, slaves got little joy from the Fiscal when they complained about the amount of work they were required to do or about being put to jobs they did not like or which were beyond their skills.[27]

The best results they got was complaining about working on Sundays. Being worked on Sunday was a clear breach of slave regulations and was an issue on which the Fiscal knew that abolitionists took a keen interest. On occasion, the desire by the Fiscal to make sure that slaves did what they were told ran up against their determination to make sure enslaved people did not work on Sundays. On October 14, 1822, Sally, from Plantation Sandvort, complained that she was forced by the manager to wash coffee on the previous day, which was a Sunday. When she refused, she was flogged. The manager noted that she gave "insolence" to him and to the driver, Nicholas. He commented that "there was 3,000 pounds of coffee in the house liable to be injured by lying without washing" and that is why he asked Sally to work on a day specified for rest. The Fiscal hedged his decision. He accepted that the coffee needed to be washed that morning and reprimanded Sally for not obeying an order that needed to be complied with. But he was worried about the precedent of allowing Sunday work. He threatened the manager that "if it ever could be proved in future that he punished one of the negroes under his charge on a Sunday, he would be prosecuted before the honourable Court of Criminal Justice."[28]

Slaves in Berbice shared many of the same issues over work that were common throughout the Caribbean and which affected all enslaved people. Slaves everywhere were forced to work long hours in unsatisfying work, especially in sugar production, without either enough food to provide their necessary energy needs or else the spare time to devote to other activities except plantation work. What was different in Berbice was that enslaved people did not work set hours, as had been common in older British Caribbean slave societies in the eighteenth century, but worked according to a task-work system, in which slaves were given specified tasks measured in terms of distance, area, or volume.[29]

Tasks were meant to equate to the number of hours worked in a day, defined as beginning at 6 am and finishing between 2 and 3 pm, though often planters inflated tasks so that enslaved people worked until 6 pm, meaning they had relatively little time to cultivate their own provision grounds. There was generally a two-hour break between 11 am and 1 pm. The break was a double-edged sword. As Mary Turner explains, 11 am often was the start of what she called the "11 o'clock flog." Managers, especially new ones wanting to increase productivity, surveyed what enslaved people had done at work half way through the work day and if less than half the task had been completed they would order slaves to be flogged for poor work. Notionally, task work was meant to be beneficial to those slaves who displayed good work habits. It rewarded the industrious with free time and penalized the lazy with having to work longer. In practice, as Turner notes, "it allowed managers to set tasks which filled the regular working day and then measure and punish shortfalls without necessarily taking into account weather and soil conditions which affected the quality of labor needed."[30]

What enslaved people had to do varied a great deal, but in Demerara slaves were expected to do 500 yards of weeding and molding, or two-feet-wide trenching. In Berbice, slaves on coffee estates were expected to clean ninety to hundred coffee trees. Task work did not suit some occupations, notably watchmen, fishermen, or domestics, who worked according to set hours. The hours worked were meant to decline after 1823 through legislation introduced banning work on Sundays and allowing slaves to attend markets on Saturdays. It is difficult to know whether there was much decline in work hours in Berbice after 1823—statements from slaves to the Fiscal suggest that many planters and managers ignored legislative restrictions on how many hours enslaved people worked. The nature of the climate in Berbice, for example, aggravated slaves' work hours on sugar estates because cropping could extend throughout the year rather than being confined to January through June. Berbice slaves cropped for longer than six months, especially after the introduction of steam-powered mills and improved boiling techniques. No figures have been compiled for the hours worked for Berbice slaves, but the hours worked before the 1826 amelioration reforms were undoubtedly onerous, probably closer to the 4,000 hours of work per annum estimated for Jamaican slaves in the early nineteenth century rather than the 3,200 hours that Barbadian slaves worked. Barry Higman notes that West Indian slaves worked longer than British factory workers in 1830 (2,900 hours) and rural slaves in antebellum America (3,000 hours). He notes that "the slaves with the longest annual work times also performed the heaviest tasks, worked the longest continuous spells, and most often had to produce their own food outside the time spent in estate labor."[31]

The amount of work to be done on plantations was set by custom, but custom was often in the eye of the beholder in a relatively recently settled colony full of freshly arrived Africans. Task work, in short, was an area of constant negotiation between managers and workers. In part, as Da Costa points out, tasking was impossible because there were so many variations in individual abilities, the nature of the soil, the stage of growth of plantation products and weather conditions affecting the amount of work that women could be expected to achieve in a specified time. McDonnell went into detail about what enslaved people could or could not do. If a woman was asked to weed and mold young canes—a light but dangerous and tedious task usually assigned to women—sometimes they could do one-eighth of an acre a day and sometimes one-ninth. If they were assigned to carry "megass" (the fibrous residue left after the extraction of sugar from sugar cane) the amount they could carry depended on variables such as whether the logie (storage building) was close or far away from where the cane was ground. Women were given smaller picking quotas than men—they were expected to gin thirty pounds of cotton a day compared to males' fifty pounds. But managers, many inexperienced, were unpredictable in how much work they gave to enslaved people, often not adjusting for gender, let alone age or sickness.[32]

Other confrontations between enslaved people and managers concerned "rights" that enslaved people thought they had, not just to food and cloth allowances but to the products of their gardens and their animals. Enslaved people also felt that they should not be assigned to do things they were not trained to do. The Fiscal was resolutely unsympathetic to these issues. What slaves were most concerned about were violations of customary norms or "rights," whether it was over labor performance, allowances or medical assistance. A typical example of women being concerned about unfairness came in 1829 when five women belonging to plantation Le Repentir but working on plantation La Pénitence complained that their task to take megass from the mill to the logie was too difficult and meant they worked all the time without time to eat. When asked to do the task a third day in a row, they refused, claiming that others should do it "as it was the custom that those who carried megass should, after doing that duty for two days running" be excused from doing it again because, they claimed, carrying megass was the hardest job on a sugar estate.[33]

In this case, very unusually, their manager was punished. The manager and the overseer were called to give evidence, and each supported the other in claiming that the women had to be assigned to take away the megass for a third day because otherwise the machinery would be damaged. But the engineer on the estate admitted that though he thought the women had caused the mill to seize up because the megass had begun to accumulate, that they had no chance of doing the job properly. The engineer admitted that "the megass comes from the mill too fast; it is a large mill; while I looked after them and hurried them, they worked as fast as they could; but I do not know if they did so when I turned away." The Protector of Slaves decided that the manager had acted against regulations about slave management put in place after 1826 and fined him 200 guilders for each slave, or 1,000 guilders in total. That was not an inconsiderable sum—£71—but was the lowest penalty stipulated by the regulations.[34]

The best testimony regarding task work in the Fiscal's and Protector of Slave's records is the complaint by Carolina from Plantation Everton on 26 November 1830 against her manager, Thomas Edgelow. She gave lengthy evidence to the Protector, including a considerable back story about how she had been given a task to do weeding with another woman and then was asked to do the task alone. When Carolina complained, according to her testimony, the manager told her to "shut her mouth." Later, he called her a "damned bitch" when she looked at him in what he considered to be an insolent manner, leading her to snipe that "are people not to look any more?" She compounded her problems on Everton by telling Edgelow that while she was willing to take the punishment (being put in stocks) she insisted that she "had done no harm." Her fellow slave, Grace, confirmed that "Carolina did not leave her work and did not use insolent language." The Fiscal refused to hear the evidence from the other witness, Rose, because she was Carolina's daughter. Edgelow, however, talked at length about Carolina's "insolence" and how she gave him "the grossest abuse, telling me she would make me repent as soon as she came from the dark-house," where she had been confined. Edgelow was convinced there was a conspiracy among enslaved women to reduce their workload "so that he was compelled to have the greater part of them alternately confined within the public stocks." The Protector agreed that such a "combination" existed and that Carolina was the "principal" villain because her husband, the driver, had been "broken by the present manager, who has not been long on the estate." He dismissed the case and reprimanded Carolina severely.[35]

Much of the work that enslaved people did remained unchanged over time, notably the heavy demands of working in plantation agriculture. Throughout the period under study enslaved people worked very hard in unsatisfying jobs under extremely trying conditions. Indeed, to an extent conditions worsened over time, as improved management techniques and increased mechanization led managers and owners to push slaves harder to improve productivity and profits. But the nature of slave work also changed over time, notably in response to imperial pressure from the mid-1820s because of abolitionist agitation. As Mary Turner argues, the imperial government began in this period to dismantle the most reprehensible aspects of the slave labor system that had existed for 150 years in the British Caribbean, with better regulated work place discipline, greater recognition of customary rights and more oversight of how managers and owners treated enslaved people. This oversight was performed by a Protector of Slaves, who was empowered to act in the interests of slaves more than had been the case with the office of the Fiscal, whom the Protector largely replaced as someone to whom enslaved people could complain.[36] In Berbice, the significant piece of legislation came in October 1826 with the passing of a new set of slave laws called the Amelioration Act. This was enacted in the teeth of planter legislation and only after the colonial secretary of state, Lord Bathurst, had given an ultimatum to the Berbice Council to either pass a satisfactory slave law ordinance or to have a proclamation enforcing the amelioration laws on them whether they liked it or not. The Berbice Council folded in the face of such high-level imperial intervention, though their capitulation was bitterly resented by many resident planters.[37]

The Amelioration Act, or the Berbice Slave Code, initiated far-reaching reforms in Berbice work practices. Some of these reforms were administrative, such as the replacement of the Fiscal, who acted in his capacity of arbitrator over slavery only part-time, with a full time Protector of Slaves, alongside a raft of assistant protectors of slaves in newly created districts based on divisions established in the eighteenth century by the previous owners, Dutch, of the colony. These men had a more active role in regulating slave work conditions than did the Fiscal, being enjoined to visit estates in person to make sure that the Slave Code was being enforced. That active role was important because, as David Power, the new Protector of Slaves, commented to Bathurst, it would go against the "uniform experience of mankind" to expect that "legislation so novel and so opposed to the ordinary prepossessions of those upon whose instrumentality its efficiency mainly depended" would work just by promulgation.[38] A more active establishment ensued, with the number of cases dealt with by the Protector of Slaves almost doubling from the days of the Fiscal with more owners and managers referred to criminal courts. This increase in cases reflects, in part, increased attention from government to making planters deal properly with enslaved people. But it also indicates that enslaved people were increasingly prepared to challenge planter prerogatives. As Governor Basil D'Urban of Demerara wrote to Governor General John Murray of Berbice in April 1830, "nothing can be more keenly observant than the slaves are of that [which] affects their interests."[39]

The new code had several important clauses affecting the labor conditions of slaves. It limited the use of the whip, especially in the field. It eliminated the ability of planters to carry a whip in the field, meaning that slaves could no longer be whipped while they were at work or during the 11 o'clock break. Women could no longer be flogged but instead were placed in solitary confinement and in the public stocks as punishments. Women could also be punished through enforced wearing of handcuffs, distinctive dress or lightweight collars. One result of the new regulations was that fewer slaves, especially fewer men, complained about how they were punished compared to before 1826. Turner argues that the new laws had a significant impact on the intensity of workplace punishments, even if the number of punishments—now revealed through an insistence that every plantation keep a record of them—was extraordinarily high.[40]

In addition, the Slave Code mandated the customary expectations for enslaved work hours in legislation. The standard work period was twelve-hour days, six days a week, with some exceptions for special circumstances, the most important being work needed for the "preservation of crops." It was the latter caveat that justified managers forcing enslaved women to carry megass out of the mill house so that engines were not required to stop. Moreover, the 1826 code ruled that if slaves in sugar production worked overtime they would get paid in cash. Turner notes that "making wages for slaves a legal requirement in certain circumstances precisely paralleled the abolition of flogging for women and both innovations planted a marker pointing the way to replacing an archaic with a modern system of labour exaction."[41]

The effects of the implementation of the 1826 Slave Code can be seen in some of the complaints brought before the Protector of Slaves in which enslaved women moved toward collective action, intended to defend customary rights and the moral economy of work laborers, rather than concentrating on trying to find remedies for individual grievances. For example, eighteen women at Plantation Overyssel went on strike in 1830 and refused to begin weeding a space-defined task that the driver measured out claiming they would do "no more than in Mr. Downer's time." Downer was their previous owner. They claimed that they were protecting customary expectations of workload. Protector Power visited the estate and interviewed the women, as well as the manager and driver. As was invariably the case when disputes occurred between slaves and managers about the extent of work to be done by enslaved people, Power sided with the manager in his claim that the task work could be done in seven hours' work a day. Unusually, however, the striking women did not accept the Protector's decision and continued to protest. It led Power to lock up fourteen of the women in the darkroom under threat of losing their Christmas privileges. He also, for the only time in the cases that have survived from the Fiscal and Protector's records, sent four women to work on the innovation in punishment introduced into Berbice after 1826, the treadmill, a device that required those sentenced to it to stride on steps for long periods of time. His harsh treatment of these women achieved its purpose: the women completed the task they had been allocated; the threat of losing Christmas privileges was withdrawn; and the four women sentenced to work on the treadmill gave Power an apology for their conduct. Power had succeeded in crushing what he considered a conspiracy or "collaboration" intended to reduce workloads. But what was significant was less that the conspiracy to keep workloads within limits was defeated than that women had absorbed the tenets of the 1826 Slave Code, especially that slave workloads had been regularized.[42] The many post-1826 cases noted above indicate that managers continued to mistreat enslaved women and continued to fail to recognize that they were not just involved in production but also in reproduction, as Laura, cited above, had made abundantly clear.

Slave narratives and slave testimony are usable sources for understanding slave experience if we recognize the conditions of their creation and the limitations of how they might be used. The literary theorist Nicole Aljoe has provided a useful overview of how we might look at textual representations of British West Indian slave experiences. The standard complaint about slave narratives is that every West Indian slave narrative is mediated in some way, either by a white editor, transcriber or translator and that each therefore is a collaborative text. Scholars writing on West Indian texts who are familiar with American slave narratives tend to take the view, common in work on self-authored American slave narratives, that they are autobiographies in which a highly individuated self is explained and asserted. It makes scholars wary of the extent to which slave testimony, such as that found in Berbice court proceedings, can be used. The types of sources we have available that purport to describe West Indian slavery are hybrid and polyvocal. It is difficult for a single voice, especially the voice of an illiterate slave, to emerge from the cacophony of voices involved in the production of the fragmentary evidence we have available. For some critics these multiple voices prove an insuperable problem, meaning that "the slave's voice does not yet control the imaginative forms which her personal history assumes in print."[43]

But, Aljoe insists, just because we cannot recover the historical individual through the fragments available to us does not mean that the narratives need to be discarded. As Aljoe argues, "calling the slave's dictation 'a mere body of data' from which the editor spins out another story seems woefully inadequate" and, it might be added, contrary to Mikhail Bahktin's instructive insights into how language cannot be owned by just one person and is always mediated in an active process of expropriation.[44] It may be that the collaborative necessities that were involved in creating slave testimonies "violate the very notion of a singular, autonomous author." Nevertheless, they are all we have as evidence and if read sensitively (with what Aljoe calls "a method of strategic reading and critical hearing") then the testimonies embedded in the Fiscal's records allow us to recuperate a little bit of the slave's perspective. Sometimes we can even hear them speak.

Notes

1 Michael Craton, *Searching for the Invisible Man: Slaves and Plantation Life in Jamaica* (Cambridge, MA: Harvard University Press, 1978).

2 Joan Scott, "Gender: A Useful Category of Historical Analysis," *American Historical Review* 91, 5 (Dec., 1986): 1053–1075. For an extensive bibliography of recent woks on gender in British Caribbean history, see Marisa Fuentes, "Power and Historical Figuring: Rachel Pringle Polgreen's Troubled Archive," *Gender & History* 22, 3 (Nov., 2010): 564–584.

3 Demerara was the bigger and more dynamic, senior partner to Berbice. Donald Wood, "Berbice and the Unification of British Guiana, 1831," in *Imperialism, the State and the Third World*, ed., Michael Twaddle (London: British Academic Press, 1992), 67–79.

4 Bridget Brereton, "Family Strategies, Gender, and the Shift to Wage Labor in the British Caribbean," in *Gender and Slave Emancipation in the Atlantic World*, eds., Pamela Scully and Diana Paton (Durham: Duke University Press, 2005), 143–161.

5 The slave narratives drawn on for this study are dictated testimony and thus are the spoken rather than the written word. Charles T. Davis and Henry Louis Gates, eds., *The Slave's Narrative* (New York: Oxford University Press, 1985), xii; Joan Anim-Addo, "Sister Goose's Testimony: African-Caribbean Women's Nineteenth-Century Testimony," *Women: A Cultural Review* 15, 1 (2004): 35–57. Robert Stepto reminds us that "in their most elementary form, slave narratives are full of other voices, which are frequently just as responsible for articulating a narrative's tale and strategy" as the enslaved person's voice. Robert B. Stepto, *From Behind the Veil: A Study of Afro-American Narrative*, 2nd ed. (Chicago, IL: Chicago University Press, 1991), 256.

6 J. R. Oldfield, *Transatlantic Abolitionism in the Age of Revolution: An International History of Anti-Slavery, c.1787–1820* (Cambridge: Cambridge University Press, 2013). For a succinct analysis of slaveholders' ideological assumptions, see Alvin Thompson, "'Happy-Happy Slaves!:' Slavery as a Superior State to Freedom," *Journal of Caribbean History* 29, 1 (1995): 93–119.

7 James C. Scott, *Domination and the Arts of Resistance: Hidden Transcripts* (New Haven, CT: Yale University Press, 1990).

8 Fiscals' Reports. Part 1, 1819–1823. C.O. 116/138/appendix 17–18, National Archives, UK.

9 For these records, see Trevor Burnard and John Lean, "Hearing Slave Voices: The Fiscal's Reports of Berbice and Demerara-Essequebo," *Archives* 27 (2002): 37–50.

10 Mary Turner, "The 11 O'clock Flog: Women, Work and Labour Law in the British Caribbean," *Slavery & Abolition* 20, 1 (1999): 45.

11 Ibid., 41.

12 A similar exploration of such sources has been made in, John Edwin Mason, *Social Death and Resurrection: Slavery and Emancipation in South Africa* (Charlottesville: University of Virginia Press, 2003).

13 Jennifer L. Morgan, *Laboring Women: Reproduction and Gender in New World Slavery* (Philadelphia: University of Pennsylvania Press, 2011).

14 Lucille Mathurin Mair, "Women Field Workers in Jamaica during Slavery," in *Slavery, Freedom and Gender: The Dynamics of Caribbean Society*, ed., Brian L. Moore (Kingston: University of West Indian Press, 2001)' 183–196.

15 Bridget Brereton, "Searching for the Invisible Women," *Slavery & Abolition* 13, 1 (1992): 89.

16 Alexander McDonnell, *Considerations on Negro Slavery, with Authentic Reports, Illustrative of the Actual Condition of the Negroes in Demerara*, 2nd ed. (London, 1825).

17 Douglas Hall and Sidney Mintz, *The Origins of the Jamaica Internal Marketing System*, Yale University Publications in Anthropology (New Haven, CT: Yale University Press, 1960).

18 E. P. Thompson, "The Moral Economy of the English Crowd," *Past & Present* 50, 1 (Feb., 1971): 76–136; James C. Scott, *The Moral Economy of the Peasant: Rebellion and Subsistence in Southeast Asia* (New Haven, CT: Yale University Press, 1977); Sidney Mintz, "Was the Plantation Slave a Proletarian?," *Review* 2 (1978): 81–98; and Mintz, "Slavery and the Rise of Peasantry," *Historical Reflections* 6, 2 (1979): 215–242.

19 Trevor Burnard, "A Voice for Slaves: The Office of the Fiscal in Berbice and the Beginnings of Protection in the British Empire," *Pacific Historical Review* 87, 1 (Winter, 2018): 30–53.

20 Emilia Viotti da Costa, *Crowns of Glory, Tears of Blood: The Demerara Slave Rebellion of 1823* (New York and Oxford: Oxford University Press, 1997), 73–74.

21 McDonnell, *Considerations*, 153 and Da Costa, *Crowns of Glory*, 58–60.

22 *Further Papers relating to Slaves in the West Indies (Demerara and Berbice)* (London: House of Commons, 1825), 66.

23 Fiscals' Reports. Part 1, 1819–1823. C.O. 116/138/appendix 15–16.

24 Fiscals' Reports. Berbice, Reports of protectors of slaves, 1827–1828. C.O. 116/144.38–40; Fiscals' Reports. Berbice, Reports of protectors of slaves, 1832. C.O. 116/150/11–12.

25 J. H. Lean, "The Secret Lives of Slaves: Berbice, 1819–1827" (unpublished PhD dissertation, University of Canterbury, 2002), 59, 61.

26 Fiscals' Reports. Part 1, November 15, 1820–. C.O. 116/138/.

27 Lean, "Secret Lives of Slaves," 72–73.

28 Fiscals' Reports. Part 1, 1822. C.O. 116/138/133.

29 B. W. Higman, *Slave Populations of the British Caribbean, 1807–1834* (Baltimore, MD: Johns Hopkins University Press, 1984), 179 and Justin Roberts, *Slavery and the Enlightenment in the British Atlantic, 1750–1807* (Cambridge: Cambridge University Press, 2013).

30 Turner, "The 11 O'Clock Flog," 43.

31 Higman, *Slave Populations of the British Caribbean*, 179–188 (quotation 188).

32 McDonnell, *Considerations*, 147–167.

33 15 July 1829. C.O. 116/145/232.

34 Da Costa, *Crowns of Glory*, 67–68.

35 Fiscals' Reports. Berbice, Reports of protectors of slaves, 1830. C.O. 116/147/131–133.

36 Turner, "11 O'Clock Flog," 2.

37 Neville Thompson, *Earl Bathurst and the British Empire 1762–1834* (Leeds: Leo Cooper, 1999), 177.

38 Parliamentary Papers, House of Commons, 1829 XXV 335, Protector of Slaves Reports, David Power to Henry Beard 1 September 1828, British Library.

39 Eric Williams, ed., *Documents on British West Indies History, 1807–1833* (Trinidad: Trinidad Publishing Company, 1953), 189.

40 Turner, "11 O'Clock Flog," 50.

41 Ibid., 53.

42 Parliamentary Papers, House of Commons, Abstract of Offences, March 29, 1830.

43 Stepto, *From Behind the Veil*, 262.

44 Mikhail Bakhtin, *The Dialogic Imagination: Four Essays*, ed., Michael Holquist (Austin: University of Texas Press, 1981), 299–300.

10 "An Anomalous Population"

Recaptive Narratives in Antigua and the British Colonial Archive, 1807–1828

Anita Rupprecht

The state of African captives freed in the early nineteenth century from illegal slaving ships in the Caribbean shocked British naval officers who had given chase. As their accounts of these captured slave vessels began to filter back to England, members of the antislavery group, the African Institution became concerned that there might be a necessity for "further legislative provision for the care and disposal of captured Negroes." Their minds were focused by a letter from Commander Anthony Maitland of HMS *Pique*. Maitland requested advice about how he might recover £2,500 that he had been forced to pay for urgent maintenance and medical assistance when his ship had captured the Spanish brig *Carlos*.[1] The *Carlos,* "partly American property," had sailed with an extraordinarily large crew of eighty-two men from Havana to Bonny in September 1813. The 190-ton vessel had then made a return transatlantic crossing with 512 African men, women, and children crammed aboard. On entering the Caribbean and being pursued by the *Pique,* eighty captives had been jettisoned into the sea and left to drown. Once captured, Maitland was so alarmed at the "bones coming through the skin" of those remaining aboard that he ordered for the *Carlos* to put into the nearest island, Guadeloupe. The captives were disembarked, a 'large house' was secured for them, and medical assistance was procured. Despite his strenuous efforts, Maitland reported that a further fifteen or sixteen Africans died. Over a fifth of the captive cargo had perished by the time the ship finally arrived in Antigua in early 1814 where it was condemned as an illegal slaver by the Vice Admiralty Court.[2]

When the Abolition Act came into existence in 1808, and naval ships were tasked with intercepting those flouting the new law, the precise fate of the Africans who were taken from illegal slavers had not been fully considered, especially in relation to those who would be intercepted toward the end of the Middle Passage in the Caribbean rather than as it began off the coasts of West Africa. After the triumph of the passing of the 1807 Act, abolitionists turned their attention to the prospects for the development of Sierra Leone. It was not until around the time that the *Carlos* was captured that they began to think seriously about the human consequences of the new laws as they were being enacted in the slaveholding colonies of the British Caribbean. Whether those who had survived this unspeakable crossing understood what had happened to them, or, indeed, what was going to happen next, especially when reembarked aboard the same ship where the horror had occurred, is unanswerable. When the *Carlos* was condemned in March, 1814, the Abolition Act legislated for two possible fates for the rescued captives. Many were immediately enlisted into the British military forces. Others were indentured for a maximum of fourteen years.

In 1821, the British government dispatched a Royal Commission to the Caribbean to assess the 'state' and 'condition' of the 'Captured Negroes'. Over the next five years, three successive sets of Royal Commissioners traveled to eight sugar colonies and accounted for some 3,500 African born and Creole peoples who had fallen under the abolition laws, most of whom had been enlisted or indentured.[3] The ninety men and women who had been aboard the *Carlos,* and who had been indentured were among the 285 people who appeared before the Commission in Antigua. The term 'Captured Negroes' referred not only to those who had been disembarked from illegal transatlantic slave ships but to enslaved peoples who had been otherwise seized in the colonies and condemned under laws that prohibited the intercolonial transfer of enslaved peoples across the Caribbean itself. As a result, the official inquiry also swept up enslaved peoples who had been 'seized' from vessels not necessarily dedicated to transatlantic slaving or who had been apprehended along island harbor fronts by local Customs officials. Often dislocated and stranded, this 'condemned' group of people included 'free' African sailors, enslaved women who had been smuggled between colonies as 'legitimate' domestic servants, enslaved Creole artisans illegally sold away, and covertly transported enslaved children.[4]

Most significantly, unlike any other metropolitan inquiry associated with the Caribbean colonies in the last decades of slavery, the commissioners interviewed the diverse subjects of their investigation. This chapter examines the archival remains of the Commission's inquiry in Antigua in order to recover some of the individual stories behind the abolition policies. As the commissioners used the original legal documents produced at the time of the Vice Admiralty court trials to organize the schedules of interviews, it is possible to trace individual trajectories of many of the recaptives from ship to shore, and beyond, in ways that the anonymizing and commodifying records of the legal transatlantic slave trade simply obliterated. Most significantly, the documents provide an extremely rare, if highly mediated, glimpse into the ways in which the 'condemned' peoples responded to the circumstances of their rescue from enslavement. Many historians have noted that the recaptive, or later 'Liberated,' Africans, who arrived in the Americas in this manner, lived lives little better than if they had been enslaved, implying that the difference between slavery and 'apprenticeship' was in name only. As many of these testimonies reveal, however, the legal difference certainly mattered to the recaptives themselves. They understood the specific terms of their indenture—that they be taught a trade and provided with an allowance, clothes, food, and shelter—very clearly.

A young "Ebo" man, who had survived the Middle Passage aboard the *Carlos*, and who had been named Owen Robinson was indentured to learn the craft of masonry.[5] At the time of the inquiry, Robinson had no masonry skills. He was living with his employer's impoverished widow and could "take care of a horse." His 'wife', another African apprentice, supplied his food. His words were interpreted on the page as, "[h]is mistress is good to him when she has it in her power."[6] A shipmate of Robinson's, an "Ebo" woman named Fanny Buller, had been indentured as a house servant. She said that she was 'married' to an enslaved man. She reported that she "received no allowance of money, food or clothes, either for herself or children." Buller's attempts to find an independent means of income for herself had evidently threatened her employer who, she stated, would not allow her to work for her own support. She complained about the lack of food to George Wyke, Antigua's Collector of Customs, who was the Crown official legally responsible for the indenturing of rescued Africans and their welfare. He had done nothing to alleviate the servant's distress other than suggesting that she and her employer go before a magistrate. Buller told the commissioners that her mistress had refused the suggestion and that she had not felt able to petition the magistrate herself. The multiple contradictions produced by the policy of indentureship—as a method of colonial 'improvement'—at the heart of a society dependent on slave relations register in Robinson and Buller's scant testimonies. Like most of the apprentices, they were living by means that had little to do with the legal terms of their unenslaved, though bonded, labor. Kinship connections were vital to their ability to survive. Robinson and Buller both said they were married though neither marriage had been legally recognized. Indeed, the commissioners commented on "the familiar use made of the terms *husband* and *wife* by the apprenticed Africans, at the examinations" while lamenting that these marriages were hardly ever legally sanctioned.[7]

The number and nature of ways in which people came before the Commission were varied. Between 1811 and 1814, Antigua's Vice Admiralty Court condemned—along with the *Carlos*—another two Spanish slaving vessels and two French vessels, carrying 1,388 captive Africans. Eighty-six people died before they could be apprenticed or enlisted. Prior to the end of the Napoleonic wars, most recaptives taken to Sierra Leone or seized in the West Indies were enlisted into the army or navy to fight for the British imperial interest. As Antigua was garrisoned,

1,017 African men who were condemned on the island were enlisted into the army or the navy and subsequently moved to other sites around the Caribbean. A further 233 women joined the men as wives or were indentured as servants to the families of officers. Commissioner Patrick Gannon thought these Africans were least in need of "anxious investigation" given that it "was not to be apprehended that persons, who had lived for some time as British soldiers, would afterwards lose sight of their privileges, or relapse into a state of slavery."[8] In the end, the Commission was recalled before any attempt was made to trace the new military recruits and their families. In 1820, a French brig, *Louise*, with a further 128 captives aboard, was seized while in port by customs officials after having allegedly mistaken Antigua for Guadeloupe. Sixty women from the *Louise* were sent to Trinidad almost immediately at the request of Trinidad's Governor Woodford, while the remaining 29 women and 39 men were indentured in Antigua.[9]

While visiting the island, the Commission accounted for 285 recaptive servants. They should not be viewed as representative of all recaptives who disembarked in the Caribbean in the early days of suppression even though the possible life-ways prescribed by the Abolition Acts were narrowly delimited. Indeed, it is clear that no generalized and consistent policy existed. The social, economic, political, and environmental contexts of the islands in which recaptives were disembarked shaped their individual experiences, while the subsequent trajectories of each African were as contingent on the particular colonial prejudices and visions of the individuals who were charged with their oversight as they were on the numbers and intensity of arrivals. Moreover, the Commission documents do not account accurately for everyone disembarked on the islands that they visited. The metropolitan officers were working with incomplete or corrupt documents and defensive and often hostile local officials, and their task remained unfinished when they were recalled to London.

Prior to the arrival of the Commission, only two of Antigua's large plantation owners had taken any interest in employing the recaptives. Nearly everyone had been indentured in white colonial households in urban St. John's as Owen Robinson and Fanny Buller had been. As an abolitionist measure, the 1808 Orders in Council had prohibited fieldwork for the apprentices and stipulated the gendered division of labor. Some effort had been made to indenture men to local coopers, masons, carpenters, cobblers, tailors, blacksmiths, and barbers to that purpose. Others were employed along the docks, or as fishermen and mariners. Nevertheless, many men were laboring at menial tasks or in domestic contexts. Women were employed as domestics, seamstresses, cooks, and washerwomen, or they were sent out by their masters and mistresses to huckster dry goods around the town and the surrounding countryside. Many were without official indenture papers.

Colonial merchant families employed groups of apprentices in their households and hired them out. For example, Mrs. Kentish, a member of a prominent merchant family in St John accounted for ten apprentices who were all employed as house servants and hucksters. John Trott, another merchant, employed six men as porters, sailors, and coopers.[10] Miss Clarke apprenticed four women as domestics, seamstresses and hucksters. Local Customs officers also employed large groups of apprentices as cooks, washers, grooms, and hucksters. Others were indentured individually to local professionals, shopkeepers, tradesmen, artisans and among the free colored petty-trading population.[11]

As the enquiry unfolded, it became apparent that George Wyke, Antigua's Collector of Customs, had not fulfilled his duty in strict accordance with abolitionist policy. The commissioners found that employers of a large number of recaptive men and women had not been required to sign official indenture contracts and that many recaptives were no longer working for their original employers. Exposed, Wyke defended himself by explaining that he had not been able to find colonials who were prepared to employ Africans because of their insubordinate behavior. He had, however, acquired for himself and his fellow customs officers, a large "irregular gang" of recaptive Africans who were put to work in and around the busy Customs House. Given that the Collector received funds from Britain for their maintenance—known as the "King's Allowance"—this was a lucrative enterprise. The unindentured Africans labored at the backbreaking work of ramming sugar into hogsheads; unloading, reloading, and stacking goods and stores; repairing boats and tackle or in general maintenance and cleaning the yard. When not working, they slept in what was known locally as the "African Hospital." This motley group, who were effectively homeless, arbitrarily exploited, and at the mercy of their dubious legal status, became something of a lightning rod for the visiting metropolitans insofar as it was perceived that they represented the abuses to which the Abolition laws could be put. That the Collector of Customs—the official responsible for organizing all enlistments and indentureships and for their subsequent oversight—was at the center of this questionable arrangement became a key concern shaping the Commission's investigation in Antigua.

Approaching these Commission documents for what they might reveal about the recaptives' own views about their experiences is fraught with difficulties.[12] Read from above and as an abstract historical source, the archive certainly accords with Ann Laura Stoler's description of commissions as constituting a particular "genre of documentation" that employs "certain writerly conventions, techniques of persuasion, and forms of evidence that combined a passion for numbers with the numbing bulk of repetition and the pathos of vignette."[13] As a form of colonial power, this commission provides a vivid reminder of the ways in which imperial interest, instrumental economic imperative and racialized fantasies framed official visions of appropriate colonial subjectivity during the years leading up to emancipation. As an enactment of imperial surveillance, it was produced in situ. The documents supply a veneer of colonial order and precision evinced by multiple "schedules," tables, calibrations, and taxonomies. Brushed against their grain, and read together with the copious peripheral documentation, it is possible to unpick the multiple temporalities of the Commission's practice, and the ways in which its presence on the islands disturbed the complacencies of colonial power. It quickly becomes clear that the indentured Africans knew that the enquiry represented metropolitan abolitionism and that tensions existed between their employers, local authorities, and the visiting officers of the Crown. They were, it seems, largely reticent about speaking out in the formal enquiry, however, they exploited the fault lines and divisions that opened up around its edges finding other spaces in which to tell their stories and to seek redress.

The formal enquiry was held in the Long Street courthouse in St John. The imposing stone neoclassical building, used for Council and Assembly meetings, charity balls, official dinners and lectures, as well as for the prosecution of colonial law, added to the disciplinary atmosphere of its investigative proceedings.[14] While it is not clear exactly how the hearings were organized spatially, the commission secretary collated the original information in tabular form on extremely large sheets of paper that were folded carefully into ledgers. A long table would certainly have been required to support these large and unwieldy manuscripts, and for the clerk to be able to move across them as he filled in each column. Prior to its arrival in Antigua, the commission had descended into such acrimony about how best to conduct the enquiry that one commissioner had resigned and the other had been recalled. One of the central issues had been whether masters or mistresses and their servants should be in the enquiry room at the same time when each were questioned.[15] Antigua's commissioners were aware of this earlier dispute and they were careful to describe clearly their method of proceeding in their report. They decided that the examinations of apprentices and their masters or mistresses should be conducted entirely separately. Apprentices were to be called before the Commission first. Once their examination was completed, the masters or mistresses would be questioned.[16]

Names, age, and distinguishing features, or "marks"; residence; and the "trade or business" to which the servants had been indentured were noted on the schedules. For example, Mary Ann Damer, who had been aboard the *Carlos,* is recorded as being five feet and six inches tall, twenty-four years old, and "marked on the temples." Her indenture was to "Mrs Seares; after to Mrs. Hill." Her employment is registered as "domestic." The date of her first indenture is listed as 8 May 1814, the second is "to Mrs. Hill for fourteen years from 9 June 1814." In the column entitled "If the trade be taught according to the indenture; and if not, how the Apprentice is employed," the record simply states, "Can wash."[17] Damer is recorded as having no children. In the column "Religion," Damer's entry notes that she had been "baptised," "instructed" and that she worshipped at the Moravian church. In the next column, "Party's Account as to Present Condition, Local Attachments &c.", Damer's interview is transcribed thus:

> Mrs. Seares did not treat her well; Collector removed her, and placed her with Mrs. Hill; was removed from Mrs. Hill in consequence of quarrelling with the other servants; was then for a few months with Mr Chipchase; is now in the Collector's hospital, and receives the allowance.

Once the interview had been completed, apprentices were asked to leave the room so that the master or mistresses or "another person qualified to answer" could be questioned out of earshot of the servants. They were invited to give an "opinion" on the "ability" and "character" of each African as to "the proficiency, habits of industry, general conduct" and the "prospect of future employment." These findings are transcribed in columns immediately adjacent to the "Party's Account." In the column entitled "Account given by other Persons," the record for Damer reads,

> The Collector says this is a turbulent person. Mr. Hill, son of Mrs. Hill, says that Damer was so riotous, it became necessary to remove her; another was substituted from the hospital.

As if it were the arithmetical sum of the two statements by master and servant, the next column in the schedule is entitled "Actual Condition of the Apprentice; proficiency in Trade, Craft, or Employment; Character, &c. as collected by this Inquiry." Damer is described here as "Healthy and active; can wash, but is quarrelsome." This judgment is followed by a final statement in the last column, "What probability of finding Maintenance at the expiration of the Apprenticeship." Mary Ann Damer's apparent "turbulence" clearly threatened her future prospects. The entry reads, "Could maintain herself if kept employed."[18] The formal organization of the records confirms the "state and condition" of the Africans as matter of demeaning calculation and moralizing judgment. As Mary Ann Damer's entry indicates, most of the exchanges were flattened into third person fragments of prose. Cumulatively, they add up to little more than truncated narratives denoting either colonial improvement or failure.

However, the scraps of testimony contain multiple gaps, expressive contradictions and imprecisions as well as moments of unpredicted elaboration or subsequent qualification. At times, they are evocative of the moment in which they were heard, infused with the drama of the enquiry. In this sense, as Arlette Farge has suggested in another context, they can be interpreted as "events" that register as "fragmented expression[s] of being … still ringing with the echoes of the world that surrounded [them]." At times, verbatim snatches of speech were transcribed. These moments vividly dramatize the everyday and arbitrary violence of the slave colony.[19] For example, Caroline Dewar, indentured as a domestic to James Norman, one of the Customs House officers, was in the middle of an ongoing and violent dispute with her employer when she appeared in the Court House. Her furious testimony begins thus:

> Went out on Wednesday morning … to buy a dog's worth of bread for her breakfast; was not long out; when she returned, her mistress had locked the gate, and complaining that she (Caroline) had been too long away, was fretted, and took up a sweeping brush and struck her. Mrs Norman's daughter (a girl 15 or 16 years of age) came up to her and saying, 'you must not chat with my mother', boxed her on the face. Mr. Norman was sent for to the Customs House; when he came home, he asked her what was the matter? Hollo! Hollo! He struck her on the face; locked her up; let her out on Thursday morning … [20]

While most of the testimonies are certainly shaped by the limited and limiting questions the colonial administrators put to the indentured Africans, as Caroline Dewar's protest makes clear, the indentured servants did not simply answer the questions put to them. They turned the inquiry into a forum for ongoing protest or festering complaint. Tyrone Juxton, for example, was indentured to a local blacksmith, Samuel Nelson. Unlike most recaptives, he had been taught blacksmithing, but he had not always received the weekly "allowance" to which recaptives were entitled. He reported that he had complained to the Collector and that the 'irregularity' had been rectified. Juxton, however, also argued that he possessed specialist skills demanding appropriate recompense by noting in the enquiry that he was dissatisfied with its paltry amount.[21]

His shipmate, Jack Gibbs, had been indentured to a butcher but reported that he worked "hauling fish, cutting wood and burning lime," and that he was hungry. He complained that he received "nine "little" pints of corn meal a week" and was only allowed to keep "small fish for himself." His master thought he was "rather idle." John Roberts, indentured to a cooper, stated that he was sick. He simply said he was "treated as well by his master as any other apprentice is." Thomas Trott, the cooper, did not believe that Roberts was ill. He thought he was "very sullen and insolent."[22] George Jolter, indentured first to a school-master and then to a sailor, knew something of barrel-making although he was laboring in obtaining ship's ballast and "moving houses." He stressed the relentlessness of his work by saying that he labored "even on Sundays." He stated that he received no clothes, no lodging, and an irregular allowance. When asked how he survived, he suggested networks of solidarity when he said that "his countrymen assist him."[23]

Sam Touchwood was indentured to a mason, James Baker. He was furious with his lot, saying that he was given one suit of clothes at Christmas, and "old clothes at other times." He said that he had a "bad master and leads a dog's life" and that Baker "punished him for trifling causes." He had had enough of the menial domestic work, stating that he had walked away from Baker a week earlier. It is not possible to tell whether the Commission's presence in the town had emboldened Touchwood to leave but Touchwood said of Baker that "he tied him up and licked him but does not know how many lashes; says he licked him with the belt of a gun last Saturday and turned him off; has not returned to his master since."

The Bakers clearly thought that some gratitude was warranted from Touchwood. Their statement also registers the time it had taken to mend, if at all, from the physical suffering that the Africans had endured aboard the *Carlos*. In their defense, they began by saying that it had taken Touchwood two years to recover from his ordeal aboard the ship, during which time they had paid for his medical attention, and placed him under the Moravians "for his discipline." They linked this arrangement to their perception that he had "behaved himself very well for a few years." Touchwood's current alleged "insolence" and "disrespect" was put down to the "evil example of his fellow apprentice, George." Mr. Baker said that he could not recall having exercised any "systematic cruelty upon him" although he admitted that when Touchwood's "ill behaviour" had "merited correction," a switch or a cane had been used. Apparently, Touchwood had repeatedly fought back.[24]

The *Carlos* had sailed from the Bight of Biafra and on disembarkation in Antigua, everyone was given the ethnic label of either "Moco" or "Ebo" except for Peter Rumford who had been about fifteen when he arrived and Wellington who had been sixteen. They were too young to enlist into the army and so were indentured. Peter Rumford was "tattooed on the breast," twenty-three years old and his "nation" is recorded as "Guinea." Wellington was a year older than Peter, carried "no marks," and is recorded as "Coromantyn." The stories of these two men highlight the fact that some of the indentured servants sought redress by petitioning the commissioners privately outside of its formal hours, and away from the Court House.

Peter Rumford was aggrieved. He had first been put to work as a sailor—without indenture—under a man named Nowell. Nowell formally bonded him only after having extracted his labor for four years, and then for the maximum term of fourteen years. Nowell had passed him onto Grenion, a struggling shoemaker in St. John who professed to be Nowell's attorney. While Peter said that he "understood" shoe-making, he was working as Grenion's house servant. Pressed about his current situation, Peter simply said that he was "well treated" and "satisfied." Grenion, on the other hand, reported that Peter was a "very indifferent character" who was "addicted to drink," "light-fingered," and no good at shoemaking. The record reveals little beyond the unhappy arrangement except that Peter was facing eighteen years of bonded servitude rather than the maximum of fourteen years and that Grenion was exploiting Peter's labor to which he had no legal right at all. It is impossible to know whether it was Peter's experience at the enquiry that changed the frame of reference by which he conceived of his position but, a few days later, he called at the commissioners' private lodgings and complained that Grenion had mistreated him. He told his story while holding a piece of broken chain in his hand as proof. A hastily written letter from George Wyke, the Collector of Customs—no doubt to cover the fact that he had turned a blind eye to the irregularity of Peter's employment—illuminates something of the violence of Peter's world that he had withheld in the enquiry room earlier. Apparently, Peter had stolen a pig and had been rescued from a severe beating in the street by Grenion's slaves. Peter then drowned his sorrows in a bottle of rum that Grenion later took from him and smashed. Peter's response was to be "very abusive to his master" after which Grenion had chained him to a stool in his room. The Commissioner was unimpressed by the story of Peter's humiliation but even more unimpressed by Grenion's slandering of Peter's character in the enquiry room. Gannon later noted that the courtroom investigation had not revealed that "laborious services were performed by this African" and that his "master was of that class of employers who are accustomed to profit by the labours of their Apprentices more than the latter receive of benefit in care or improvement."[25]

As the above narrative makes clear, Commissioner Gannon's sympathy with the Africans fluctuated according to the social and class position of their employers. Grenion was a poor white artisan whose violence was deemed to be excessive. When the relatively wealthy colonial customs officers—who had clearly monopolized the labor supplied by the rescued Africans without formally indenturing them—were under scrutiny, he was less ready to criticize their beatings and less amenable to listening to the plight of the servants.

This class prejudice was evident when Wellington called privately at the Commissioners' lodgings to complain that he had been beaten. He had originally been indentured to a cabinet-maker who had put him to "keep sheep." Accused of killing one of the animals, he was taken to the cage in St. John to receive "thirty-nine lashes," the maximum arbitrary punishment for an enslaved person. A magistrate had intervened, ruling the flogging illegal, and "ordered him to be set at liberty." Having been released from his bond, Wellington was homeless so he returned to the

Custom House where many of his fellow Africans lived. He was not rein-
dentured but was passed between Customs officers and put to work as a
house servant and groom. Wellington complained about this treatment
and stated hopefully that he "could do some work as a joiner and thinks
he could support himself in that way."

Later at the Commissioners' lodgings, Wellington, and a fellow apprentice, said they had been flogged with a "cat," and displayed marks
on their backs as proof. They "declared their intention not to return
anymore to the service of this master." A "cat" is shorthand for a "cat
o'nine tails" which was a multistranded whip used to inflict severe physical punishment. As a result of this private petition, Gannon noted that
the customs officer had acted "improperly" but that Wellington's insubordinate disposition was such that it could provoke the anger a "man of
good nature but warm temper" as he believed the respected official to
be. As far as he was concerned, the official's violence was "unbecoming"
but understandable. Despite their efforts, the Commissioner did nothing
to remove the two Africans even though there were no official indentures
in place.

If the testimonies of the African men are marked by the violence they
endured and by the fact that they had, by and large, not been appropri-
ately apprenticed to learn trades that might have enabled them to become
self-sustaining, the testimonies of the African women who had been
aboard the *Carlos* speak to the restrictions of domestic service against
which many of them struggled. They also reveal more about the kinship
and other social relations of the African apprentices. Servants and mistresses had different ideas about what regular 'payment' meant in relation to domestic service. Moreover, in the eyes of colonial employers, the
kinship connections forged by the African women further complicated
the issue of who exactly should pay for their financial support. As a
result, Mary Copley, a washer, married to another apprentice, said that
she was "allowed food sometimes from her mistress's table" but that she
did not receive her allowance regularly.[26] Mary Ann Bacon, a domestic,
reported that she had never received an allowance, even at Christmas,
and that her clothes allowance had been stopped once she had married
an enslaved man named Prince.[27] Sylvia Cotton, who had given birth to
three children, two of whom were dead by the time she was interviewed,
was cooking in Mrs. Slaney's household with no indenture to prove her
bond. She reported that she received no regular allowance but that she
was occasionally paid "2 dogs or half a bit" when she washed the house.
Mrs. Slaney thought Sylvia was a "very dissatisfied woman" and noted
that she paid her "in money" or "fed her from the table" only when she
worked regularly.

Confined within the intimate spaces of the household, apprenticed female domestics had limited opportunities to escape the oversight of their
employers, and like their enslaved counterparts they were particularly

vulnerable to sexual and physical abuse. Clara Corbet managed to extract herself from her first employer but only after seven years "owing to having been ill-treated and refused her weekly allowance."[28] Juliet Cook, seventeen years old, and whose facial "marks" were apparently so remarkable they are noted twice, had married an enslaved man who provided her support. She lost four children in infancy. Apprenticed at English Harbour as a washer and cook, Juliet reported that her first master had "treated her very ill" and that her "present master and mistress have chastised her very severely, once or twice."

Employment in huckstering afforded apprenticed women greater mobility and provided women with opportunities to earn extra money. In the enquiry, the indentured women registered their preference for forms of labor and living that enabled them to inhabit spaces beyond the surveillance of their employers. Eliza Carr, employed to make beds and sell dry goods, spent her money hiring her own room in town. Maria Bowyer was indentured to a Mr. Sheriff who lived across the island at Fort Byam. He paid her no allowance so she resided in town with her husband, and earned her living by washing clothes. Mrs. Kentish sent out her three domestic servants to market dry goods. They were not permitted to live with their husbands, all soldiers in the First West India Regiment, but she clearly did not mind that the men contributed to their wives' subsistence.

The urban laboring positions allocated to the indentured African men and women carried some social prestige among enslaved and freed peoples in Antigua, as elsewhere in the Caribbean. These gendered occupations were also subject to customary hierarchies of skin color such that skilled artisanal work and domestic laboring positions were usually occupied by those with mixed ancestry. That newly arrived, unacculturated Africans should occupy these positions, and that they were not enslaved, threatened long-established racial, gender, and class hierarchies and boundaries that were reflected in relationships among African descended people.[29]

The testimonies given by Mary Byam and her mistress, Charlotte Kalman, a free colored woman, register the complicated racial hierarchies of island life, and the social tensions that developed among St. John's enslaved and free population as they accommodated the indentured Africans. Mary was indentured as a washer but she said that she had received no allowance for the last few months, and that she was living with her husband, a soldier, in the local barracks. In front of the Commissioners she stated boldly that she "prefers living with her man ... to remaining in her mistress's service." Charlotte Kalman clearly saw Mary's 'preference' as a form of inappropriate defiance and ingratitude. She said that she had complained to the Collector several times that Mary was "idle," that she could not "keep her at home, though she had a room to stop in" and finally, that she could wash but requires "a driver" to "keep her to her business." Kalman's use of the term 'driver' carried derogatory racial, social, and cultural connotations, suggesting that Mary was only fit to be treated as if she was enslaved. It is a reminder of the multiple prejudices endured by the newly arrived Africans who were widely perceived to be backward and certainly not fit to be working in the house. Nonetheless, the multivocal nature of the archive offers a sense of a more molten landscape within which the indentured Africans lived and worked. The boundaries between peoples were not indelibly fixed by the intersections of racial and class prejudice. Nelly Bayntun was in the domestic service of the Wills, a free colored family. She was able to do very little work other than carry water. Mrs. Wills reported to the Commissioner that she took care of Nelly "more from motives of humanity, than for any service that she performs."[30]

The Commission was also tasked with enquiring into the fate of enslaved Africans and Creoles who had been otherwise seized in the colonies or condemned to the Crown because of their 'illegal' transfer between Caribbean colonies. The Commissioners found a large group of such individuals laboring among those who had arrived aboard illegal transatlantic slavers in the Collector, Wyke's, Custom House. Three skilled African sailors had been stranded in Antigua for eight months, as a result of the Abolition laws, when they appeared in front of the Commissioners. All reported that they had been seized from the British schooner *Ocean*, when it had put in for water, and that they had since been detained at the Custom House. A customs officer, Simpson (after whom one of the men had been renamed), confirmed that they had been "libelled and prosecuted as slaves" and condemned to the King by the Vice Admiralty Court but neither he nor the sailors referred directly to the circumstances under which the seizure had occurred, or to how the men came to be aboard the British ship when it departed from Senegal or whether they had, indeed, been enslaved. After their condemnation in Antigua, they had not been freed or indentured, and neither were they receiving wages. The Collector clearly recognized the labor value of all three men, and especially Pierre Farah's expert maritime knowledge and linguistic dexterity. He took Farah to crew on his own thirty-ton "fine topsail schooner," *Poetess*, aboard which he regularly entertained the island's elite planters, visitors, and dignitaries.[31] George Bliss and Robert Simpson had not caught Wyke's eye, however. They were laboring at packing and repacking hogsheads in the Custom House. Despite their release from enslavement, all three men were aggrieved, dislocated, and homesick. During their interviews before the Commission they stressed their prior freedom in West Africa, and their desire to return home. They made it clear that they had not forgotten their old lives, livelihoods, or their families.

Pierre Farrah spoke French and English fluently, and said that he had been baptized by a French clergyman. He confirmed that he was from

Senegal and, marking the distinction between his situation in Antigua and home, he said that he had been "free in his own country." In Senegal, he worked aboard one of the first steam boats that had begun plying the Senegal River as trade expanded with the French reoccupation of the region after Napoleon's defeat.[32] He stated that he wished to go back to his "mother, brother and sister" and that he would "willingly work his own passage back to Africa if he was permitted."

George Bliss, also an experienced sailor from "Guinea," said that when he arrived at the Custom House, he had been first employed aboard a drogher by "a free coloured man" during which time he had not been paid regularly. He was currently receiving an allowance from the Collector. Alongside the arduous task of repacking sugar, he was also doing the heavy work of portering. He made it clear that he disliked the work and would "prefer the life of a sailor." He also stressed that he had been "free in his own country," that he had a wife and three children there, and that he wished to return home.

Robert Simpson remembered his previous free life in Sierra Leone, explaining that he had traveled the river and creeks in his canoe "trafficking in various articles" such as rice, camwood, and palm oil. It is not clear how long he had worked aboard the *Ocean* before being seized in Antigua but he reported that he had made a voyage to England. Presumably, it was while aboard this vessel, or another, that his spoken English became "excellent." Simpson stated that, since he had been stranded in Antigua, he had been occasionally employed as crew for the Custom House boat but most of the time he was packing sugar. He stated that he "wished very much to go back to his country, Sierra Leone."[33] Despite the fact that the testimonies of these three men are frustratingly brief, they allude to the diversity of the many displacements wrought by the suppression campaign, and their impact on the lives of peoples caught up in its imperial wake. There was no official mechanism by which these men would be returned home. While it is certainly the case that other enslaved peoples successfully retraversed the Atlantic, it is probably impossible to tell what became of Farah, Simpson, and Bliss.

James Wright, described as a "Creole of Antigua," was also caught up in Wyke's Custom House gang. He had an enslaved wife and children living on an estate in the country, and was embroiled in trying to extract himself from the Collector having been subject to the blunt instrument of Abolition laws. Before the Commission he told a detailed and extraordinary story of his struggle to secure his *own* freedom under the Abolition laws that had been designed to prohibit planters and other slaveowners engaging in the local intercolonial trade. His remarkable story illustrates how knowledge regarding shifting legal lines circulated as the imperial state moved toward ending slavery in the Caribbean.[34] Wright's owner, Steele, smuggled him to Demerara for him to be sold. In the enquiry, Wright said that Steele's decision had been provoked because they "did not agree." In Demerara,

Steele arranged for a middle man named Stevenson to sell him to a carpenter, Childers, who took him to the coast. After three months working at Childers' carpenter's business, Wright told how he "escaped," traveled to George Town and "stated his case" to Governor Murray. He explained that he had been sold illegally and that he wanted to return home. Murray did not refer him to the courts but simply gave him a pass and told him to find his own passage back to Antigua. Meanwhile, Childers discovered Wright's plans, apparently took the pass from him and forwarded it to Steele. Desperate to return home, Wright risked sailing for Antigua anyway and was "immediately reclaimed by Steele."

Wright knew that Steele's opportunism was illegal and that, when discovered, it should have released him from bondage. He made sure to tell the Commission that he was "aware of his civil condition." Steele next petitioned Antigua's governor, Basil D'Urban. This time, Wright's case was brought before the Vice Admiralty Court, and Steele was forced to relinquish ownership of the carpenter. The court did not simply release Wright, however, nor did it furnish him with freedom papers. The law made no distinction between local Creoles and the Africans rescued from illegal slaving ships. He was handed over to the Collector of Customs. A few days after the verdict, Wyke left for England, so Wright went home to his wife and children, "to his own place, and worked for himself." When Wyke returned, however, he sent for Wright and insisted he live in the Custom House Hospital, and work for him as a ship's carpenter. Wright's testimony concludes with the phrases, "Would wish to work for himself" and even more pointedly, "Has no complaint to make of the Collector, but prefers his freedom, being entitled to it."

After years of struggle, Wright took to the stage provided by the Commission to tell the story of his (illegal) transportation for sale, the risk he took by escaping, his confronting of colonial authority, and then how he found a way to return to Antigua and his family. Despite being reenslaved, he knew that he was entitled to his freedom as a consequence of his owner's criminal activities and that this freedom was being withheld by Wyke.[35]

As far as the Collector was concerned, the condition of Wright's moral character overshadowed any legal rights he might claim to possess. He stated that Wright was a repeated runaway and a vagrant. He reported that, once condemned, Wright had not gone home but "taken himself off without … his knowledge or leave, and secreted himself somewhere in the country." He said that he had "ordered him to the Custom-house, to be put upon his list for support and kept from vagabondizing about the country." Wright, he claimed, was perfectly able to earn his livelihood "if he will work" but that he was "much addicted to drink."

That the commission provided a space where Wyke's colonial privilege—exemplified by his claim to know Wright's moral disposition—could be called into question is a reminder of the ways in which the inquiry disturbed the embedded inequities of the island. Moreover, Wyke knew that his struggle with Wright was being watched closely by the apprenticed Africans and he wrote to the commissioner Gannon to that effect.[36] A few days later, after his appearance at the official enquiry, Wyke attempted to exert his power over Wright again. He ordered him to oversee a group of Custom House Africans in building a boathouse. The workers had quarreled, Wright later said, "because they objected to him being placed over them," and he had walked away from the yard. Wyke finally caught up with him and imprisoned him—in irons—in the "Sick House."[37] Wright immediately complained at his ill-treatment to the Attorney General. An extensive peripheral enquiry into Wyke's unauthorized punishment ensued during which time the Custom House officers rallied to his defense. Meanwhile, the Commissioners recommended that Wright should be given a certificate of his "civil condition." Determined to resist having his authority even further traduced, Wyke did not inform Wright of this decision. He wrote to the Commissioners that he could not release Wright because a "partial liberation" of those on his 'Hospital List' would "excite great jealousy and discontent" among the rest. He claimed to be at his wits end, complaining that "the Africans on this island have become more turbulent and insolent, and unruly since the arrival of your Commission with us, than they were before," and that lately, "the Africans had positively refused to be bound out, and declared their fixed determination not to serve anyone."[38] On hearing about the dispute, Antigua's Attorney General charged the Collector, at length, with being a "despotic master" who wielded "monstrous power" over the Africans.[39] The two Commissioners did not offer their judgment on the affair. They had fallen out between themselves on account of which they were abruptly recalled to London at the end of August, 1824.[40]

There may be a good reason why this archival cache has been almost completely ignored to date. If historians tend to take account of Commissions when their outcomes are deemed to be significant then this one can certainly be classified as a failure and an embarrassment. The documents preserve an extremely rare collection of Caribbean-based recaptive testimonies, however. The Commission required hundreds of men and women to survey their circumstances from a fixed standpoint, and to deliver up scraps of detail about their lives. In this sense, they might be understood, in some senses at least, as analogous to what Carolyn Steedman terms the "enforced narratives of the self" that thousands of the poor delivered to the Poor Law Magistrates in England.[41] If this is the case, the documents tell us a good deal about the trafficking between colony and metropole in the making of modern raced and classed colonial identities, and about the ways in which they were produced by imperial ambitions to possess, and then to dispossess, recaptives with certain desired qualities and attributes.

The Commission records are not documents of slavery; rather, they record a significant moment in slavery's unraveling. The testimonies shed light on how the confrontation with abolitionist policy on the ground was shaped as much by local and immediate circumstances as by any elaborate design to help the recaptives forge new lives. As in Sierra Leone, rescue from enslavement meant forced military service or a legally ambiguous form of bonded servitude that would last long into an unknown future. Settlement in the Caribbean, prior to the ending of slavery, however, meant that recaptives had to endure a different, and complex, set of circumstances and prejudices. Yet, beyond the oppressive paternalism that came with abolitionist surveillance, and beyond the fury of the colonials who viewed their unquestioned white supremacy as under attack, Antigua's recaptive Africans developed relationships with their shipmates, found their countrymen and women, forged new connections and families and clearly understood their legal condition. Drawing meaning from the archival fragments is certainly difficult but it is possible to know that the indentured African and Creole men and women repeatedly spoke back, claiming that their labor was theirs, that they wanted their labor back, that they desired to work on their own terms, and that they desired forms of being that were excessive to, and incompatible with, the colonial terms of industry. Most generally, the testimonies shed light on the complexity of everyday struggles from below and on the ways in which they were shaped and reshaped as the imperial state began to control the direction of Caribbean labor in the run up to emancipation.

Notes

1 *Ninth Report of the Directors of the African Institution* (London: Ellerton & Henderson, 1815), 46

2 *Ninth Report*, 47; Thomas Buxton, *The African Slave Trade and Its Remedy* (London: John Murray, 1840), 109; and James Walvin, *Crossings: Africa, the Americas and the Atlantic Slave Trade* (London: Reaktion Books, 2013), 180.

3 Reports by Commissioners of Inquiry into State of Africans apprenticed in West Indies I: Papers relating to Captured Negroes, *Parliamentary Papers* [hereafter *PP*], 1825 (114), XXV.193. According to accounts laid before the British Parliament in 1821, "there appeared to be 3,207 Captured Negroes in the West Indies." The National Archives of the UK [hereafter TNA] CO 320/5. The first set of Commissioners were John Dougan and Thomas Moody, who traveled to Barbados and Tortola. In 1824, Commissioners Bowles and Gannon were appointed to go to Saint Kitts and Nevis and Antigua, and Charles Wyndham Burdett and John Kinchela were appointed to investigate the Winkel Establishment of Crown Slaves at Berbice. For the original documents of the entire Commission see TNA CO 318/82-3; CO318/85-93.

4 For key texts in the debate about the role of the intercolonial slave trade and its imbrication in the process of reform prior to emancipation see Eric Williams, "The British West Indian Slave Trade after its Abolition in 1807," *Journal of Negro History*, 27, 2 (Apr., 1942), 175–91; David Eltis, "Traffic

in Slaves between British West Indian Colonies, 1807–1833," *Economic History Review*, 25, 1 (Feb., 1972), 55–64; Seymour Drescher, "The Fragmentation of Atlantic Slavery and the British Intercolonial Slave Trade" and Hilary McD. Beckles, "'An Unfeeling Traffick': The Intercolonial Movement of Slaves in the British Caribbean, 1807–1833," in Walter Johnson, ed., *The Chattel Principle: Internal Slave Trades in the Americas* (New Haven, CT: Yale University Press, 2004), 234–274.

5 The process of recording approximations of the Africans' birth names was uneven around the Atlantic. Antigua's Vice Admiralty Court officials made no attempt to document birth names. The names by which the apprentices are identified in the commission records are new names given on arrival in the colony.

6 Papers relating to Captured Negroes: Appendix to Report on the State of Apprenticed Africans at Antigua, *PP*, 1826–1827 (553), XXX.349, "Schedules," 46–47. The original ledgers are in the National Archives CO318/81. The schedules were later printed as Parliamentary Papers. Hereafter, references are to the (identical) printed versions.

7 Papers relating to Captured Negroes, Report on the State of Apprenticed Africans at Antigua, "Mr. Gannon's Report," *Parliamentary Papers* (hereafter *PP*), 1826–1827 (355), XXII.287, 10.

8 "Mr. Gannon's Report," *PP*, 1826–1827 (355) XXII.287, 5.

9 Rosanne Marion Adderley, *"New Negroes from Africa": Slave Trade Abolition and Free African Settlement in the Nineteenth Century Caribbean* (Bloomington: Indiana University Press, 2006), 135–136.

10 "Mr. Gannon's Report," *PP*, 1826–1827 (355) XXII.287, 16–18.

11 "Mr. Gannon's Report," *PP*, 1826–1827 (355) XXII.287, 20–21.

12 The problems of approaching the archive of transatlantic slavery in an attempt to access something of the experience of those captured and reified are now well documented. An often-cited meditation on this archival (im)possibility is Saidiya Hartman's "Venus in Two Acts," *Small Axe*, 26, 2 (June 2008), 1–14. See also Marisa J. Fuentes, *Dispossessed Lives: Enslaved Women, Violence and the Colonial Archive* (Philadelphia: University of Pennsylvania Press, 2016).

13 Ann Laura Stoler, *Along the Archival Grain: Epistemic Anxieties and Colonial Common Sense* (Princeton: Princeton University Press, 2009), 142. See also Lauren Benton and Lisa Ford, eds., *Rage for Order: The British Empire and the Origins of International Law, 1800–1850* (Cambridge, MA: Harvard University Press, 2016), 56–82; Clare Anderson, *Subaltern Lives: Biographies of Colonialism in the Indian Ocean World, 1790–1920* (Cambridge: Cambridge University Press, 2012); and Oz Frankel, *States of Inquiry: Social Investigations and Print Culture in Nineteenth-Century Britain and the United States* (Baltimore, MD: Johns Hopkins University Press, 2006).

14 For a contemporary colonial description of St. John including the court house see, Fredrick William Naylor Bayley, *Four Years Residence in the West Indies: During the Years 1826, 7, 8, and 9* (London: W. Kidd, 1833), 310.

15 Anita Rupprecht, "'When He Gets among His Countrymen, They Tell Him that He is Free': Slave Trade Abolition, Indentured Africans and a Royal Commission," *Slavery & Abolition*, 33, 3 (2012), 442.

16 "Mr. Gannon's Report," *PP*, 1826–1827 (355) XXII.287, 15.

17 *PP*, 1826–1827 (553) XXII.349, "Schedules," 52.

18 *PP*, 1826–1827 (553) XXII.349, "Schedules," 53.

19 Arlette Farge, *The Allure of the Archives* (New Haven, CT: Yale University Press, 2013), 80.

20 *PP*, 1826–1827 (553) XXII.349, "Schedules," 55.

21 *PP*, 1826–1827 (553) XXII.349, "Schedules," 49.

22 *PP*, 1826–1827 (553) XXII.349, "Schedules," 42–43.

23 *PP*, 1826–1827 (553) XXII.349, "Schedules," 45.

24 *PP*, 1826–1827 (553) XXII.349, "Schedules," 47.

25 'Mr. Gannon's Report,' *PP*, 1826–1827 (355) XXII.287, 61.

26 *PP*, 1826–1827 (553) XXII.349, "Schedules," 58.

27 *PP*, 1826–1827 (553) XXII.349, "Schedules," 58.

28 *PP*, 1826–1827 (553) XXII.349, "Schedules," 69.

29 Natasha Lightfoot, *Troubling Freedom: Antigua and the Aftermath of British Emancipation* (Durham: Duke University Press, 2015), 35–46.

30 *PP*, 1826–1827 (553) XXII.349, "Schedules," 65.

31 Henry Nelson Coleridge, *Six Months in the West Indies in* 1825 (London: J. Murray, 1826), 265–274.

32 Philip Curtin, *Economic Change in Precolonial Africa: Senegambia in the Era of the Slave Trade* (Madison: University of Wisconsin Press, 1975), 128.

33 *PP*, 1826–1827 (553) XXII.349, "Schedules," 93.

34 The classic account of the ways in which knowledge circulated via the Black Atlantic is Julius C. Scott, *The Common Wind: Afro-American Currents in the Age of the Haitian Revolution* (London: Verso, 2018).

35 *PP*, 1826–1827 (553) XXII.349, "Schedules," 103.

36 George Wyke to Gannon and Bowles, June 21, 1824. TNA CO318/81.

37 James Wright, "Sworn Testimony," August 26, 1824. TNA, CO 318/81.

38 George Wyke to Gannon and Bowles, June 21, 1824. TNA CO318/81.

39 William Musgrave to Gannon and Bowles, September 14, 1824. TNA CO 318/81.

40 "Gannon's note," CO 318/81. The Africans at Antigua's Custom House continued to struggle with Wyke for years. He eventually hired a large vessel to act as a prison hulk, forced the Africans aboard, and moored it in the harbor. See "Information Received from the Island of Antigua Respecting Acts if Insubordination by Liberated Africans," *PP*, 1826 (351) XXVI.453, 3.

41 Carolyn Steedman, *Dust* (Manchester: Manchester University Press, 2001), 48.

Conclusion
Slave Testimonies: The Long View

Emily Clark

This volume accomplishes many things, freedom the greatest of them all. Not the freedom from slavery that was sought and sometimes gained by those whose testimonies unspool over the preceding pages, but the liberation of historians from the grip of the slave narrative genre of the Anglophone Atlantic and the historiographical cul de sac it spawned.

The autobiography that moves from enslavement to resistance to deliverance along a route guided by Enlightenment principles of freedom and equality has defined what a slave narrative is for so long that it is hard to see and make sense of testimonies of the enslaved that have no such storylines to offer. Cugoano, Equiano, and their literary and ideological heirs tell a story of politicization and triumph that confirms abolitionist Theodore Parker's 1853 declaration that the arc of the moral universe bends toward justice. When Martin Luther King, Jr. rescued Parker's words from obscurity in 1968 he did more than supply hope to the Civil Rights Movement. He also inspired historians who had just begun to mine classic slave narratives to write a new history of slavery in which the enslaved, like King, emerge as powerfully eloquent crusaders for the freedom of their people.[1] No wonder, then, that historians have not rushed to push beyond the heroic voices that emerge from traditional slave narratives to unearth and engage testimonies from women and men whose lives had no happy ending.

The scholars who contributed to this volume are both intrepid and brave in their willingness to grapple with material that does not fit neatly with long-standing expectations for what slave testimonies should be like. More often than not, the testimonies that we encounter in this collection were written about the enslaved, not by them. They present us only with fragments and snapshots of lives that typically ended in continued enslavement, suffering, or death. They rarely have an edifying moral to communicate or even a satisfying resolution. Some offer glimpses of how a self-conscious quest for the Enlightenment ideal of liberty evolved among enslaved people, but most reveal episodes of struggle and resistance that arose from the quotidian, the circumstantial and the contingent. Frustratingly, they seem to tell us more about the history of slavery and the perspective of the enslavers than they do about the people whose voices we want most to hear. In comparison to classic slave narratives, what we have here may seem at first blush both deficient and disappointing.

If we allow the testimonies to make a case for themselves, however, they offer one reward after another. Manon in New France and Marguerite in Louisiana did just that, in fact, breaking free of the prescriptive interrogatories of the French colonial judiciary to blurt out information solicited neither by the prosecutor nor the historian. Scholars long conditioned by the contours of the classic narrative ask questions thrown up from within the boundaries of the genre and the Anglophone Atlantic world that produced it. The sources presented in this volume, both individually and collectively, open avenues of interrogation that push those who engage them well beyond the borders of where they would have looked otherwise.

The boundaries most obviously traversed are linguistic and imperial. The classic slave narratives originated and developed in the Anglophone Atlantic. Expanding the inquiry beyond the genre immediately frees historians to consider sources produced in languages other than English. There are obviously many from which to choose, but French makes sense because it and English are the two languages that dominate the archives of North America and the Caribbean, the geographic focal points of slave historiography. On the mainland, the archives of New France and Louisiana offer a counterpoise and complement to those of the thirteen British colonies. Saint-Domingue and Martinique, both considered in this volume, are only two of the places that offer the possibility of supplying balance to a Caribbean historiography of slavery dominated by studies of the British sugar islands.

There was long an assumption shared by many historians of early continental North America that slavery under the French was not as harsh as in the British mainland colonies. While recent scholarship has quite soundly disproved this, it has also shown that the apparatus of enslavement and some aspects of the experience of the enslaved *were* different, though probably not as different as one might presume. Even the divergent archival regimes and judicial systems of the British and French Atlantic do not so much produce differences in what we learn about the experience of the enslaved who lived under them as they do differences in the register of the voices that come to us through them.

The French archival regime and judicial system were, indeed, quite different from those that produced the archives of the British Atlantic and provide a body of trial testimony that is voluminous and detailed. The essays of Dominique Rogers, Brett Rushforth, Cécile Vidal, and Sophie White, drawn from the judicial archives of the French Caribbean, New France, and Louisiana, show how much difference legal culture makes to the quality of the enslaved voices available to us through them. French law privileged testimony above all else, so its criminal procedure called for the careful, verbatim, in extenso recording of the words of the accused and all who were called as witnesses, enslaved and free. Trial transcripts were long and detailed—Jupiter's trial for burglary took fifteen days and produced over 150 pages of testimony in the records of the Superior Council of Louisiana. Much of what the enslaved said in such trials was structured by the prescribed prosecutorial interrogatories, but occasionally the witnesses interjected comments "without being asked" that render the voices, if not the thoughts, of the enslaved speakers startlingly immediate. Marguerite's sarcastic mimicry of her mistress in a New Orleans courtroom takes us aback as surely as it must have her French examiners, and we can imagine the voluble Manon exclaiming breathlessly in Montreal, "Oh my God! It wasn't me who took them ... and I don't know who might have taken them."

Such flashes of personality and passion are startling for historians used to the measured cadences of classic slave narratives, where a carefully curated repertoire of emotions is invoked to arouse the particular kind of sympathy best suited to advancing abolition. The words that Manon and Marguerite blurted out survived, however, because they upheld slavery, not because they might hasten its demise. An insubordinate outburst showed just why enslaved transgressors had to be kept in line with brutal justice. The willingness of an enslaved woman to incriminate someone who shared her bonded state offered comforting evidence that prosecution and the threat of punishment were as likely to prevent the formation of dangerous group loyalty as to promote it. It is tempting to praise the French for a legal culture that uniquely, if unthinkingly, preserved such outbursts. But, as the essays of Margaret Newell and Linford Fisher show us, the British left behind trial testimony, too. The records that preserve the proceedings involving Indian Ann, Ben, Elisha and Pardon Ned quickly demolish any essentialist claims that might be made about the superior nature of French judicial archives. While the enslaved people of New England did not have the same scope as those in the French Atlantic to craft their stories to achieve exoneration, clemency or leniency, their testimony, nonetheless, makes many details of their lives poignantly visible. Taken together, the French and British sources confirm the similarities, not the differences, in the experience and administration of slavery under two different imperial regimes.

Outbursts like Manon's and Marguerite's are tantalizing for historians who long for an aperture onto the subjectivities of the enslaved, though all the contributors to this volume know the perils of such a quest. Every word that survived long enough to be considered in the foregoing pages has been mediated to some degree. Beyond that is the problem of seeking individual consciousness in a world that was only beginning to recognize a self that was distinct from the collectives of which it was a part. Cécile Vidal rightly cautions that since "judicial archives offer a repertoire of daily interactions between people of all conditions, they call for a relational social history of slavery rather than for an impossible quest of individual subjectivity."

All the same, most of the testimonies that inform the essays in this volume offer glimpses of some of the feelings and ideas that made up a conscious self, even if the expression of that self was fragmentary and evanescent. Marguerite was not sad or resigned in the face of her mistress's suppression of her sexual expression. She was outraged and inspired to coin a brilliant simile that reveals a laser-like intelligence. When Castor defecated at the entrance to a sugar mill in Saint-Domingue, it is true that he claimed the protection and status he thought due him because his master was socially superior to the man whom the act offended. It was a claim that was, indeed, relational. Choosing to express his defiance in such a shocking way in the first place, however, gestures at a unique personality, if not an elaborated subjectivity.

The most compelling evidence that some of the enslaved experienced a sense of self comes from stories that relate attempts to escape it. Patience Boston, Joseph Quassan, Peter Rumford, and Manon disclose an acute, painful consciousness of themselves in the actions they took to suppress that awareness with alcohol. Joseph Quassan, born a Wampanoag but raised among the English, despaired when he attempted to return to his people but failed because he could not speak his native tongue. Alienated and alone, he sought escape in drink. Patience Boston set fire to her master's home three times. In her conversion narrative she described herself as a "mischievous and rebellious Servant," but what is most revelatory in her testimony is her description of her social life. Patience was part of a network of people of all races, free and bound, who drank. Drinking—and presumably numbing intoxication—was so central to Patience's life that she followed one of her enslaved drinking buddies to Maine. African Peter Rumford was indentured in Antigua in 1813, the fate of all recaptured Africans taken in the British naval dragnet that enforced the abolition of the slave trade. Peter's relationship with the shoemaker who held his indenture was fraught and he drank to drown his sorrows. It broke down completely when the shoemaker grabbed the bottle of rum from which Peter was drinking and smashed it.

A few testimonies suggest that some enslaved Africans believed that they had individual souls that were destined to be judged by the Christian God after death. The enslaved driver of Dame Romieu in eighteenth-century Saint-Domingue declared at his trial that "Since he was about to stand before God, he did not want to lie." Locked in a dungeon in Guadeloupe for twenty-two months and thinking that she would die there, Lucille asked that a priest come to her to administer last rites so that she could "die at least a Christian." And Jupiter proclaimed at his capital trial in Louisiana "that he does not fear death because he says the truth," and "gives his soul to God and his body to justice." Such declarations can certainly be understood as words carefully chosen to elicit sympathy, but in all three cases they were spoken by individuals who knew that their deaths were likely imminent and as such may reveal a belief in individual fate.

None of these examples comes close to the subjectivities delineated in classic slave narratives, where the existence of an individual soul is central to the case for freedom and abolition. That element of the genre may be what makes it difficult to detect clues about the nature of the subjectivity of the enslaved people who flit across the archival stage in the variety of testimonies gathered in this volume. Historians have been conditioned to look for evidence of the kind of self-realization that sparked a quest for individual freedom. What the archives have yielded up instead is a succession of stories about people with more ambiguous ambitions for themselves and, if they believed in them, for their immortal souls.

Among the most significant things to emerge from the essays in the aggregate is a complex sense of the chronology of the practice and experience of slavery. The corpus of classic slave narratives was produced between the last third of the eighteenth century and the outbreak of the civil war. Developed to advance the abolition of the institution, the focus of these works is on the places, processes, people and period that exemplify the institution at its strongest and most cruel. This has the effect, among other things, of offering narratives that provide no sense of change over time. The narrator experiences an evolution in both his awareness and his state, to be sure, but slavery comes across as a curiously atemporal phenomenon.

Since Peter Wood published *Black Majority,* historians have participated in dismantling the notion that slavery was monolithic and unchanging. Ira Berlin's *Many Thousands Gone* supplied a framework and a vocabulary to describe the progression from a "society with slaves" to a "slave society" that continues to inspire—and provoke—new inquiries into the evolutionary path of slavery in settings distinguished by location, geography and relationship to imperial timelines.[2] This volume adds three new analytical strands to a history of slavery sensitive to chronology. The first is a consideration of the massive enslavement of indigenous people in North America before 1700 and its relationship to the evolution of Black slavery, the second a consideration of changes in patterns of mobility, both in terms of the physical mobility of enslaved people and movement into and out of slavery. Finally, the essays render visible a shift from the concept of the moral economy of slavery as a touchstone for slave agency and resistance to the emergence and growth of Enlightenment discourse and ideas about freedom and equality which marked the birth of political consciousness.

As Margaret Newell has pointed out, before 1700 most of those who were enslaved in the Americas were people of native descent and they remained a significant proportion of the population held in bondage well into the eighteenth century. "Europeans enslaved Indians from Quebec to New Orleans, and from New England to the Carolinas," Newell observes, lest any early American historians are tempted to think that their region was the exception to this phenomenon. Africans and African descended people eventually outnumbered indigenous people among the ranks of the enslaved in North America, but in the mid-eighteenth century they constituted roughly equal numbers in New England, where there were 1,500 Africans and 1,000–1,500 Native Americans.[3] The enslaved indigenous people at the center of the essays in this volume by Linford Fisher, Margaret Newell, and Brett Rushforth lived alongside African and African descended people. Some of them formed families with them, which increasingly imperiled their own freedom and that of their children in the eighteenth century, as the legitimacy of enslaving Natives diminished nearly to the vanishing point at the same time that African birth and descent came to signify the enslaved state unless proved otherwise. The process by which any enslaved person proved her free status arguably originated in freedom petitions like Indian Ann's, which carefully traced the accidents of fortune and mobility that she claimed led to her wrongful enslavement. The narration of a biography like Indian Ann's, offering details of a birth in freedom coupled with a story of capture, enslavement, and forced migration to a distant site of bondage, may have supplied the template for the stories of capture and enslavement which became the typical starting point in classic slave narratives.

Indian slavery came first, Rushforth points out, and was the laboratory in which the legal, religious and social apparatus needed to construct and maintain slavery was worked out. The same laws and institutions erected to govern the lives of enslaved Native Americans and make race were applied to African and African descended people as they entered the bonded population. Slavery was "equally terrible whether one was of Native or African descent," he observes. The two groups shared the misery of slavery and deployed similar strategies to survive it. If we want to understand the evolution of slavery as an institution and an experience, we must study the Native diaspora as carefully as the African.

The essays that make the indigenous enslaved focal show that bridging the historiographical divide between Native and African slavery is possible, though it may prove an elusive goal in the short term, at least among historians who work and are read primarily in the United States. Black slavery and its social and economic legacies are potently central to American politics. While it is true that white supremacy is a toxic influence in the lives of both contemporary Native and African descended people, carving out a space for the indigenous in the historiography of American slavery that is commensurate with the role it played in the making of the history itself will remain a challenge. The essays of Fisher, Newell and Rushforth make an impressive start at taking it on.

The mass migrations produced by the Middle Passage and the internal slave trade of the nineteenth century are both familiar and well-studied examples of the mobility of captive and enslaved people. The essays in this volume demonstrate that there are episodes of mobility at a smaller scale that are equally valuable to gaining purchase on the multifarious nature of both the Indian and African diasporas. They also expose a different kind of mobility. The journey between freedom and slavery has generally been imagined as a linear one, from freedom to enslavement and, if one was lucky, from enslavement into permanent freedom. There were, we discover, other itineraries that were shaped by specific historical developments.

Newell and Fisher offer case studies that entered the archival record in New England but which offer especially valuable insight into the impact on indigenous slavery of Caribbean raiding and the Indian wars of the southeast. Conflicts in the Carolinas between 1701 and 1716 produced Native captives who were sold north. Paradoxically, some of them may have found themselves enslaved because of voluntary travel that took them far from their homelands on trading and other missions, putting them in the crosshairs of conflict-driven slaving activity. Indian Ann may exemplify such a case. James Spaniard's bondage in New England resulted from British slave raids in the Caribbean that conveyed captives to Charlestown for sale and export northward. Indian wars converged with privateering and piracy in the early eighteenth century to produce captives sold via the Carolinas into New England, a class loosely labeled "Spanish Indians." Specific historical circumstances pulled people like Indian Ann and James Spaniard across space and at the same time pushed them back and forth between freedom and bondage.

Miranda Spieler's exploration of freedom suits from the Paris Admiralty Court introduces us to a later historical moment that produced similar phenomena. The Seven Years' War (1756–1763) triggered a burst of mobility across and around the Atlantic for the free and enslaved alike and offered a new path to personal freedom in Metropolitan France. The war produced circumstances that brought people held in slavery to the Continent in unprecedented numbers and the Court of Admiralty in charge of regulating the enslaved in France was forced to create new law and procedures to cope with the swollen population. As it had in early eighteenth-century North America, the chaos of war introduced uncertainty into the question of who could legitimately be considered enslaved. Ultimately, proof of status lay in one's personal history, so the narration of one's life was the key component in the freedom suits brought before the court. Spieler observes that, "[N]ever before had it been possible for a person of color to obtain freedom papers in exchange for his autobiography." A rash of mobility launched by a different historical contingency in the nineteenth-century British Caribbean was to produce a similar deployment of life stories.

The end of the international slave trade and the gradual abolition of slavery introduced new vectors of both mobility and testimony for the enslaved in Britain's islands. Anita Rupprecht fruitfully mines the recaptive narratives rendered before the Royal Commission that was sent to the Caribbean to determine the condition of the African and African-descended people rescued from illegal slavers. Here, too, a quest for liberty turned on a biography that convincingly demonstrated life begun in freedom. Of course, nearly all of the women and men kidnapped into slavery to feed the transatlantic trade began their lives as free people, but the 1807 abolition changed two things. It created a novel itinerary for thousands who would otherwise have known only the awful migration that terminated in enslavement. They went from an aborted Middle Passage to an odd sort of middle ground, finding themselves indentured and apprenticed, far from home and equally far from the unambiguous free status to which many felt entitled. The decades between 1807 and 1834 also produced new vehicles for testimonies of the enslaved. The Royal Commission received those of recaptured people, who narrated poignant tales of enslavement and mistreatment in what was usually a vain attempt to regain their full freedom and a return to their homeland. Thousands who would have gone unnoticed and unheard only a decade or two earlier left traces of their voices in the archives because of a specific historic event.

The chronological and geographic range of this volume makes it possible to map two different discourses of enslaved agency and resistance across time and space, as significant for the historiographical contribution it makes as for the questions it poses for future study. The earliest of the testimonies introduce us to what Trevor Burnard calls the concept of the moral economy of slavery by which enslaved people believed their servitude was, or should be, governed. Aaron Fogleman traces the emergence of the second discourse in the last third of the eighteenth century, which revolved around the Enlightenment concepts of liberty and justice that animated the Revolutionary age. Once again, considered together, the essays collected in this volume reveal nothing so simple as a linear progression from one of these conceptual frameworks to the other. Testimonies shaped by the notion of a moral economy of slavery crossed the Revolutionary divide and thrived decades into the nineteenth century, appearing side by side with the classic slave narratives infused with Enlightenment discourse.

Cécile Vidal's vivid portrait of Jupiter reveals the operation of a moral economy of reciprocal expectations between enslaved and enslaver in 1740s Louisiana. Jupiter called out the ways that his master, Pradel, overstepped what was reasonable and just. When Jupiter was sent into town to sell produce and did not return with the amount of money his master had set as his unreasonable quota, Pradel whipped him. Jupiter included this information in his testimony because he believed—or at least hoped—that the court would recognize Pradel's transgression of the moral economy and exercise mercy in its judgement of his crime. As was to prove true in similar cases we meet in this volume, Jupiter's hopes were disappointed and he was sentenced to death. Nonetheless, his testimony makes it clear that he believed that a moral economy existed and that it was recognized, if not honored, by the enslavers. Two decades later, Marguerite's testimony in the same courtroom reveals the same expectations and sense of justice remained at work in French Louisiana, despite disappointments like Jupiter's.

Fogleman's analysis of an expanded corpus of slave narratives supplies a welcome chronological sensitivity to the history of slave testimonies. He pinpoints to the Revolutionary era the emergence of the rights discourse that was central to the classic genre. Slave narratives emerged in the 1730s, but it was only after 1770 that they employed Enlightenment ideas about liberty and equality to make their case for an end to the slave trade and slavery. Miranda Spieler's analyses of the cases brought before the Paris Admiralty Court after the Seven Years' War suggest that this ideology may have informed the laws that made space for this litigation, but it is impossible to know whether those seeking their freedom through the Admiralty Court were aware of these ideas, let alone consciously chose to invoke them. That is a feature that is restricted to the slave narratives produced in the British Atlantic.

Revolutionary activity was not the only thing that prompted the appearance of a rights discourse in slave testimonies, according to Fogleman. Christianity, which was increasingly embraced by the enslaved after the Great Awakening, as well as the eighteenth-century Muslim antislave trade jihad in Africa contributed to the appearance of a new emphasis on freedom and equality in the autobiographical slave narrative genre. An irony emerges from this observation. The only critique of the slave trade that emerged from Africa itself was the Muslim prohibition against enslaving one's coreligionists, an objection that figures in Ayuba Suleiman Diallo's 1734 narrative. Diallo remained a devout Muslim, but the African and African-descended narrators who subsequently emerged abandoned the parameters of the African-born Muslim objection to the slave trade for the universalist condemnations premised on Christian and Enlightenment principles. The limited African legacy supplied by Islam was to be eclipsed after 1770 by the religious and political ideologies that originated with the enslavers. There seem to have been no exceptions. Ibrhm Abd ar-Rahaman was born a Muslim in the late eighteenth century, but it was his conversion to Christianity that initiated his antislavery career in 1827.

The Great Awakening and the Revolution produced a fault line in the nature of the slave narrative genre. There was, however, no clear break in the deployment of the concept of a moral economy of slavery, which the essays of Dominique Rogers, Anita Rupprecht, and Trevor

Burnard demonstrate remained a prominent feature in other forms of slave testimony in the nineteenth-century. Intriguingly, unlike the explicit Enlightenment discourse that appears only in Anglophone sources, the concept of fairness in master-slave relationships emerges in both the British and French Atlantics. The cases of Jupiter and Marguerite show it at work in pre-Revolutionary Louisiana and Dominique Rogers offers several examples from the post-Revolutionary French Caribbean. When Lucille was locked in a dungeon in Guadeloupe in 1840 for a crime that she claimed she did not commit, she railed not so much about unjust accusation and punishment at the hands of her master as against his denying her the comfort of a priest when she faced death.

In the decades between the cases of Louisiana's Jupiter and Marguerite and Guadeloupe's Lucille, there were others in the French Atlantic that suggest continuity in the use of the concept by the enslaved. In late-eighteenth-century Saint-Domingue, the failure of a white man to pay an enslaved cooper for his work was widely acknowledged as unfair. More striking are cases brought in the 1770s and 1780s by groups of ten or more enslaved people in Saint-Domingue who accused their masters of abuse. These may have been inspired in part by the percolation of Enlightenment ideas, which influenced the passage of legislation in 1784 and 1785 that aimed to reduce the brutal treatment of the enslaved. Yet, as Rogers points out, it is not possible to tell if exposure to the new European discourse was what prompted the complaints. They, and the campaign for a three-day workweek that led to revolt in Saint-Pierre, could just as easily have been inspired by the long-standing moral economy concept.

It is intriguing to consider the possibility that the principles of fairness and reciprocity that limned the concept of a moral economy may have been at least partly a legacy of Africa. The origins of Enlightenment ideas were clearly European, but it is all but impossible to make the case that the other moral framework that emerges in slave testimonies was equally indebted to the West. Perhaps Louisiana's Marguerite and Janot shared, reinforced and sustained a moral paradigm from their native Congo. In Saint-Domingue, the pattern of the slave trade suggests that the agitators in Saint-Pierre and the groups that brought complaints against abusive owners were likely to have been African born. Their concepts of what was just may well have had roots in their homeland.

There can be no question but that Enlightenment ideas changed things in the British Caribbean, where they propelled the abolition of the slave trade in 1807 and the end of slavery in 1834. These historical processes produced the testimonies preserved in the records of the Royal Commissioners in Antigua and the Fiscal in Berbice that Anita Rupprecht and Trevor Burnard mine so imaginatively and productively. They may also, at least indirectly, have prompted and informed the complaints that the enslaved brought before these British officials. Burnard notes that after whipping women was forbidden in the British colonies in 1825, enslaved people began to lodge complaints specifically against this form of mistreatment. In the course of making a complaint to the Royal Commissioners in Antigua about mistreatment, a recaptured African man named Peter learned that he was being illegally kept in indenture beyond the stipulated term and sought redress for it.

There are other cases from the same period that do not necessarily reflect consciousness among the enslaved of the new Western ideas. A recaptured woman indentured on Antigua complained that she was given no food either for herself or her children, another that she was beaten for no good reason. Rupprecht observes that although these testimonies were heavily mediated, limited by the interrogatories of the white authorities to whom the recaptured Africans reported their grievances, "the indentured servants did not simply answer the questions put to them." The content and formulation of their complaints were not, then, necessarily crafted to speak to and exploit the reformist ideas that created a forum for their testimonies. They may, instead, have been rooted at least partially in a sense of what was just and right that originated in their previous lives in Africa.

Similar invocations of the moral economy of slavery appear in the testimonies preserved in the records of the Fiscal in Berbice during the final decades of slavery. A mother who complained about not being able to leave the field to nurse an ailing child may have known that there were authorities who were required to listen to her grievance, but her sense of what was right reflects the notion of a moral economy of slavery rather than Enlightenment concepts. Another enslaved woman in Berbice was put in the stocks for complaining to her manager for overworking her. While she thought her punishment unjust, she told the manager that she was willing to submit to it, though she "had done no wrong."

Classic autobiographical slave narratives offer a window into the subjectivity of the enslaved and examples of the politicization of individuals. Historians prize these things as powerful evidence of agency and victory over the annihilation that enslavement threated and often achieved. Most of today's descendants of the enslaved cannot claim one of these triumphant men and women as an ancestor, but the slave testimonies that inspired this book tell the stories of people who might have been one of their forebears. Dominique Rogers reflects on contemporary Martiniquais who attend workshops at which they are introduced to the histories of the ordinary enslaved people from whom they are descended. School children and adults alike learn about things that happened in places that are familiar to them and people whose names they share or know.

The testimonies at the center of this volume do not tell stories that ended with the triumph of freedom, but they reveal the complexities that defined the lives of most of the enslaved, where there was both suffering and agency. More than anything, they are stories of survival that can arm today's descendants with the fortitude it will take to dismantle the structures and politics of white supremacy that continue to oppress them. Brett Rushforth observes that Lorena Gale's play about the enslaved woman executed for arson in eighteenth century Montreal links "the deeper past of slavery to present injustices." A Martiniquaise woman who attended a conference organized for descendants of the enslaved offers one of the most powerful testimonies in this volume. "If my female ancestor managed to survive overworking and too often raping, who, as a women, am I not to try to overcome day to day difficulties in the twenty-first century, and like her reconstruct myself, my family, and my social life the way I want it?"

Today's descendants face daunting individual challenges, but they are also confronted with systemic racism that requires yoking individual resolve to collective political action. Here, too, the testimonies offer stories to inspire them. Trevor Burnard has uncovered women in the British Caribbean who organized themselves into groups to approach the Fiscal with complaints against enslavers, revealing the emergence of a collective political consciousness among the enslaved. It is a precious example.

Though historians may be disappointed that sources like the Fiscal do not yield "autobiographies in which a highly individuated self is explained and asserted," the evidence of collective action that this and the other sources so skillfully interrogated in this volume challenges the premise that discovering and describing the individual subjectivity of the enslaved is the only, or even the greatest prize worth seeking. The ultimate triumph over slavery and its legacies, after all, lies in the way the descendants of the enslaved—whether indigenous or African descended—asserted and continue to assert their collective power to dismantle the politics of white supremacy. Together, the slave testimonies in this volume illuminate that process more brilliantly than the catalog of classic slave narratives ever can.

Notes

1 Theodore Parker, *Ten Sermons of Religion* (Boston, MA: Crosby, Nichols and Company, 1853) 84–85, https://books.google.com/books?id=sUUQA AAAYAAJ&printsec=frontcover&source=gbs_ge_summary_r& cad=0#v=onepage&q&f=false, accessed 2 October 2019; "We shall overcome because the arc of the moral universe is long but it bends toward justice," formed part of the speech that King gave at the National Cathedral in 1968. Martin Luther King Jr., "Remaining Awake Through a Great Revolution," Speech given at the National Cathedral, March 31, 1968. https://www.si.edu/spotlight/mlk?page=4&iframe=true, accessed 2 October 2019; Mychal Denzel Smith, "The Truth About 'The Arc of the Moral Universe," *Huffpost*, 18 January 2018, https://www.huffpost.com/entry/ opinion-smith-obama-king_n_5a5903e0e4b04f3c55a252a4?guccounter=1, accessed October 2, 2019.

2 Peter Wood, *Black Majority: Negroes in Colonial South Carolina from 1670 to the Stono Rebellion* (New York: Random House, 1974) and Ira Berlin, *Many Thousands Gone: The First Two Centuries of Slavery in North America* (Cambridge, MA: Harvard University Press, 1998).

3 Brett Rushforth, citing Andrés Resendez, *The Other Slavery: The Uncovered Story of Indian Enslavement in America* (Boston, MA: Houghton Mifflin Harcourt, 2016) and Margaret Newell, "The Forgotten Slaves," *Chronicle of Higher Education*, December 11, 2016 (quote). Margaret Ellen Newell, *Brethren by Nature: New England Indians, Colonists, and the Origins of American Slavery* (Ithaca, NY: Cornell University Press, 2015) and Wendy Warren, *New England Bound: Slavery and Colonization in Early America* (New York: Liveright, 2016).

Contributors

Trevor Burnard is Wilberforce Professor of Slavery and Emancipation at the University of Hull. He is the author of *Jamaica in the Age of Revolution* (2020); *The Atlantic in World History, 1490–1830* (2020); *Britain and the Wider World, 1603–1800* (2020); and, with John Garrigus, *The Plantation Machine: Atlantic Capitalism in French Saint-Domingue and British Jamaica* (2016). He is the editor of the *Oxford Online Biography in Atlantic History*. He works on plantation societies in Jamaica, Maryland, and Berbice from the mid-seventeenth century until the abolition of slavery in the 1830s.

Emily Clark is Clement Chambers Benenson Professor in American Colonial History at Tulane University. She specializes in the French Atlantic and circum-Caribbean. She is the author or editor of five books, *New Orleans and Saint-Louis, Senegal: Mirror Cities in the Atlantic World,* with Ibrahima Thioub and Cécile Vidal (LSU Press 2019); *The Strange History of the American Quadroon: Free Women of Color in the Revolutionary Atlantic World* (UNC Press 2013); the multiple prize-winning *Masterless Mistresses: The New Orleans Ursulines and the Development of a New World Society: 1727–1834* (UNC Press 2007); *Women and Religion in the Atlantic Age, 1550–1900* (with Mary Laven, Ashgate, 2013); and *Voices from an Early American Convent: Marie Madeleine Hachard and the New Orleans Ursulines, 1727–1760* (LSU Press 2007). She is currently at work on the biography of Noel Carriere, the commander of the New Orleans free black militia. Her work has been supported by the American Council of Learned Societies, the Louisiana State Board of Regents, the Historic New Orleans Collection, and the Pew Foundation.

Linford D. Fisher is an associate professor of history at Brown University. He is the author of *The Indian Great Awakening: Religion and the Shaping of Native Cultures in Early America* (2012) and the coauthor of *Decoding Roger Williams: The Lost Essay of Rhode Island's Founding Father* (2014). Fisher is the PI of a digital project titled The Database of Indigenous Slavery in the Americas. He is currently finishing a book-length project, tentatively titled *America Enslaved,* on

Native American enslavement in English colonies in North America and the Caribbean and, later, in the United States, between Columbus and the American Civil War.

Aaron Spencer Fogleman is a Distinguished Research Professor in the History Department at Northern Illinois University. His research and teaching interests include forced and free transatlantic migrations, revolution, slavery, religion, and gender in the Atlantic World and Early America, and he has written many books and articles on these topics. Currently, he is the chief editor of a project entitled "A Catalog of Narratives by Africans Enslaved in the Transatlantic Slave Trade, 1586-1936," which will appear first in cloth, followed by on-line digitization. He is also preparing a monograph on four centuries of forced and free transatlantic migrations from Europe and Africa to the Americas, tentatively entitled "Immigrant Voices." He has been a Fulbright Distinguished Chair at the Goethe University in Frankfurt, an Alexander von Humboldt Fellow at the Max Planck Institute for History in Göttingen, and a Guggenheim Fellow.

Margaret Ellen Newell is Professor of History at the Ohio State University. Major works include *Brethren by Nature: New England Indians, Colonists and the Origins of American Slavery* (2015), which won the Organization of American Historians' James A. Rawley Prize for the best book on race relations in America, and the Peter J. Gomes Prize from the Massachusetts Historical Society, and *From Dependency to Independence: Economic Revolution in Colonial New England* (1998; rev. ed. 2015). She is working on runaway slaves in eighteenth- and nineteenth-century America.

Dominique Rogers is maîtresse de conférences in early modern history, at the université des Antilles. She is the author of a Ph.D. dissertation on the free people of color of the two capitals of French Saint-Domingue at the end of the eighteenth century. She has recently edited two volumes with Boris Lesueur, *Sortir de l'esclavage, Europe du sud et Amériques (XIVe–XIXe siècles)* (Paris: Karthala, 2018) and *Libres après les abolitions? (Statuts et identités aux Amériques et en Afrique)* (Paris: Karthala, 2018). As part of the EURESCL project, she has also worked on slave voices and edited *Voix d'esclaves: Antilles, Guyane et Louisiane françaises, XVIIIe–XIXe siècles*, Collections sources et documents (Paris: Karthala, 2015).

Anita Rupprecht is a principal lecturer in the School of Humanities at the University of Brighton in the UK. She has published on the British and American slave trades, abolitionism, slavery, resistance, and empire. She is currently working on a Leverhulme funded monograph project, 'Indenturing Re-Captured Africans in the Caribbean, 1807–1828.'

Brett Rushforth is an associate professor of history at the University of Oregon. He is the author of *Bonds of Alliance: Indigenous and Atlantic Slaveries in New France*, which won the Merle Curti Book Award, the Boucher Prize, the FEEGI Biennial Book Prize and the Wylie Prize, and was nominated for the Frederick Douglass Book Prize. He is is co-author, with Christopher Hodson, of the forthcoming *Discovering Empire: France and the Atlantic World from the Age of Exploration to the Age of Revolutions* and is currently writing a book about the 1710 and 1717 Gaulet Rebellions in Martinique, provisionally titled *Rebel Slaves, Rebel Planters: Informal Economies and Negotiated Power in Eighteenth-Century Martinique*.

Miranda Spieler is Associate Professor of History at the American University of Paris. She is completing a global history of slaves and slave masters who lived in the eighteenth-century French capital. She is the author of *Empire and Underworld: Captivity in French Guiana* (2012).

Cécile Vidal is directrice d'études (professor) at the École des Hautes études en Sciences Sociales, Paris. Among her many works on French Atlantic history are *Histoire de l'Amérique française* (with Gilles Havard, 5th edition, 2019 [2003]), the edited volumes *Louisiana: Crossroads of the Atlantic World* (2013) and *New Orleans, Louisiana, and Saint-Louis, Senegal: Mirror Cities of the Atlantic World, 1659–2000s* (with Emily Clark and Ibrahima Thioub, 2019), and the monograph *Caribbean New Orleans: Empire, Race, and the Making of a Slave Society* (2019).

Sophie White is Professor of American Studies at the University of Notre Dame. She is the author of two monographs, *Voices of the Enslaved: Love, Labor, and Longing in Colonial Louisiana* (Omohundro Institute of Early American History and Culture for the University of North Carolina Press, 2019) and *Wild Frenchmen and Frenchified Indians: Material Culture and Race in Colonial Louisiana* (University of Pennsylvania Press, 2012), both of which were supported by fellowships from the National Endowment for the Humanities. In addition to her articles and essays, she is developing a digital humanities project on slave testimony which will be featured on the Omohundro Institute's OI Reader platform, and is writing a new book on red hair that examines the intersection of genomics, culture, and the construction of otherness.

Index

Note: *Italic* page numbers refer to figures and page numbers followed by "n" denote endnotes.

Made in the USA
Las Vegas, NV
06 September 2022

54783932R00146